RENT CONTROL
MYTHS & REALITIES

RENT CONTROL
MYTHS &REALITIES
International Evidence of the Effects of Rent Control in Six Countries

Contributors include
Milton Friedman, Friedrich Hayek,
and Basil Kalymon

Co-edited by Walter Block
and Edgar Olsen

THE FRASER INSTITUTE
1981

Canadian Cataloguing in Publication Data
Main entry under title:
Rent control, myths & realities

(Fraser Institute housing and land economics
series ; no. 7)
Bibliography: p.
ISBN 0-88975-033-5

1. Rent control - Addresses, essays, lectures.
2. Housing - Addresses, essays, lectures.
I. Block, Walter, 1941-   II. Olsen, Edgar,
1942-   III. Friedrich, Milton, 1912-
IV. Hayek, Friedrich A., 1899-
V. Kalymon, Basil A., 1944-   VI. Series:
Fraser Institute, Vancouver, B.C.   Fraser
Institute housing and land economics series ;
no. 7
HD7287.5.R457   333.5   C80-091222-5

Contents

PART TWO—THE THEORY OF RENT CONTROL

Chapter 2: A Short Course in Housing Economics

M.A. Walker, *Director,*
The Fraser Institute

Chapter 3: The Presumed Advantages and Real Disadvantages of Rent Control

Richard W. Ault, *Acting Assistant Professor,*
Louisiana State University

PART THREE—THE PRACTICE OF RENT CONTROL

Chapter 4: Roofs or Ceilings? The Current Housing Problem

Milton Friedman, *Paul Snowden Russell Distinguished Service Professor of Economics, University of Chicago, and Senior Research Fellow, Hoover Institution, Stanford, California*

Chapter 5: Questions and Some Answers about Rent Control: An Empirical Analysis of New York's Experience

Chapter 6: The Effects of Rent Control and Rent Stabilization in New York City

PART FOUR—CONCLUSIONS

Chapter 14: Alternatives

Edgar O. Olsen, *Associate Professor of Economics,*
University of Virginia

M.A. Walker, *Director,*
The Fraser Institute

Chapter 15: Postscript: A Reply to the Critics

Walter Block, *Senior Economist,*
The Fraser Institute

The theoretical analysis of rent control rests on some principles which are quite elementary, indeed distressingly so. They are so obvious that one would feel the greatest reluctance to repeat them on the pages of a professional journal were it not that a great public policy has been erected upon either ignorance or a repudiation of them. If we were to ask a competent sophomore what would happen if consumers' real income increased some 60 percent while the price of a service of more than zero income elasticity were held constant, we should be justified in expecting him to answer that the quantity demanded of the service would become greater than the quantity supplied and the market would be in disequilibrium. And the sophomore who met our expectations would thereby have uncovered the central element in the housing problem, about which so much has been written and spoken and over which many families have experienced great annoyance and no little hardship.

If our sophomore were something more than competent, if he had a touch of affection for the subject, he would go on to express a doubt that much new investment would be attracted to the production of the service in question, that, instead, investment would look for richer pastures in those areas of the economy where maximum prices were not fixed. He might then, warming to the problem (and perhaps seeing an "A" shimmering before him), go on to say that buyers would engage in a scramble for the service fixed in price with the distribution of it becoming a very haphazard affair. In all this, he would be most correct. But if it then were asked of him whether the theoretical observations applied when rental housing was the service in question, he would, like most members of the human community, draw himself up sharp before the heartlessness of applying the elements of supply and demand analysis to so tender a thing as home and hearth. *He would revert to phrases about, 'Housing is a necessity'... 'Rents in a free market would be exorbitant'... 'People would have no place to live'... 'Landlords would make enormous profits out of the poor.' He might so recoil at the thought of free rents that he would go to the library and there discover that the removal of rent control would be inflationary, that it would lead to strikes, that it would reduce the purchases of durable consumer goods and hence lead to unemployment. But for all of his instinctive (and commendable) sympathies, his original remarks still would be correct.*" (emphasis added).

W.S. Grampp, "Some Effects of Rent Control"

Preface

In the United States, rent control has been a local phenomenon, except during and immediately after the World Wars and in the early 1970s, when it was a part of the Economic Stabilization Act. It is all too often initiated without clear understanding of its effects or consideration of alternative means to the same ends. Although there is much evidence of the effects of this legislation, it is not easily accessible to concerned citizens and their representatives and, hence, has had little influence on the fate of proposed ordinances. Since rent control can have major effects on the well-being of individuals, this failure is particularly unfortunate. The Fraser Institute is publishing *Rent Control: Myths and Realities* to help fill this information gap.

It is often said that rent control is inevitable in a democracy because tenants greatly outnumber landlords.

Yet, at least until recently, rent control has been the exception rather than the rule in the United States. In Europe, where it has been pervasive since World War I, governments have been moving slowly toward decontrol for more than a decade. Therefore, it would seem more accurate to say that the introduction of rent control is politically feasible only in areas with no recent experience—because only an electorate uninformed of its consequences will support it.

UNEXPECTED UNANIMITY

This book contains a narrow range of views concerning the desirability of rent control. The reason is simple. Economists who have researched its effects are virtually unanimous in their assessment. The extent of their agreement is indicated by the remarks of the 1974 Nobel Prize winners in economics, Gunnar Myrdal and Friedrich Hayek, whose ideological views on matters other than rent control are, to say the least, quite different. Paul Samuelson, 1970 winner of the Nobel award, described their general views as follows: "In no sense has their work been joint. Indeed, their policy conclusions if followed literally would be at loggerheads and self-cancelling."[1]

Gunnar Myrdal, whom Samuelson described as an important architect of the Swedish Labor Party's Welfare State, had the following low opinion of rent control and those who implement it: "Rent control has in certain western countries constituted, maybe, the worst example of poor planning by governments lacking courage and vision."[2] And, says Friedrich Hayek, author of the best selling *Road to Serfdom* and one of the most respected intellectual defenders of free choice as the basis for human conduct:

> "If this account seems to boil down to a catalogue of iniquities to be laid at the door of rent control, that is no mere coincidence, but inevitable....I doubt very much whether theoretical research into the same problems carried out by someone of a different politico-economic

persuasion than myself could lead to different conclusions. Therefore, if theory brings to light nothing but unfavorable conclusions, it must indicate that though the immediate benefits of rent control, for which it was introduced in the first place, are obvious to everyone, theory is needed to uncover the unintentional consequences which intervention brings in its wake."[3]

Thus, although the reader will not find any support for rent control in the present volume, the essays do reflect the widest consensus within the economics profession.

THE ROLE OF THE ECONOMIST

The responsibility of the economist in analysing public policy such as rent control is to objectively assess the likely course of events in the presence and absence of intervention; to determine its likely effects in this manner; and finally, if intervention is clearly justified on economic grounds, to outline its most constructive form.

Very often the economist's attention focuses on government policies after the fact, largely because many of them are undertaken for purely political reasons and, hence, are not initially scrutinized for their economic impact. In other cases, a harmful intervention is so pervasive or of such long standing that it has become institutionalized. These circumstances greatly complicate the task of objective assessment, for the economist is then confronted with the task of proposing policy action that will be regarded as "politically impossible."

But the more deeply a harmful government program is entrenched and, thus, the more politically impossible it is to change it, the greater the need there is for the economist to speak out. It is in precisely this sort of case that expert economic analysis is most needed. If the economist kowtows to uninformed popular opinion in such cases, the citizenry can never learn the truth.

The same principle applies in the health field. It may be "medically impossible" to convince people to do something, but the doctor who remains silent for this reason is derelict in his duty. For if a *doctor* will not oppose poor health habits, how can the public ever learn of the evils? The health professional, and the economist, must lead the layman—and not be deterred by his uninformed prejudices. To the extent that the economist as policy analyst fails in this task and permits political expediency to affect his policy recommendations, he completely renounces any claim to special standing and expertise. More important, he undermines the public interest. This is why it is crucial that the truth be told about rent control, however unpopular this may be in some quarters.

WHAT IS THE PROBLEM?

The present volume is organized into four parts: "The Politics of Rent Control," "The Theory of Rent Control," "The Practice of Rent Control," and "Conclusions." Batting off in first place is Ted Dienstfrey, whose "The Politics of Rent Control in the United States: A Program at the Yellow Light" provides an up-to-date, in-depth analysis of the political realities operating in the rent control arena. Surveying the court battles, tenant organizations, rent strikes, and landlord responses now taking place from Connecticut to California, Dienstfrey contributes an illuminating survey of the attempts—both successful and otherwise—to enact rent control legislation in some two dozen American states and local communities. Covering the related political behind-the-scenes-machinations, he is able to focus on certain highly irregular practices, as well as on the activities of Jane Fonda, Tom Hayden, Howard Jarvis, Paul Gann, and other actors on the rent control stage. Dienstfrey unearths several unexpected opponents of controls, such as the liberal Senator Thomas Eagleton (Missouri) and *The Amsterdam News,* a widely respected black-owned newspaper in New York City, and maintains that the prospects for the continuing spread of rent control are at a "flashing yellow traffic light."

The theoretical section that follows features "A Short Course in Housing Economics" by Michael Walker. This essay provides answers to questions such as "What is a housing shortage?" "How are rents determined?" "What are rent controls?" and "What are their effects?" Defining such terms as "basic shelter," "present discounted value," and "scarcity," and then applying them to economic analysis, Walker objects to "the existence of local minimum housing quality standards because they reduce the choice of some consumers." He concludes that housing shortages are the result of inappropriate and artificially maintained price (rent) controls.

Richard Ault, in a masterful analytical essay, utterly annihilates several claims made on behalf of rent control: that it protects the poor, stops inflation, stabilizes neighborhoods, benefits racial minorities, prevents rent "gouging," and reduces slums. Instead, he casts rent control as the villain of the piece, discouraging rental housing construction, reducing maintenance, eroding the tax base, shifting the burden to homeowners, cutting labor mobility, increasing housing costs, and unsatisfactorily redistributing income.

HOW HAS RENT CONTROL WORKED?

Part Three, "The Practice of Rent Control," marshalls the evidence distilled from the experience of six different countries over more than half a century. Beginning with the United States, Milton Friedman and George Stigler, in "Roofs or Ceilings?" compare two methods of dealing with housing shortages. The first, the price system, was used in the San Francisco earthquake of 1906 which decimated that city's housing stock. Rents were allowed to rise freely, but not even a single mention of a housing crisis was made in the first newspaper published after the earthquake—available a short five weeks later. The second method, rent control, was utilized in the far less serious housing shortage suffered by San Francisco in 1946. This time, rents were *not* allowed to rise freely. The result was a chronic housing crisis of epic proportions which continued until the demise of controls several years later.

The Olsen and Kristof articles are companion pieces,

dealing with New York City rent control before and after 1969, respectively. Edgar Olsen points out that New York might be considered the rent control capital of the world, at least as far as research is concerned, for (1) this program was in operation in the late 1960s when the econometric techniques necessary for an empirical study of its effects came into their own, (2) good data for analysis is available there, and (3) the New York City government, anxious to learn of its effects, commissioned several studies. Olsen definitively shows that, at least as far as the Big Apple is concerned, rent control exacerbates rather than solves a housing shortage. He maintains, moreover, that this program is a "grossly inefficient and inequitable income redistributive device."

THE NEW YORK CITY FINANCIAL CRISIS

The Kristof contribution, an updating of his *Fifteenth Interim Report to the Mayor* for the Temporary Commission on (New York) City Finances, reports that rent control, although originally conceived as a temporary measure, has been anything but short-lived. Instead, it has been marked by an unparalleled number of housing abandonments, the deterioration and utter devastation of large portions of the City's housing stock, and consequent destruction of the tax base—all of which has contributed to the City's financial decline and near bankruptcy. Frank Kristof regards the rent stabilization program of 1969 (a "moderate" form of rent control) as a "shabby betrayal of trust"—all post-1947 rental units were guaranteed control free in the future—"which led to a virtual cessation of private new rental construction."

A CANADIAN EXAMPLE

In "Apartment Shortages and Rent Control," Basil Kalymon reports a smooth operation of the rental market in Toronto—until the advent of controls in 1975. Then, with negative landlord expectations, low vacancy rates could no longer call forth the increased supply of dwelling units necessary to abate rent rises. Instead, the government stepped into the breach, and subsidized rental housing starts rose from 13 percent in 1974 to a staggering 91 percent three scant years later.

Based on his statistical analysis, Kalymon is highly critical of the view that rent decontrol must wait for high vacancy rates. This argument "puts the cart before the horse," because "low vacancy rates cannot be alleviated *until* rents are allowed to rise."

EUROPEAN RENT CONTROL

Earlier versions of the next several essays, the ones covering Great Britain, Austria, France, and Sweden appeared in *Verdict on Rent Control* published by the Institute of Economic Affairs. Taken as a group, they show that the shattering effects of rent control are by no means limited to the North American continent.

F.W. Paish begins by offering a tour of rent restriction legislation in England, stretching back to 1915. We are dismayed to learn, as only one instance in a long record of inequities, injustices, and abuses, that, according to the law, "if a house was last let in 1815, then the rent paid at the time of the battle of Waterloo is the standard rent today." Other problems include a doubling of all other prices from 1915 to 1939, while rents stayed constant, resulting in inadequate maintenance, reduced tenant mobility and a sharp fall in dwelling space offered to let.

Tracing the British practice from the 1950s to the present, F.G. Pennance details a litany of further misallocations in the residential rental market. These were ignored by the Report of the Francis Committee which concluded, instead, that "the system is working well." To this, Pennance replied:

"It is no surprise to find that it 'works.' Rent Officers are no doubt sensible, hard-working and conscientious. They have a National Association, write papers, hold conferences: in short, they behave much like other responsible public officers required to produce valuations according to statutory rules. They would probably have no difficulty at all in fixing a 'fair' rent for Buckingham Palace if need be. But this proves nothing except that operational rules can be invented for any situation as long as the operators are under no compulsion to consider the economic facts of life or the effects of their decision.''

We have already seen Friedrich Hayek's conclusions concerning rent restrictions. The basis upon which he reaches them is illustrated by the operation of the rent law in Austria: the resulting inability of neighboring manufacturing firms to attract Viennese workers fearful of losing protected tenancies—despite high central-city unemployment rates; the misallocation of private investment funds to areas which need them less than housing; the unnecessary public housing works which ensue.

Rent restrictions in France, reports Bertrand de Jouvenel, have brought things to such a pass that "a month's rent for a large family of six costs as much as eleven packets of cigarettes." At such levels, rents absorb only 1.5 percent of the average worker's budget, one-third of the amount spent on entertainment, and equal to the transport costs to and from his job. The repercussions are just as stark: "bootleg" apartments, housing disrepair, virtually no new construction.

Rent control in Sweden has pursued a somewhat different path than elsewhere because of the existence of (1) a National Association of Tenants which bargains collectively with landlords, much in the manner of labor unions, and (2) a landlord association of local municipal authorities, which controls the largest block of apartment units, and which is politically motivated to charge below-cost rentals. But the results, says Swedish economist Sven Rydenfelt, are distressingly similar to those elsewhere: "inadequate funds for maintenance, gradually deteriorating accommodation, growing slum areas, and declining quality of life for the dwellers of rented units."

Michael Walker concludes this historical section with a study of the effects of rent decontrol. He argues that the magnitude of any subsequent rent rise "depends upon the severity and duration of the rent control ordinance and changes in other factors such as population and real income." Examining the experience of fourteen U.S. cities which underwent decontrol in late 1949, Walker reports that short-term rent rises were not as serious as widely feared: they ranged from a low of 2.9 percent to a high of 26.7 percent, with an average increase of only 11.6 percent. He cautions, however, that his assumptions of adequate housing quality under controls and the absence of a decontrolled rental sector are not always met in the real world and, hence, extrapolation from his findings is problematical.

BENEVOLENT INTENTIONS

In the last section of the book, Walker and Olsen cite three factors as the origins of rent control: tenant activism, housing shortages and hardships (real or imagined), and the widespread belief that governments "can't do nothing" in the face of rising rents. But the dismal results are the same no matter what the motivation: housing deterioration, haphazard income redistribution, racial discrimination, tax base loss, reduction in labor mobility—and a *worsening*, not an improvement, in the initial housing shortage (if indeed there ever was one).

Given the basic nobility of a concern for the well-being of low-income households, rent control is *still* just about the worst possible means to this worthy end. For this program, argue Walker and Olsen, unjustifiably aids middle-and-upper-income families. Moreover, a disproportionate weight falls unfairly on the backs of a small number of people who own rental property—not on society as a whole. The alternative offered is a housing allowance designed to protect people from the hardships associated with the rising cost of *basic* shelter. It would be made directly to the recipient, *not* through the type of inequitable grants-in-kind currently made available through conventional U.S. public housing programs.

Which way out of this mess? State the authors, "the best way to achieve an uncontrolled housing market is to resist rent control in the first place." But if stuck, Walker and

Olsen recommend "a gradual but specific decontrol program," coupled with tenant subsidies to overcome temporary hardships. Instantaneous decontrol runs the risk of political backlash, and a too-gradual phase-out is unlikely to attract potential investors.

This volume draws to a close with "Postscript: A Reply to the Critics," in which Walter Block considers several widely held but fallacious arguments on behalf of rent control. Debunked myths include the claim that the rental housing market is monopolistic, earns "excessive" profits, "exploits" tenants, is marked by an absentee landlord "menance," and places profit above human needs. Holding no brief for the landlord, however, Block finds "a grain of truth" in the critic's castigation of unscrupulous practices on the part of some real estate managers.

Lastly, *Rent Control: Myths and Realities* addresses itself to the often-made claim that rent control—and fire bombing—have similar effects on the urban landscape (see the statement by Assar Lindbeck cited by Sven Rydenfelt on p. 213). Each of the fifteen essays is illustrated with a photograph of *either* a "bombed-out" *or* "rent controlled-out" city, otherwise unmarked. The reader is invited to identify the two categories (for the correct answers, see p. 320).

In view of the rising interest in rent control on the part of many tenants—and given what can only be called the "disastrous" experience of many countries with this program—the Fraser Institute is pleased to publish this book of essays, the seventh in our Housing and Land Economics Series. However, owing to the independence of the authors, the views expressed may or may not conform severally or collectively with those of the members of the Institute.

W. Block

NOTES

1 Paul Samuelson, *New York Times,* 10 October 1974.
2 See "The Rise, Fall, and Revival of Swedish Rent Control" in this volume, p. 201.
3 See "The Repercussions of Rent Restriction," in this volume, p. 171.

Part One
The Politics of
Rent Control

Chapter One
The Politics of Rent Control in the United States: A Program at the Yellow Light

TED DIENSTFREY

1. Bomb Damage or Rent Control? See page 320 for the answer.

THE AUTHOR

TED DIENSTFREY graduated from the University of Chicago in 1960 and was appointed to the US Foreign Service. Eighteen months later, he was dismissed in large part over policy differences concerning the growing military involvement of the US in Southeast Asia and the sluggish recognition that historical behavior on racial issues needed to be changed. At that time he wrote an article for *Commentary* on the founding of the student Non-violent Coordinating Committee.

Several years later he attended planning school at the University of California, Berkeley, and worked on a major study of new towns. His financial model of new towns, described in the *Journal of American Planners* and *The Community Builders* by Edward Eichler, indicated that most new towns would be financially unsound investments.

Recently he has reviewed various political strategies for improving air and water quality in *The Public Interest*.

Since April 1975 he has been Director of Research and Planning for the California Housing Council, which is a statewide trade association of apartment owners and managers. He currently serves on numerous state and regional committees that are trying to understand the objections to continued economic growth and economic opportunity.

Chapter One
The Politics of Rent Control in the United States: A Program at the Yellow Light

TED DIENSTFREY

*Director of Research and Planning,
California Housing Council*

WHAT WILL HAPPEN TO RENT CONTROL?

One can characterize a political program that has no effective opposition as being at a "green light." The various anti-redlining efforts and further redistribution of goods and services to the elderly are cases in point. At the other end of the spectrum are programs to which opposition is nearly universal. They could be described as facing a "red light" and, at least for the time being, going nowhere. Examples include mass transit and employee participation in management (the German codetermination program). In the middle are programs with an uncertain immediate political fate. These can be viewed as being at the "yellow light." Rent control, in the United States, for various reasons explained below, could increase or decrease in its importance. It is therefore at a flashing yellow light.

Rent control can have enormous effects on private rental housing, a sector which provides about 35 percent of all dwelling units in the United States and over 90 percent of all rental housing. Nor are families living in owner-occupied housing free of its consequences. What happens to rent control programs over the next few years will depend upon many things, including the economic evidence. But political factors can be expected to play an important role as well. The purpose of this essay is therefore to describe the current politics of rent control in the United States, and to consider its prospects.

THE RENT CONTROL POLITICAL DEBATE

Elsewhere in this book, the detailed *economic* arguments and *historical evidence* of the effects of rent control are presented. However, since rent control is a *political* issue as well, it is of some importance to know the arguments raised in this sphere. It is important to understand that neither proponents nor opponents of rent control are a unified, ideologically "pure" group. Each side includes individuals trying to understand both their own and society's best options.

The most common argument for rent control assumes that all, or at least most, landlords receive "exorbitant" profits and that government is therefore needed to curtail such greed. Profit limitation is urged more on moral grounds than on any real conception of its actual level. The major political support for rent control probably rests on our fundamentally ambiguous views toward profit, privately owned wealth, and the "social good."

Another view is that rents *ought* to be related to costs. This too is a moral position and it dates back at least as far as the medieval debates on "just price." Housing, according to this argument, is so important that it cannot be left to the unfair marketplace.

What the press calls "horror stories" provide another argument that has great emotional appeal and political importance. Most of the rental units in the United States are owned by small, nonprofessional, part-time landlords who often do not actively raise rents to the current market level. Many believe they are doing their tenants a favor. However, sometimes these below-market units are sold to an owner who tries to raise rents to market levels in one jump. The newspapers cover this by showing elderly tenants being evicted in the winter. They label this "irresponsible" and "gouging." Although statistically insignificant, such cases can have a tremendous political impact.

Also in vogue is the tenant organizing phrase "housing for people and not for profits." It is not always clear if the desire is to turn private rental housing into a utility type industry with government guaranteed profit, or if the goal is some form of public ownership. Perhaps the reason for the ambiguity is the voter's fear that the government cannot provide adequate rental housing—let alone outperform the private sector. This is probably coupled with a basic opposition, on the part of many rent control advocates, to private ownership of rental housing *per se*.[1] But Ernest van den Haag explains why so many university oriented intellectuals believe it would be in their own best interests to enact such programs as government rent control: "Intellectuals have often designed wishful utopias, generated by reason and desire, though bereft of reality or even possibility. They would reward morally valuable activities—their own kind of activities—rather than economic ones."[2]

Rent control is recognized, even by some of its supporters, as an ineffectual tool to provide needed rental housing. Nevertheless, it is viewed as a good organizing tool. The hope is that tenants will move from rent enactments to regulation of financial and corporate institutions, and to a radical reordering of the priorities of society.[3] Rent control, for these proponents, is merely a form of "consciousness raising," which is important only if it leads to further political action. Whatever the merits of this position, it is hard to see much evidence that rent controls have led to such a "radicalization" of the tenants.

Recently, rent laws have been favored by some of the organized, older voters. These people are on fixed incomes and see inflation eating away their savings. Many feel that the deterioration of housing caused by rent control will occur slowly and will, therefore, not be noticeable until after they have died.

And finally, there is a silent support from a group of great political importance, the upper-middle and middle-income "no growthers." These individuals see controls as a socially and politically acceptable way of preventing construction of additional rental units in their community.

Opponents of rent control have as diverse a set of political priorities as proponents. More often than not, the majority of small landlords declare, or at least believe, that any tampering with their right to do with their property as they see fit is "unAmerican" and just one more step toward the end of individual freedom and risk-taking as we know it. This is basically a moral argument with limited political appeal in jurisdictions with large numbers of tenants. A further problem is that its landlord proponents are not as articulate as their university educated opponents.

A second argument is that rents have not increased as fast as costs and that rents ought to be higher. Indeed, one can even use the federal Consumer Price Index (CPI) figures to justify this position.[4] There is a danger with this argument, however. It is similar to the *pro*-rent control position that rents of existing units should be a function of government determined cost estimates.

Then there is the argument that, while controls may start as a minor irritant to the private rental housing industry, they quickly become unreasonable bureaucratic nightmares. New York City once was the prime example of this problem. The so-called second generation of modern rent controls have now given us Fort Lee, New Jersey, where 1973 rents and property taxes were still in litigation five years later.[5]

Opponents of rent control argue quite successfully that controls which reduce rents must result in housing disinvestment. Often tenants seem less impressed with detailed, hard-to-understand economic analysis than with the two questions they were asked during a rent control election:

1. Would they want their own or their parents' savings or pension fund invested in rent controlled housing?
2. If they owned a rent controlled building, what would they do to maintain it?

If one believes that controls decrease the number of rental units in a housing market, it is clear that the poor or minorities will be hurt. There is endless anecdotal information of the wealthy or well-connected tenant making illegal payment to obtain a vacant rental unit. And there are a growing number of advocates for the poor who have begun to understand the negative implications of a program that results in fewer rental housing units. Editorialized a leading black newspaper in New York:

> "We would be vigorously supporting the continuance of rent control if that concept and that ideal had moved minority groups toward better and less expensive housing. But unfortunately, this has not been the case.... The result is that the property, no matter who owns it, goes steadily downhill to eventually become another war-torn hollow shell—a victim of the war of rent control."[6]

Also telling is the argument that higher rents would lead to additional rental units and—via filtering—result in better housing for the poor. While this may be economically valid, to date it has had limited political impact. First, there is the burgeoning no-growth movement which opposes any new construction. And second, the proponents of rent control are not overly swayed by economic logic.

It is oft-times maintained that rent control reduces labor mobility and is therefore actually a disguised "tax" on moving. But this argument is politically irrelevant. For the individuals most hurt by this "moving tax,"—future immigrants—do not yet live in the community and can thus have no effect. However, in university communities, often characterized by tight housing markets, students do seem to understand that rent control will make it harder for them to find housing after the next summer vacation.

One of the most important political arguments against rent control deals with the ensuing property tax shift to homeowners. Tax law, at least prior to the California Jarvis/Gann referendum, ensures that decreased rents lead to lower assessments; but this results in lower city services or *higher taxes for homeowners.*[7] Homeowners believe this argument and, at least prior to Jarvis/Gann, voted in large numbers against rent controls.

A most disarming argument admits that the poor and the elderly on low, fixed incomes are not "adequately" housed. But since rent control is an untargeted subsidy, it will not solve these real political problems.[8] Dramatic cases in point are the $60,000 per year Mayor Koch of New York who retains his rent controlled apartment, and the highrise luxury tenants of Fort Lee who grumble about air conditioning and swimming pool maintenance.

Moreover, rent regulations pose less hardship to large corporations which can hire lawyers and accountants than they do to thousands of small, part-time owners. Proponents of rent control argue that, since the small landlord is undercapitalized, and nothing more than a "front" for the financial institutions in any case, wiping him out would be of minimum social importance. But in fact these small ownerships provide an entry into capital accumulation for upwardly mobile minorities. This is hardly irrelevant.

Last but not least is the claim that rent control leads to a New York-type abandonment problem (the South Bronx is a vivid example). Some believe this will occur immediately upon enactment. Others argue that the New York City housing mess has taken years to develop. Moreover, it must be conceded that other cities, such as Philadelphia and Detroit, have an abandonment problem and no rent control.

Whatever the merits of blaming New York's abandonment on rent control, proponents of rent control will go to any length to call a program by which the government controls rents anything but rent control. The concept of rent control may be politically attractive, but the term "rent control" is definitely not an aesthetic one. Opponents of rent control claim that if a rose by any other name smells the same, so does an onion.

THE CURRENT STATUS OF RENT CONTROL IN THE UNITED STATES

New York City

While rent control is the law in over a hundred communities

in New York state, attention is usually focused on New York City's *two* separate rent programs: *rent control*, first passed in 1942 as a "temporary" measure, and *rent stabilization*, enacted in 1969.

Currently, as rent controlled apartments are vacated they are moved into the stabilization program. As of 1977, there were more units under "stabilization" than "control." The basic difference between the two is that stabilization stipulates an orderly annual increase in rents with relatively little red tape attached, while controls, which cover only pre-1947 buildings, and which originally provided for no annual increase in rents at all, now provide for smaller increases with greater difficulties under the "maximum base rent" program.

Stabilization, although a so-called modern, second generation, more flexible rent control program, has caused grave damage to New York City, for the original program exempted post-1947 units from controls "forevermore." But 1969 saw the rent "stabilization" of units built since 1947. Henceforth, *no investor anywhere in the United States could rationally believe in the reliability of any local rent control program's guarantee of permanent exemption for new construction.*

While Congress considered requiring New York City to abandon rent control as a precondition for federal financial support needed to prevent bankruptcy in 1977, it never pursued this position. Congress has, however, issued a report from the Senate Committee on Banking, Housing and Urban Affairs, which states:

"Interestingly enough, there is no evidence to show that rent control benefits the poor. Quite the contrary, it helps a small, privileged group of long-time residents, largely middle class, while driving up rents in uncontrolled units."[9]

New Jersey

In the late 1960s and early 1970s many sophisticated investors saw that the New York City residential market was deteriorating. They perceived a pent-up demand for better apartments, neighborhoods and maintenance. Units were accordingly built in nearby New Jersey, and New York City tenants were duly attracted. But rent control followed them across the Hudson River: over 100 communities in New Jersey have some form of this legislation.[10]

There is no evidence that rent control, once enacted as a temporary measure by tenant majorities, will ever be repealed, or even reduced in severity. In fact, year by year, the rate of permissible rent increases tends to decline. While Fort Lee's initial law permitted rent raises equal to that of the CPI, they have been subsequently reduced to 2.5 percent, or to the CPI rate, whichever is lower.

Two interrelated situations are developing in New Jersey. First, every rent control law in the country provides for "a fair return." The courts have indicated that anything else would be a violation of due process and constitute an uncompensated taking. However, most enactments have failed to define this term. Until the New Jersey Supreme Court rules on this matter, it will be impossible to determine what the New Jersey rent control laws really mean.[11]

Secondly, there is the movement toward the development of a statewide rent control law. The property owners are willing to settle for a law that would prevent extraordinary rent increases upon the sale of a building and thereby prevent the "horror stories" the press covers periodically. The tenants are asking for an enabling law which defines fair return as 40 percent of the gross rent for debt service and profit. As of now, neither side seems to have the votes in the State legislature to pass a bill.

Massachusetts

In 1970, Massachusetts passed an enabling law which permitted cities to enact rent control. Boston, Lynn, Cambridge, Brookline, and Summerfield passed such laws. Lynn later repealed it. The 1970 enabling law expired in 1974. Prior to expiration of the enabling law, the

Massachusetts legislature commissioned Harbridge House to study its effects. The report recommended extending and expanding the enabling law.[12] But Harvard economist John Kain testified to the Massachusetts legislature that the Harbridge House conclusions were unsupported by its own data. Said he:

> "The evidence and analyses presented in the Harbridge House report simply do not support its recommendation that Chapter 842 should be extended any more than they support its repeal. Most of the data and analyses contained in the Harbridge House report are simply irrelevant....The major weakness of the Harbridge House report is the absence of any framework or conception of how urban housing markets work. As a result, the report is a jumble of largely irrelevant or misleading statistics in search of a framework for their interpretation."[13]

The Massachusetts legislature permitted the enabling law to lapse in 1974 but allowed for continuation of rent control in the four concerned communities.

In 1977, the chairperson of a pro-rent control Boston City Council Committee contracted for an economic analysis to be made on the effects of this legislation. Without any publicity, an economist from The Massachusetts Institute of Technology was given the task of compiling such a study. But, to the great chagrin and disappointment of the City Administration, the findings were very critical of rent control. They were therefore never released to the public.

There is, however, a move to end controls in Boston, which, by the way, has a high vacancy rate. In fact, for over a year, the city has had vacancy decontrol, in which a unit is controlled only as long as the present tenant remains. Furthermore, the Mayor has suggested exempting all owner-occupied buildings with fifteen or fewer units and has indicated that a new more favorable rate of return formula must be developed. Concluded the "Report of the Mayor's Committee on Rent Control," submitted to the Honorable Kevin H. White, Mayor, City of Boston, September 1977:

"If there is a lack of housing at rents which low and moderate income households can afford, it is a problem national in scope, which is particularly acute in older, urban areas. The problem can only be addressed through a national housing policy which focuses on this need. It cannot be resolved at the local level through rent control.

In general, the present housing crisis is not one brought on by a tight market, uncurbed speculation, rapidly spiralling rents and displacement, as was the case in the late sixties. Rather, it is one characterized by disinvestment, deferred maintenance, erosion of the housing stock and tax base; and *it is one aggravated by keeping a lid on investor's revenue while rising operating costs push up cash outlays.*" (emphasis added)[14]

Connecticut

Connecticut is interesting because of a little-known type of compulsory arbitration triggered by a tenant complaint. Instead of a control board setting all rents, it sets them only upon a tenant complaint. Such a regulation permits the control board to consider the rents of comparable apartments. It is so little known that in 1977, after eight years of such controls, several *large* Connecticut lending institutions were unaware of its existence.

The Connecticut or "Stamford Plan" seems to have the same detrimental effects as the New Jersey-New York variety. Units are converted to condominiums, and new construction is minimal. The "Fair Rent Commission Annual Report, Fiscal Year 1977-78," City of Stamford, Connecticut, finds that during 1976-77, the city lost at least 533 rental units due to fire, condemnation, demolition and condominium conversion. In the past five years, moreover, 1306 units were converted to condominiums. The report reluctantly concludes: "If landlords are not permitted to make reasonable profits, they will convert their buildings to either office space or condominiums resulting in loss of more rental units."

Washington, D.C.

The District enacted rent control in the early 1970s with Congressional approval. Since that time, Senator Eagleton, chairman of the Senate District of Columbia Committee, has publicly come out against rent control. Eagleton says, "The sad truth is that rent controls—enacted for the best of motives to protect middle and low-income tenants—actually work against the very people they were designed to aid. Washington's rent control program has driven apartment owners, large and small, out of business.... A government worker who owns four rental units told our committee how he went to the rent commission on his lunch hour, intending to register his modest properties quickly. Instead, he was given 15 pages of forms which were so complex he had to seek legal help to complete them."[15]

In late 1977, the District voted to extend controls for three more years. In 1978, rents may increase from 2 to 10 percent, in 1979 and in 1980, rents will be tied to the CPI.

Maryland

Several communities adopted and then phased out local rent controls. Prince George County permitted rents to increase by 10 percent. Since the market, at the time of controls, would not absorb a 10 percent rent increase, the controls in question did not result in an overall reduction in rent and, therefore, served no economic function for most renters.[16]

Florida

Miami Beach enacted a local rent control law, but after extensive lobbying in 1977, the City Council permitted the law to lapse. A move was started to place the measure before the voters as an initiative. However, the State legislature passed an enabling bill that made controls much less desirable.

In 1976, the Florida legislature passed a bill which held rent control to be a statewide concern and it could not therefore be enacted by a local government. This was vetoed by the Governor.

In 1977, the legislature passed a law allowing any community to enact rent legislation for one year—given a court finding of a housing emergency. The municipality could control only those units renting for less than $250 per month.[17] This removed the ability of middle and upper-income tenants to lower their rents through local controls and has effectively eliminated any immediate move toward rent control.

California

Prior to the Proposition 13 (Jarvis/Gann) election in June 1978, no apartments in California were continuously subject to local rent controls, except for a Stamford, Connecticut, type of control for mobile homes in one small town.

Significantly, a series of local rent control intitiative elections were defeated by the voters in this period, and city councils had continually refused to enact such legislation. The pre-Jarvis/Gann history is as follows:

- *Berkeley*
  In 1972, Berkeley became the first California community in the post-World War II period to enact a rent control law. The proposal was rejected by the City Council but enacted via an initiative vote of 27,000 to 25,000 at the height of the antiwar student protests. An injunction prohibiting enforcement was granted, and the case worked its way through the courts. In June 1976, the State Supreme Court, in the *Birkenfeld* case, ruled that although the specific Berkeley law was unconstitutional, there was nothing in existing state law to prevent a local community from controlling rents, as long as they permitted some undefined fair return. Stated the Court:

  > "It is suggested that the existence of a serious public emergency should be constitutionally required for rent controls because they create uncertainty about returns from capital investment in rental housing and thereby

discourage construction or improvement of rental units, exacerbate any rental housing shortage, and so adversely affect the community at large. Such considerations go to the wisdom of rent controls and not to their constitutionality. In determining the validity of a legislative measure under the police power *our sole concern is with whether the measure reasonably relates to a legitimate governmental purpose and 'we must not confuse reasonableness in this context with wisdom.' "* (emphasis added)[18]

In April 1977, a new rent control scheme was presented to the Berkeley voters. It was opposed by the League of Women Voters, the Berkeley Black Council, as well as a large number of individuals and groups within the industry. Over 1,000 individuals worked in the campaign against rent control. Not only was the initiative defeated by 21,000 to 14,000, even though ⅔ of the Berkeley housing units are rentals, but every candidate for city office (four, including one very popular incumbent) and every school board candidate who endorsed rent control was defeated. Both winners and losers agreed that this measure was the deciding issue in all the elective positions.*

- *Palo Alto*
  In 1974, this Stanford University town defeated a rent control initiative by three to one. Early polls indicated that homeowners were indifferent and that the measure would pass. But the local NAACP opposed it on the grounds that, if passed, there would be a greater shortage of rental units which would make it easier for property owners to discriminate.

- *San Diego*
  In 1977, a compulsory arbitration rent control plan, similar to that adopted in Stamford, Connecticut was presented to the City Council. Only two out of nine council

---

*The Fraser Institute's *Rent Control: A Popular Paradox* was reported as influential in this campaign.—Ed.

members supported it. Proponents filed a notice of intent to circulate petitions for an election but failed to collect enough valid signatures for a 1978 election.

- *Los Angeles*
  During 1977, a Los Angeles City Councilman proposed a local rent plan. At a final committee vote in the spring of 1978, rent control along with an antispeculation proposal was filed (i.e., killed) by two to one. At that time the Mayor had indicated that rent control would be a disaster and that he would not support such controls. When brought to the council, rent control received six out of eight votes needed for the city attorney to draft a proposal. As of the June 1978 elections, petitions were being circulated for a May 1979 election.

- *Long Beach*
  In January 1978, an effort began to qualify rent control. It was unsuccessful.

- *Cotati*
  In March 1978, this small community of 2,000 voters adjacent to Sonoma State University held a rent control election. It failed by a vote of 501 to 415.

- *Seaside*
  In this community of 30,000 adjacent to Monterey, an unsuccessful attempt was made to qualify a rent control initiative for the June 1978 election. Proponents argued that they would attempt another effort if Proposition 13, the Jarvis/Gann initiative, passed in the June election.

- *Santa Barbara*
  In June 1978, the voters of Santa Barbara defeated rent control by 62 percent to 38 percent. Santa Barbara is the home of the training camp for Jane Fonda's and Tom Hayden's political organization, the Council for Economic Democracy—one of the statewide organizations which views housing as a "right" and wishes to convert the housing industry into a public utility.

- *Santa Monica*

  In the fall of 1977, a signature drive to qualify an initiative in this community was started. Success was expected, as 80 percent of the dwelling units are rentals and 70 percent of the voters are tenants. As of January 1978, much to everyone's surprise, it was nowhere near qualifying, and its leader threatened to stop participating. The Hayden organization took over leadership of this rent control drive and qualified the initiative. But in June, the voters astonishingly defeated the proposal by a vote of 55 percent to 45 percent.

On 6 June, with the passage of the Jarvis/Gann initiative, the politics of rent control in California abruptly changed. Proposition 13, which was passed by a two-to-one margin in a statewide election, limits property taxes to 1 percent of the 1975 assessed fair market value if a property had not changed hands since 1975, or to 1 percent of the sales value if the property is resold. Most homeowners expected that the passage of Jarvis/Gann would result in an initial 60 percent reduction in current property taxes.

While renters were not specifically mentioned, Jarvis himself, and his supporters implied that passage would result in substantial and immediate rent reductions. For a number of reasons, not the least of which is the unresolved constitutionality of Jarvis/Gann, rents continued to increase at the same rate as before the election.

Newspapers ran front page stories and editorial cartoons of landlords refusing to immediately share the expected future Jarvis/Gann savings. Since Jarvis is the head of a small apartment trade association, many who voted for the initiative were angry at landlords for their seeming duplicity.

The outcome of this surge of illwill toward landlords was a six-month rent freeze enacted by the Los Angeles City Council at the end of August 1978 and a series of initiative elections in San Francisco, Berkeley, Palo Alto, Santa Cruz, and Davis in Northern California. No one, supporters or opponents, fully understands the long-term implications of Jarvis/Gann for rent control in California.

It is interesting to note that Milton Friedman was a

principal spokesperson for the Jarvis/Gann proposal. He argued that the reduction in property tax costs would make apartments more valuable and thereby attract more investment for new construction, but he did not consider the political importance of the no-growth movement or the latent forces supporting rent control.

Rent control elsewhere

In 1976, rent control was defeated for the second time in two years in East Lansing, Michigan, home of Michigan State University. In 1977, an initiative was defeated by a six-to-one vote in Madison, Wisconsin, which is both a university town (one-third of the voters are students at the University of East Lansing) and the state capital. An effort has been made to put an initiative on the ballot in New Orleans, but the courts have ruled that the specific proposal was unconstitutional. In 1977, in Chicago the mayor set up a special committee to study rent control which reported that it was unworkable. A Seattle City Council, in 1977, rejected a similar enactment. Currently, the Philadelphia City Council has asked for a study of rent control.

The federal government

The Department of Housing & Urban Development (HUD) is the agency with the most impact on rent control. With its spread to New Jersey, Massachusetts, and elsewhere, HUD found itself in the position of granting permission for greater increases than the local rent control boards. In 1975, Regulation 403 was issued, which states that HUD will set or pre-empt the rents on any building it owns or subsidizes with below-market interest rates. HUD furthermore reserves the right to pre-empt the local rent control board on any building it insures.[19] This pre-emption has been upheld in federal courts in Massachusetts, New Jersey, and New York. In 1976, the Carter administration indicated it would retain the pre-emption regulation. Pro-rent control congressmen from New York and New Jersey have indicated they would attempt to legislate a congressional reversal of federal pre-emption.

THE FUTURE OF RENT CONTROL
IN THE UNITED STATES

There are many tenant organizers and property owners who believe that political pressures are such that rent control is inevitable. The former believe such controls will herald a bright new day, and the latter wonder who will invest in new rental units or maintain existing ones.

Given the evidence presented elsewhere in this book, it is hard to imagine that elected officials and voters would decide to experiment again and again with a program that aggravates our real housing problems. The real question that has to be decided is whether we base our political decision for or against rent control on the known effects of such programs or on the emotional desire to find some "free fix" to lower rental housing costs to the consumer.

If the decision is made at the city council level, it is easier to see why rent controls might be adopted. Los Angeles has over 600,000 rental units, and, if even 1 percent of tenants decide to demand controls, the council would have to face over 6,000 angry voters. If as few as 5 percent of the tenants of a major city should decide to attend a council meeting, the political pressures might be overwhelming.

But the situation is not hopeless. Local elections in California, Michigan, Wisconsin, and elsewhere have shown that rent control can be defeated even in the so-called radical communities, or in ones with large student or tenant majorities.

The questions that must be asked of anyone suggesting rent control are:

- Can we improve the housing of tenants, particularly low-income tenants, without building more rental units?

- Would rent control encourage or discourage construction of private rental units?

- Do we want, and can we expect, the government to provide rental units?

- Would he or she want personal or parents' savings or pension fund invested in rent controlled housing?

- If he or she owned a rent controlled building, what would be done to maintain it?

Proponents of rent control can count on widespread hostility toward landlords. The case against rent control is based only on the economic reality of how housing is built and managed. Whether the voters will decide on dreams or reality remains to be seen.

EPILOGUE

The above paper was written in the Fall of 1978. By the Fall of 1979, the political situation had changed dramatically.

First some facts. Rents in the United States were still at bargain basement rates. The Consumer Price Index for August 1979 showed the following changes listed in Table 1:

TABLE 1
CONSUMER PRICE INDEX, SELECTED ITEMS—
MAY-AUGUST 1979

	August 1979	May 1979	% Change
	1967 = 100		
All items	221	193	15
Food	236	209	13
Medical Care	241	217	11
Home Ownership	268	221	21
Rents	178	162	10

Source: US Department of Labor, Bureau of Labor Statistics, *Monthly Labor Review.*

Tenants, at least in California, recognized that rents were still a bargain. Notwithstanding the constant media attack on landlords for not sharing the Jarvis-Gann property tax savings with tenants, a statewide poll by Mervin Field in June 1979 found that *73 percent of tenants believed that their own rents were fair.* However, perhaps in response to the constant media reporting of large individual rent increases, 81 percent of tenants felt that rents, in general, were unfair. Interestingly, 56 percent of the entire population, renters and homeowners, favored some form of rent regulation.[20]

In the Fall 1978 rent control elections in California, San Francisco, Palo Alto, and Santa Cruz rejected rent control. Voters of the university communities of Davis and Berkeley approved a one year control that covered both commercial and residential rents. (The rejected San Francisco and Palo Alto measures also included commercial rent control.)

During the Spring and Summer of 1979, voters in Santa Cruz (for the second time), Hayward, Milpitas, and Salinas rejected rent control initiatives. Santa Monica voters approved a rent control measure.

The Davis initiative was declared unconstitutional. The Berkeley law was in the courts in the Fall of 1979, but it was due to expire prior to a decision. The Santa Monica situation was under litigation.

In Santa Monica, an elected board was authorized to establish a rent control system, that is, the initiative itself gave no guidance on what would be permitted. The courts thus faced the likelihood of having to decide the Santa Monica case based on the action of the rent control board and not on the law itself. Meanwhile, individuals concerned with preserving rental housing in Santa Monica qualified a new initiative that would significantly limit the powers of the rent control board.

It was not by accident that there were a growing number of rent control elections in California by late 1979. In November 1978, Tom Hayden had told a statewide meeting of neighborhood organizers that the radical strategy should be to force endless initiative elections and to "bleed" the rental industry into submission.

City officials in three of the state's major cities, Los Angeles, San Francisco, and San Jose, adopted one year rent regulation systems during this period. All of these proposals permitted increases of at least 7 percent to tenants in place and no control for the initial rent of a new tenant. In Los Angeles a landlord needed permission to increase rents above the permitted rates, and in San Francisco a tenant could request arbitration for an increase above the permitted amount.

While these council initiated rent controls would not by themselves cause irreparable damage to the private rental sector, the apartment owners, quite justifiably, were concerned with what would come next. Rent control advocate Richard Blumberg, writing in the July-August 1979 issue of the *Housing Law Bulletin*, indicated that the Los Angeles regulation was unacceptable. In particular, he opposed turnover decontrol and permitting rent increases without cost certification.[21]

In San Francisco a group of rent control advocates qualified an initiative that would not only destroy the viability of existing rental housing but would also attempt to eliminate the local redevelopment agency. These advocates wished to fund a series of new neighborhood development corporations with the money currently allocated to the redevelopment agency.

A group in San Francisco had put together an anthology on housing which indicated favored directions for the rent control movement. We were told that,

"other longer range state measures worthy of support... include a freeze on land values and the forced sale of larger land holdings to reduce the land costs, the formation of a state bank lending public monies.... At the federal level, low-income housing construction programs need to be revived, [with]...the nationalization of the country's housing stock [and] lifetime tenure guaranteed to current residents."[22]

A statewide group of mobile home coach owners attempted unsuccessfully to qualify a statewide mandatory four year rent control measure for all residential rents. If this measure had passed, any rent increase greater than one-half of the CPI could have been challenged in court by a tenant.

Needless to say there were very few lenders currently willing to finance new private rental units in California. At one conference, a savings and loan executive stated that until the local rent control issue was resolved, a lender would have to be out of his mind to make a new loan on a rent development in California. Even Governor Brown in his 1979 *Economic Report* recognized the problem. The Governor reported,

"Although the present amount of rent regulations in effect in the California housing market is relatively small, the specter of future controls is already having an impact. Many builders are shying away from multiple unit construction because of the potential of regulation. During 1979, multiple unit construction is expected to fall about 35 to 40 percent of all residential construction, versus about 47 percent normally, partly due to rent regulation fears. Some existing owners of rental units are converting the units into condominiums for sale, partly to avoid the rent regulation problem. Thus, rent controls are not only having a direct impact in a few California communities, but an indirect effect on statewide construction and operation of rental housing."[23]

Given this new post-Proposition 13 political reality, the providers of rental housing in California reviewed their options. The choices seemed to be:

- Give up; sell to uninformed and/or high risk investors; and start a program of disinvestment.

- Continue to oppose every local rent control initiative and hope that in the process the industry would not be "bled" to death.

- Attempt once more to enact some sort of prohibition of local option rent control.

- Attempt to find a compromise solution that would alleviate some of the tenants' fears of possible future unacceptable rent increases while not destroying the private rental housing sector.

For better or for worse, the developers, owners, lenders, and construction trades opted to try to find a compromise. In 1979, this industry wide coalition drafted a state constitutional amendment that if adopted by the voters in 1980 would:

- Permit local rent control for four-year periods if each enactment is ratified by local voters.

- Permit local rent regulation boards to arbitrate rent increases to tenants in place if requested and if the rent increase is greater than the rate of inflation as measured by the CPI.

- Prohibit any regulation of rentals built after adoption of the state amendment.

Industry lenders believe that these state guidelines would prevent disinvestment in existing rental units and encourage investment in needed new construction.

Elsewhere in the country, the New Jersey State Supreme Court in the Helmsley case declared unconstitutional the then current Fort Lee rent control law permitting 2.5 percent annual rent control increases.[24] While the court sidetracked once more the "fair return" issue, it did indicate that if it ever got around to deciding what the terms "fair return" meant, it would have to take into consideration the effects of inflation on measuring return.

The New Jersey court in the Helmsley case stated that a city could have as restrictive a rent control measure as it wanted. In order to prevent confiscation, however, the more restrictive the law, the more sophisticated and elaborate must be the hardship mechanism. Since the Fort Lee law did not pass muster on this requirement, it was unacceptable. The court said:

"A municipality can constitutionally enact rent control ordinances with stringent controls like Fort Lee's. If it does so, however, it must be prepared to protect landlords' interests by providing prompt, fair, and efficacious administrative relief. Conversely, if a municipality is not prepared to support a sophisticated administrative relief system, it must adopt a more moderate rent control scheme, one which does not attempt to keep landlords' returns at the constitutional minimum."[25]

Supporters of the California fair rents guideline initiative took comfort in the closing comments of the Helmsley decision, in which the court asks for statewide guidelines. The court ended with the statement that "rent control implicates complex economic, social, and political issues. The state legislature is better equipped than most municipalities to formulate a comprehensive approach to this delicate problem. In conclusion, we endorse the New York Court of Appeals' discussion of legislative and judicial roles in rent regulation:

"...the [rent control] legislation contains serious gaps, not readily filled by interpretation based on intention, because there was none, or even by judicial construction to make reasonable and workable schemes that are self-abortive as designed. There is a limit to which courts may or should go in rectifying such statutory gaps.... Ultimate resolution requires correction at the legislative level, state or local, and not at the judicial level. The courts have limited access to the controlling economic and social facts. They are also limited by a decent respect for the separation of powers upon which our system of government is based."[26]

Immediately after the Helmsley ruling, Fort Lee activated a new rent control measure that permitted rent increases of 1.9 percent! Fort Lee property owners attempted to get the US Supreme Court to review the whole issue, but this was rejected on the ground that there was no federal constitutional issue at stake.

In a similar ruling on 26 April 1979, the Florida Supreme Court overturned a statewide mobile home rent control law on grounds that various sections "are constitutionally defective because they charge the commission with the fundamental legislative task of striking this balance between mobile home park owners and mobile home park tenant, without any meaningful guidance."[27]

Around the country in a growing number of cities, the issue of rent control was beginning at this time to be discussed and evaluated. In typical American fashion, both proponents and opponents organized national associations to explain and argue their positions. In typical American fashion, both proponents and opponents believed that their side would prevail if only they could explain to the apathetic majority the righteousness of their position. In typical American fashion, we were grouping for an acceptable political consensus.

NOTES

1 One of the best articles in defence of rent control is "The Social Utility of Rent Control" by Emily Paradise Achtenberg in Jon Pynoos et. al., eds., *Housing Urban America* (Chicago: Aldine, 1973). Achtenberg writes (p. 447), "If housing controls which are necessary to protect tenants serve to expedite the ongoing process of disinvestment by the private sector, then new forms of public subsidization, ownership, and financing must be created to take its place. To the extent that any system of housing controls can facilitate these needed changes in the housing system, its social utility is that much enhanced."

2 Ernest van den Haag, "Economics is not Enough—Notes on the Anticapitalist Spirit," *The Public Interest* (Fall 1976).

3 Chester Hartman, in "The Big Squeeze," *Politics Today* (May/June 1978): says: "The value of rent control, apart from the progressive income transfers it effectuates, is that it is an immediate gut issue around which people can organize. As they work to improve their own housing conditions, their consciousness is raised about the workings of the housing system; the demands they make on the system as a whole are sharpened. As tenant activists in New York City and elsewhere now see, the issues transcend the individual evil landlord."

4 The May 1978, Consumer Price Index reported that all items of the index had increased to 193 percent of the 1967 base year; home

ownership had increased to 221 percent, food had increased to 209 percent, medical care to 217 percent, and rent to only 162 percent.

5 For the best discussion on the legal and economic mess in New Jersey see *Helmsley vs Fort Lee*, Supreme Court of New Jersey, 13719, September Term 1977, Findings and Determinations, 1 March 1978. Judge Harvey Smith states: "This chapter of the Fort Lee rent control saga takes place along the razor's edge which separates stringent government regulation from unlawful confiscation."

6 "End Rent Control," *New York Amsterdam News*, 1 May 1976.

7 The reduction in assessed value of rentals due to rent control is cited in the Findings and Determination of the *Helmsley* case (note 5 supra) and in *Birkenfeld vs Berkeley*, Memorandum of Decision, Superior Court of California, Alameda, 14 May 1973, which states,

"There was considerable testimony by various experts that the value of an apartment house complex was fixed generally by a formula of seven times gross receipts. There was testimony indicating that since rent control was voted in Berkeley (in November 1972), the multiple has gone down to five and is declining. The County Assessor is bound by law to appraise property at its fair market value. If the value of Berkeley rental property is reducing by one-third to one-fourth, and there is no reduction in city services, and the need for tax revenue does not, therefore, diminish, it is plain to see that either the tax rate will have to increase or non-controlled properties will have to be appraised upward, or both. And, in any event, a heavier burden will fall on all Berkeley property owners."

Mathematically, a 25 percent reduction in the assessment of Berkeley apartments in buildings of four or more units would have resulted in a 7 percent increase in the tax rate. Joseph Eckert in his Ph.D. thesis, "The Effect of Rent Controls on Assessment Practices, Differential Incidence of Taxation, and Income Adjustment Mechanisms for Rental Housing in Brookline, Massachusetts" (Tufts University, 1977) found that even though the tax abatement (tax reduction) was equal to rent reduction to tenants, homeowners did not receive a tax increase due to the fact that 5 percent of the rental stock converted to condominiums and raised the total tax base.

8 The law seems clear that one cannot constitutionally target the benefits of rent control. *Property Owners Association vs Township of North Bergin*, Supreme Court of New Jersey, A-148, September Term 1976, Decided 12 September 1977, says:

"We reiterate that under its police power a municipality may in the interests of the general welfare enact ordinances to assist senior citizens, provided the relationship between the purposes and the classification is rational and sound and there is not an undue taking of property of others which amounts to constitutional confiscation. A legislative category of economically needy senior citizens is sound, proper and sustainable as a rational classification. But compelled subsidization by landlords or by tenants who happen to live in an apartment building with senior citizens is an improper and unconstitutional method of solving the problem."

9 "Report on The New York City Loan Program," Committee on Banking, Housing and Urban Affairs, United States Senate, Report 94-900, 17 May 1976.

10 The best sociological-legal review of rent control in New Jersey is "Rent Control in the 1970's: the Case of the New Jersey Tenants' Movement," Kenneth Baar, *Hastings Law Journals* 28, no 3 (January 1977). Baar, a proponent of controls, reports

"the suburban middle-class character of New Jersey tenants' movement has also played a significant role in its success. The New Jersey suburbs of New York City have a high percentage of middle income tenants who are accustomed to voting and having their desires met. Furthermore, many New Jersey tenants, unlike tenants in other parts of the country, have benefited from rent control as former New York residents. Their strength has been compounded by the fact that they tend to live in newer, larger apartment complexes which are easier to organize than small buildings. A fifth of the tenants in a three hundred-unit apartment complex can lead a demonstration which will seem large and receive publicity. A fifth of the tenants in a ten-unit building could not form a crowd."

11 See *Helmsley vs Fort Lee*, op. cit. "The cumulative effect of the 2-2½ percent limitation (on rent increases), the tax surcharge repealor and the R.B (rent leveling board) hardship formula, applied to the fiscal facts adduced during the remand hearing, renders the entire Fort Lee rent control mechanism confiscatory and invalid. The CPI (rent increase) limitation remains in effect." As of September 1978 the state Supreme Court had not ruled on this crucial lower court finding. In Massachusetts, in *Niles vs Boston Rent Control,* 1978 Massachusetts Appellate Court, Advance Sheets, 240, the court ruled that the burden of proof of confiscation rested with the individual property owner. Pro-rent control lawyers are hoping for New Jersey Supreme Court adoption of this Massachusetts approach; they want to avoid the treacherous waters of fair return theory.

12 In *A Case for Rent Control* (Lexington, Mass.: Lexington Books, 1976), Herbert Selesnick, Harbridge House, Inc., claims: "The statistical evidence and local administrative experience analyzed in this study indicate that there is no sound justification for allowing the expiration of Chapter 842 (the rent control enabling legislation)."

13 Testimony Given to the House Committee on Local Affairs, Massachusetts Legislature, 21 March 1975.

14 "Report of the Mayor's Committee on Rent Control," submitted to the Honorable Kevin H. White, Mayor, City of Boston, September 1977.

15 Senator Thomas F. Eagleton, "Why Rent Controls Don't Work," *Reader's Digest* (August 1977).

16 Sayra Walls Meyerhoff, "Rent Control in Maryland in the 1970's," unpublished paper.

17 Florida Rent Control Bill, May 1977, CS/SB 403.

18 *Birkenfeld vs Berkeley*, Supreme Court of California, SF 23370 on 16 June 1976.

19 Part 403, Local Rent Control, Federal Register, Vol. 40, no. 205, 22 October 1975.
20 Mervin D. Field, "Poll Finds Californians Support Rent Control," *Sacramento Bee*, 13 June 1979.
21 *Housing Law Bulletin*, National Housing Law Project, Berkeley, July-August 1979. This newsletter is edited and to a large degree written by Richard Blumberg. Blumberg helped write and defend the early New Jersey rent control laws. The Housing Law Project is a national clearing house for various federally funded legal programs.
22 Jim Shock, ed., *Where Has All the Housing Gone?* (San Francisco: New American Movement, 1979), p. 5.
23 *Economic Report of the Governor 1979*, Richard T. Silberman, Director of Finance, State of California, 26 March 1979, p. 75.
24 *Helmsley vs Fort Lee*, Supreme Court of New Jersey, A-163/164/165/166/167, September Term 1977, Opinion filed 17 October 1978.
25 *Ibid*, p. 69.
26 *Ibid*, pp. 70-71. The New York citation is 89 *Christopher Inc. vs Joy* 35 N.Y. 2d 213, 318 N.E. 2d 776, 780-81 (1974).
27 *Dept. of Business Regulation vs National Manufactured Housing Federation, Inc.,* Case no. 53,065, *The Florida Law Weekly,* 4/27/79, p. 183.

Part Two
The Theory of
Rent Control

Chapter Two
A Short Course
in Housing Economics

M.A. WALKER

2. Bomb Damage or Rent Control? See page 320 for the answer.

THE AUTHOR

MICHAEL A. WALKER is Director of the Fraser Institute. Born in Newfoundland in 1945, he received his B.A. (Summa) at St. Francis Xavier University in 1966 and his Ph.D. in Economics at the University of Western Ontario in 1969. From 1969 to 1973, he worked in various research capacities at the Bank of Canada, Ottawa, and when he left in 1973 was Research Officer in charge of the Special Studies and Monetary Policy Group in the Department of Banking. Immediately prior to joining the Fraser Institute, Dr. Walker was Econometric Model Consultant to the Federal Department of Finance, Ottawa. Dr. Walker has also taught Monetary Economics and Statistics at the University of Western Ontario and Carleton University.

Dr. Walker was editor of, and a contributor to, nine of the Fraser Institute's previous books: *Rent Control—A Popular Paradox* (1975); *The Illusion of Wage and Price Control* (1976); *How Much Tax Do You Really Pay?* (1976); *Which Way Ahead? Canada After Wage and Price Control* (1977); *Public Property? The Habitat Debate Continued* (1977, with Lawrence B. Smith); *Oil in the Seventies: Essays on Energy Policy* (1977, with G. Campbell Watkins); *Unemployment Insurance: Global Evidence of its Effects on Unemployment* (1978, with Herbert G. Grubel); *Canadian Confederation at the Crossroads: The Search for a Federal-Provincial Balance* (1979) and *Tax Facts* (1979, with Sally C. Pipes).

Dr. Walker is a regular economic commentator on national television and radio and, in addition, addresses university students and a large number of service and professional organizations on Canadian public policy issues.

Chapter Two
A Short Course
in Housing Economics

M.A. WALKER

*Director,
The Fraser Institute*

Rent control is a form of price fixing that increases the shortage of housing and ultimately reduces the ability of tenants to choose where and under what conditions they live.

Rent control is a form of tenant protection adopted because housing is a basic need like sunshine and fresh air and its provision ought not to be left to the vagaries of the marketplace.

Not surprisingly, what rent control seems to be depends on your point of view. Whatever else rent control is, it is certainly an aspect of economic policy, and in the end it will have effects that depend on people's economic behavior. Rent control, as an aspect of social legislation, cannot avoid the reality that it is, in essence, a form of price control.

This essay provides a framework for the anlaysis of rent control from the economist's point of view. What *is* the economic behavior of citizens as regards housing? How *are* rents determined? What *are* price controls and what effects *do* they have in the short term and in the long term?

THE DEMAND FOR HOUSING SERVICES

What are we talking about?

Some of the confusion that surrounds the discussion of housing market operations arises because a general agreement is not reached by the discussants about the nature of the commodity that is being bought and sold. So, let's first consider the notion of housing as a consumer product.[1]

Houses and apartments are, in general, demanded because of the services that they provide to the occupant. For instance, housing units provide shelter, privacy, and sanitary and other amenities. They also provide a source of recreation for some people and the facility to support other activities. The demand for houses or apartments is, accordingly, an expression of the demand for the services that housing units provide.

Basic shelter

It is often said that everyone has a right to decent housing, but the meaning of this sentence is elusive. To some it means that everyone should have protection from the elements. To many others decent housing involves more than basic shelter. In fact:

"There are no absolute and universal standards of housing, and it is impossible to develop such standards. For one thing, the specific requirements which need to be met in order to safeguard health and to insure a given standard of comfort vary greatly in different climates and locations; and, more important, what is regarded as an adequate standard of comfort will be determined according to local customs and local levels of income, and in response to long-term increases in real income and changes in taste and social conscience. It is easy to list the considerations that should be taken into account in determining housing standards.... To translate such a list of principles into terms of living space and facilities is a different matter. In fact, there are nearly as many housing standards as there are investigations into housing requirements."[2]

Very few housing units in the private sector are built as basic shelter. The vast majority are built as basic shelter *plus* some level of convenience or extra amenities. It is largely on the basis of the quantity of the latter that the price or rent is established. This is because the extras yield a flow of services to the occupant, either in the form of direct convenience or in the form of social prestige. The level of services provided by a given housing unit usually falls as the unit gets older, rises as renovations are made, and varies as external factors such as neighborhood conditions change. (Freeways are a modern example of such external factors.) A given housing unit is thus capable of producing a varying amount of housing services.

To take a commonplace example: the decision of a landlord to paint or wallpaper a room actually constitutes a decision to increase the flow of housing services from a given housing unit. Although this may be difficult to accept at first sight, the truth of it can be quickly seen in the fact that a newly painted apartment attracts a higher rent than an identical one that has not been decorated.

Wants and the law of demand

The desire to have access to housing is one of an almost unlimited number of human wants. The process by which wants are satisfied constitutes the general subject matter of economics. The *want* for housing services becomes the *demand* for housing services as soon as an individual has made a *choice* to spend some of his income to acquire housing services. Of course, there is no choice but to demand the basic shelter that is required to sustain life. The question of choice relates to how much more than the basics people will demand, given their income.

The decision to acquire some housing services is realized when a person rents (or buys) a particular housing unit. In essence, this reflects a decision about how much housing services that person requires or desires. Housing units of comparable size naturally yield very different flows of services because of location, age, built-in amenities, and so on, and they will bear rents (or prices) that reflect these differences. Each level of housing services has a cost associated with it and, in general, the higher the level of service the higher the rent (or purchase price).

Status-faction

Since most of us have a limited income, we must choose between alternative uses of that income. Aside from satisfying a basic need for shelter, housing perhaps provides recreation, possibly a claim to social standing, and often a level of convenience to facilitate other activities. Even the most casual examination of current housing use would suggest that "basic need" motivation is by far the smaller part in determining the effective demand for housing. This fact was noted nearly a century ago by one of the fathers of economic theory, Alfred Marshall:

> "House room satisfies the imperative need for shelter from the weather; but that need plays very little part in the effective demand for house room.... Relatively large and well-appointed house room is...at once a 'necessity for efficiency' and the most convenient and obvious way of advancing a material claim to social distinction."[3]

We can assume, then, that most of the characteristics of housing services are close competitors for other things in the typical family budget.[4] The need for status can perhaps be satisfied by buying a fancy car, a fancy boat, or a fancy house or apartment unit, depending on the person's preferences and lifestyle. The range and variability of preferences is well-illustrated by the fact that in certain circles "status-faction" flows from driving a much smaller and less expensive car than one's income could comfortably support. Recreation can flow from the facilities provided in a house or apartment, holiday trips, pub crawling, bowling nights, television, or movies. The choice that is made will depend on an individual's preferences, his total income, the price of housing services, and the price of other things.[5]

Summary

All of the foregoing has been in aid of isolating several important characteristics about the demand for housing services:

- The demand for housing services *over and above* the minimum standard will be determined by income, the price of housing services, and the prices of goods that compete with housing.

- The existence of legal minimum housing quality standards reduces the choice of some consumers, because the minimum standard may well be above the basic shelter requirement of some consumers.[6]

- The need for shelter is only one of the determinants of the demand for housing; the wants for social standing, recreation, and other things play an equally important role in determining demand.

THE SUPPLY OF HOUSING SERVICES

Current supply

The economics of the supply of housing are similar to the economics of capital intensive industries like smelting, refining or paper manufacturing. In order to sell housing services in a given year, a landlord must make a housing unit available. Whether this involves an existing structure, the renovation of an existing structure, or the construction of a new building, it always entails a large capital investment and, hence, a high capital-output ratio. (That is, the cost of a housing unit is high relative to current gross rents, which are a rough measure of "output.")

In addition to capital, the provision of housing services

entails various current costs that amount to about one-third of the total: the wages of labor (for maintenance and janitorial services), materials (oil, gas, paint, and so on) and managerial and entrepreneurial talents. The supplier/ landlord also incurs a property tax cost that is related, more or less, to the amount of housing service that he produces.[7]

Because the supply of housing is provided from a *fixed number* of houses or apartments at a given time, there is a natural tendency to regard the supply of housing services as fixed in the short run. That this is not strictly true, however, can be inferred from the fact that roughly 38 percent of the costs incurred in the provision of rental housing are current costs unrelated to the provision or maintenance of capital.[8] Thus it is possible for the supply of housing services to fall to some extent, even in the short run.[9] It is not as obvious that the supply can be very greatly increased, but some increase is possible. Lower average vacancy rates amount to increased production of services—that is, more intensive utilization of the stock—as do increases in services and amenities and reconstruction or decoration of existing suites. The proliferation of "basement suites" in tight housing markets is a case in point.

An interesting example of the extent to which the supply of housing services can rise in the short run under the pressure of events is to be found in Milton Friedman and George Stigler's analysis of the San Francisco earthquake of 1906 reprinted in this volume. During the three days that the tremors and fires lasted, the city lost about half of its housing units. And, even though there was a substantial exodus of people from the city, the half of the housing stock that survived the earthquake had for many months to absorb about a fifth of the population in addition to former inhabitants. In other words, each house had to provide shelter for about 40 percent more people than it had before the earthquake!

Increases in the supply of housing services also depend on increases in the basic stock of housing units. Investment in housing units in turn depends on a variety of factors, only some of which are determined in the housing market. In the next section, therefore, we identify some of the elements that appear to determine the level of housing investment.

Investment in housing units

There is a supply of housing services generated in the private sector because investment in the production of housing services yields an attractive rate of return. In order to isolate the principles involved we will consider the position of a landlord (or a prospective landlord) at a particular point in time. He will ask:

• What will the building cost?

• What will the market rents be during its lifetime (assuming that the property can be rented at the market rent)?

• What will the variable costs be?

• What rate of return could be realized on some other form of investment?

• What tax policy will apply in the calculation of net income tax payable on income from the investment?

Considerable uncertainty surrounds the answers to these questions. For example, the landlord must forecast the future demand and supply of the particular kind of units that he is proposing to build. In making these forecasts, landlords rely in part on their past experience and in part on hunches about future developments.

Having determined that a demand for the units might exist the landlord must then calculate prospects for the rate of return on the investment. Most often this calculation is based on current costs and current rents. A critical variable in this calculation is the rate of interest that must be paid to obtain mortgage funds. If it seems likely that the provision of more housing services will yield a profit, the landlord must then compare the net after-tax return on his equity (the downpayment) with the return he could get from other investments. Two special factors have influenced this comparison in the past: prospects for capital gain and tax deferments.

The change in capital value is the difference between the purchase price and the selling price of an asset. The price at which a residential structure will sell is determined by the discounted value of the future stream of net income that it will yield.[10] If there has been a recent record of such gains being realized, a landlord might well take this into account in calculating the prospective rate of return on his investment.

The opportunity for tax deferment arises to the extent that capital consumption allowances can be charged against total income and to the extent that the landlord has income from other sources. Thus, for example, some professional people with large incomes became landlords prior to 1971, simply because the capital consumption allowances, then permitted under Canadian Federal tax law, could be used to reduce their current tax liability.[11] In 1971, the tax law was changed to prevent the use of investment in rental accommodation as a tax deferral device.

Having made the calculation of the probable after-tax return on his capital, the landlord would then compare this return to those available on comparable investments. If a comparison between the rate of return on investment in housing and that on, say, long-term government bonds is made, the landlord would have to take into account the fact that housing investment involves greater risk and greater effort than investment in government bonds.

All of the foregoing discussion has been couched in terms of prospective additions to the rental housing stock. It is clear, however, that the outcome of the financial arithmetic might be a decision not to invest or a decision to convert existing rental housing to other uses. One method of conversion that has become popular in recent years is the sale of apartments as condominiums. A combination of consumer acceptance and the development of legal provisions has made this possible.

SOME REMARKS ON OWNER-OCCUPIERS AS LANDLORD-TENANTS

The market for housing is formed by the interaction of

supply behavior with demand behavior. In Canada, six out of ten dwellings are owner occupied.[12] So, in 60 percent of cases, both the supply and the demand for housing services come from the owner-occupier who is, in effect, his own landlord. Although there are differences in demand between owner-occupants and tenants, due to the psychic satisfaction from home ownership, and differences between landlords and tenants as suppliers of housing services, due to the income tax treatment of home ownership, these are not important for an analysis of rent control.

RENTS

The price of houses, like that of other expensive, durable commodities such as automobiles, is difficult to analyze—particularly over a period of time. In most other markets the price is readily observable and relatively easy to analyze. To take an everyday example, the price of bread in 1975 is readily observable and can easily be compared with the price of bread in 1950—the product hasn't changed.

A rent, however, is the result of multiplying a given set of housing characteristics by the price of each of these characteristics. Accordingly, a change in rents can reflect either a change in the price of some of the characteristics or a change in the composition of the set.[13]

The difficulties become obvious in comparing rents in 1950 and rents in 1975. A two-bedroom apartment in 1975 in a ten-storey apartment building with swimming pool, recreation areas, elevators, underground parking, enclosed fire escape, and so on is clearly different from a two-bedroom apartment in a three-storey walk-up which might have been considered good quality accommodation in 1950. Therefore, it would not be appropriate to compare the rents on these two units without somehow adjusting for the change in their characteristics.

A change in rent on a given housing unit implies a change in the supply-demand conditions for the characteristics of that housing unit. That is, what we have been calling *housing services* amount to characteristics of housing units, and a rent represents some flow of services (or list of

characteristics) multiplied by the price of each characteristic.

For example, location is a very important characteristic of
housing, because it influences the amount of time that
people must spend travelling to and from their place of
work. There is typically a high demand for proximity and,
for this reason, apartments near the activity centre of a city
usually have high rents relative to the amenities supplied.
For the same reason, efficient rapid transit systems usually
have the effect of reducing the price that people must pay
for proximity. That is because rapid transit effectively
increases the supply of apartments within, say, twenty
minutes of the activity centre. Number of bedrooms, height
of building, and proximity to natural environments are
other identifiable characteristics that have a more or less
well-defined price.

As the demand for and supply of these characteristics
rises and falls, the prices of the characteristics change, and
so the rents on the apartments involved change.

In terms of our supply and demand model, then, changes
in the price of housing services that lie behind changes in
rents perform two functions:

- They cause tenants to reassess their demand for housing
  services of all kinds.

- They alter rents on a given sort of housing unit and hence
  lead landlords or prospective landlords to reassess the
  supply of housing services that they bring on the market.

A HOUSING SHORTAGE?

A concept that appears regularly in the debate about
housing is that of a shortage. This concept is sometimes
misused and often confused with the notion of scarcity.
Everything is scarce owing, if not, as we are told, to the
indiscretions of Adam and Eve, then to the nature of things.
There are shortages of very few things.

One of the most remarkable aspects of North American
society is the fact that such a large variety of products is

available in about the right volume. Seldom is it that one hears of a long-standing shortage or surplus of commodities. Notable exceptions to this general rule are those commodities that are the subject of government regulation, are produced by government, or depend upon a resource that is subject to government control.

The principal reason for this remarkable fact is that price movements, in general, are permitted to "clear the market." Just as nature will not permit a vacuum to exist, a market (which is nothing more than the interaction of people wanting to sell and people wanting to buy) will eradicate surpluses and shortages if it is permitted to do so. It does this by "signalling" to consumers and producers, by means of changes in prices, that they should alter their behavior.

The notions of surplus and shortage have meaning only with respect to inappropriate prices. A surplus exists because the price is too high; a shortage exists because the price is too low.

Housing shortages produce rising rents that lead to a *decrease* in the quantity of housing services demanded and an *increase* in the quantity of housing services supplied until the shortage is eliminated. Surplus housing produces falling rents that lead to a reduction in the quantity supplied and an increase in the quantity demanded until the surplus is eliminated.[14]

PRICE CONTROLS

In general, since both shortages and supluses are the result of an inappropriate price, it is not surprising that artificially maintained prices lead to either surpluses or shortages. We are all too familiar with the effects of government price maintenance programs for agricultural producers: surplus eggs, chickens, and wheat have fed newspaper stories and legislative debates for many years. A price held above the equilibrium price (that is, the price that consumers and producers would jointly determine in the absence of controls) is bound to create a surplus. This is because it encourages consumers to demand less and producers to supply more than they would if the price were allowed to fall.

Similarly, a price that is set too low encourages consumers to buy more than they would at a higher price and producers to supply less than they would at a higher price.

A price control is a tax

Another way to look at this result is that if a price is kept low by legislation, the low price becomes, in effect, a tax on the supplier. The amount of the tax is the difference between the controlled price and the market price. The only way the supplier can avoid the tax is by not supplying the commodity or service. On the side of the consumer, the low price amounts to a transfer payment or subsidy which is equal to the difference between the market price and the control price. Furthermore, the more of the product a consumer buys, the larger is the dollar amount of the subsidy. The consumer is, thus, encouraged to buy more of the commodity or service. Can there be any doubt that such a policy, that directly taxes suppliers and gives the proceeds to consumers, leads inevitably to a widening gap between the amount demanded and the amount supplied—that is, a shortage?

That these are always the consequences of price controls follows from simple logic. If a price ceiling was set higher than the market would have determined, then the consumers in the market (who usually provide the political pressure for price ceilings) would certainly not have pressed for the ceiling in the first place. Alternatively, if both consumers and producers would have been willing to do business at a lower price (assuming that the market price was lower) they would simply have done so, and the ceiling price would have become yet another bureaucratic curiosity.

A floor (minimum) price, on the other hand (usually championed by inefficient producers), would not be effective unless it maintained the price above the market price. Certainly if the market price were above the floor price, producers would want to sell at the market price.

In the short run, price controls usually confer benefits on

one side of the market or the other. Price ceilings confer benefits on consumers, while minimum prices (commonly agricultural "support" prices) confer benefits on the producer. In each case the benefit that occurs on one side of the market is at the expense of the people on the other side.

The long-term effects of legislated ceiling prices are seldom directly observable in the case of perishable commodities. This is because effective price ceilings on perishables have never lasted for any length of time. Shortages, caused by control, either create pressures for the abandonment of the control—as happened after World War II—or black markets develop, and the control price becomes inoperative. In the particular case of rent control, the evidence on the long-term effect of control is abundant, largely because housing is durable.

The essays in Part III of this volume provide a wide range of experience with the effects that price control can have in the long term.

SUMMARY

1. The demand for housing services is determined by the wants for social standing and recreation as well as by the need for shelter. Accordingly, family income and the price of housing relative to the price of other things have a substantial impact on the housing demanded.

2. The supply of housing services arises principally from the relatively fixed number of houses or apartments in existence at a particular point in time. However, new construction, renovations (such as basement suites), and a reduction in the average time that apartments stand vacant provide substantial flexibility in the supply of services, even in the short term. The principal determinant of the supply of housing services is the expected rate of return on investment in housing relative to the expected rate of return on comparable investments. Rents are a principal determinant of the rate of return on housing.

3. The notions of "surplus" and "shortage" have meaning only with respect to inappropriate prices. A surplus exists because the price (or rent) is too high; a shortage exists because the price is too low. The concept of shortage is sometimes confused with the notion of "scarcity." Everything is scarce, but there are shortages of very few things.

4. Price control produces shortages because, if the price is kept below the market price, the control becomes, in effect, a tax on the supplier. The amount of the tax is the difference between the market price and the control price. The only way the supplier can avoid the tax is by not supplying the commodity or service. Since the proceeds of the tax are, in effect, given to the consumer, the consumer is encouraged to demand more. Thus, since price control taxes suppliers and gives the proceeds to consumers, it leads inevitably to a widening gap between the amount demanded and the amount supplied—that is, a shortage!

NOTES

1 A similar discussion, though more technical, is to be found in Richard F. Muth, "The Demand for Non-Farm Housing," in *The Demand for Durable Goods*, ed. Arnold C. Harberger (Chicago: University of Chicago Press, 1960).
2 International Labor Office, *Housing and Employment*, Studies and Reports, New Series, No. 8 (Geneva, 1948), p. 9.
3 Alfred Marshall, *Principles of Economics*, 8th ed. (London: Macmillan, 1920), p. 88.
4 The colloquial expression "house poor," for example, describes an individual or family that has displaced most recreation expenditures by committing income to the purchase or maintenance of a house.
5 The point is that the decision concerning expenditure on housing services is inextricably bound up with other expenditure decisions and will necessarily reflect the choices that an individual makes over this

range of expenditures. For example, if the difference between an apartment without a view and one with a view changes from two nights pub crawling to one night, or from ten to five nights bowling, either because pub crawling and bowling become more expensive, or because apartments with a view become cheaper, an individual may decide to move to an apartment with a view. The decision to move would reflect the judgement that an apartment with a view is preferred to one night's pub crawling or five nights bowling, but not preferred to two nights pub crawling or ten nights bowling.

6 An interesting case in point was the confrontation in 1974 between the tenants of apartments in 1601 Comox Street, Vancouver, and the City of Vancouver with regard to a new city ordinance requiring the construction of two covered stairwells or a sprinkler system in the building. The building had satisfied all requirements prior to the new ordinance, which was made retroactive. The tenants unanimously expressed the opinion that they did not feel that the modification was necessary, and that they did not want the added cost in the form of higher rent. The city council rejected the appeal of their landlord, and the tenants will be forced to occupy higher cost (higher standard?) accommodation than they would prefer. Also, since all similar accommodation is affected by the new law, they cannot avoid it by moving.

7 Property taxes are assessed on some appraised value that ultimately depends on rents, and, accordingly, an increased flow of housing services leads to increased taxes.

8 J.G. Cragg, "Rent Control Report," p. 51, Table 2. This report was commissioned by the British Columbia Rentalsman to determine what the "Allowable Rent Increase" under the province's rent control legislation ought to be. Other similar evidence on the current costs associated with the supply of housing services is to be found in L.B. Smith, *Housing in Canada* (Ottawa: Central Mortgage and Housing Corporation, 1971), pp. 16, 17.

9 It is important to distinguish between the *supply* of housing services and the *consumption* of housing services. It is possible, for example, that a landlord's reduction in janitorial services will be offset by the tenant providing more services himself. This clearly represents a reduction in the supply of services but no fall in consumption.

10 That is, since a dollar today is worth more than a dollar next year (because today's dollar would yield interest if it was invested), next year's dollar must be discounted (or reduced) by the interest rate.

11 Upon sale of the asset, the taxes on the accumulated capital consumption were recovered by the government unless the proceeds were reinvested in another rental property, which postponed the recovery until that property was sold.

12 *Perspective Canada* (Ottawa: Statistics Canada, Information Canada, 1974), p. 214.

13 See Muth, "Demand for Non-Farm Housing."

14 Take, for example, a surplus of televisions. The first indication that a surplus is developing (because of either overproduction or a fall in

demand) is a buildup in dealer inventory. Dealers, finding themselves with excess stocks, do two things. First, they reduce their orders, and, secondly, they reduce their prices.

The reduction in price causes consumers to reassess and increase their purchases of televisions. At the same time, the reduction in orders and the lowering of dealer margins causes a reduction in the production of televisions. Although all of this takes time, eventually the surplus is eradicated.

The shortage situation is a mirror image of a surplus. Dealer inventories fall, the dealers are forced to wait for shipments, and they find that they can sell all the televisions they want at or above the "suggested retail price." Radios and other sweeteners are no longer offered to purchasers of televisions, and discounts are few and far between. In other words, the effective price of televisions tends to rise.

For their part, consumers reassess their desire to purchase a television, given the effective price, and at least some decide that they can do without a new set. The net effect of these interactions is a reduction in the quantity of televisions demanded and an increase in the supply, until the shortage is eliminated. For an excellent discussion of the notion of a housing shortage, see the article by Professors Friedman and Stigler in this volume.

Chapter Three
The Presumed Advantages and Real Disadvantages of Rent Control

RICHARD W. AULT

3. Bomb Damage or Rent Control? See page 320 for the answer.

THE AUTHOR

RICHARD AULT is a Ph.D. Candidate at the University of Virginia, where he is completing a dissertation on Rent Control in New York City. He has held faculty positions at Texas A & M University and the University of Virginia, and he is currently teaching at Louisiana State University.

Chapter Three
The Presumed Advantages and Real Disadvantages of Rent Control

RICHARD W. AULT

*Acting Assistant Professor,
Louisiana State University*

PRESUMED ADVANTAGES

The number of American cities adopting rent control is increasing. Given the prospect of rent control as a continuing and expanding phenomenon, it seems appropriate to undertake a closer examination of both the claims on its behalf and the experience of cities which have adopted this policy.

Before proceeding, it is necessary to point out that a large number of widely varying programs are lumped together under the rubric "rent control." Because of these differences, arguments in favor of some programs make little sense in the context of others which are administered in a quite different manner. In its purest form, rent control is an across-the-board freeze on the price of all rental housing units at some predetermined level—generally at that which prevailed at some date prior to adoption of the ordinance.[1] However, in most cases some upward adjustments of rent are permitted as operating costs increase, as improvements are made, or as undue hardship to the landlord can be demonstrated. In addition, practices differ widely in the treatment of newly constructed and vacated units. Some jurisdictions exempt such units from subsequent control; others do not. In the following discussion, care will be taken to indicate the importance of these different policies.

ARGUMENTS FOR RENT CONTROL

Consistently, arguments in favor of rent control are initiated with the statement that "a housing shortage exists." In fact, many cities require the existence of a housing shortage, generally defined as a vacancy rate below some fixed percentage, as a condition for the implementation and continuation of rent control. Nonetheless, it seems fruitless to become involved in a discussion of what constitutes a housing shortage, because the impact of rent control will be much the same whether or not such a shortage exists. While those who base their advocacy on the existence of a housing shortage seem to imply that rent control will in some way alleviate that shortage, it is obvious that this is not the case; such legislation neither induces suppliers to make more units available, nor does it induce tenants to economize on housing. It does exactly the opposite—and by doing so adds to any existing housing shortage. Presumably, what is being suggested is that rent control will eliminate some of the undesirable consequences of a housing shortage—not that it will end the shortage itself.

A review of the popular press reveals several distinct arguments which are frequently used to justify rent control when there is a housing shortage.

Rent control protects the poor

If it were the case that tenants always have lower incomes than their landlords, the immediate effect of rent control would be to transfer wealth from these "rich" landlords to their poorer tenants whose rent payments have been reduced. In fact, individual tenants frequently have incomes which are higher than their landlord's,* and, to our knowledge, no body of evidence exists which indicates that *on average* tenants have significantly lower incomes.[2] To avoid subsidizing wealthy tenants, legislation is often written so as to preclude those units whose monthly rent exceeds some arbitrary level; but this is not a certain method of solving the problem. Small, luxurious rental units which are typically occupied by small, wealthy families sometimes have lower monthly rentals than do more spacious units, more appropriate for large but lower-income families. This being the case, high-rent decontrol cannot succeed in denying benefits to the former group without also denying them to the latter.

Even if tenants' incomes are systematically lower than landlords', rent control would still be a very inequitable way of assisting the poor because these benefits would be available only to those families able to obtain a rent controlled unit. Newcomers to an area always find it extremely difficult to obtain such units; mobile low-income groups are thus effectively shut out.

Moreover, any attempt to transfer income (or wealth) from rich to poor via rent control is flawed, because gifts in kind are always inferior to money gifts—except in the unique case where the recipient would have spent the money in *exactly* the same manner if he had a choice. Also, if there is a justification for subsidizing the poorer segments of the population, one could argue that it would be incumbent upon the *entire* population to give such support—not just owners of rental property.

While it is clear that the immediate effect of rent control is to benefit tenants regardless of their income, there are several reasons to expect these gains to be diminished as time wears on. With rents below market clearing levels, landlords are able to reduce normal maintenance and still keep their units occupied at the maximum allowable rent. As a consequence, the ensuing depreciation of rental units reduces tenant benefits by providing them with less housing services for a fixed rental price. While tenants in this

*For a good example, see de Jouvenel's paper in this volume.—Ed.

situation may elect to perform some of this maintenance themselves, any benefits are thereby reduced.

But in the usual case, neither tenant nor landlord has sufficient financial incentive to maintain and upgrade a particular building. Instead, it slides into disrepair. The decay of each housing unit, moreover, affects those nearby, and a vicious cycle comes into play. Entire city blocks, and even whole neighborhoods, have been ruined by rent control in this manner.

This is not to say that all rent controlled housing turns into slums. Deterioration will depend on a large number of factors which affect the profitability of maintenance expenditure. In cases where landlords can reasonably expect future rent increases, either as a consequence of decontrolling vacated units or completely ending rent control, maintenance is much more likely to occur. This will be particularly true if the building is located in a high-rent area, because there it is likely that larger profits can be made from a sound building. In contrast, one would expect to observe much less maintenance of rental units in slum neighborhoods or in localities where rent control ordinances provide little hope of future rent increases.

Living in a rent controlled unit not destined for deterioration can be something of a sinecure. There, the rent may be much less than that which would prevail in an uncontrolled housing market. The situation is much different for those living in units which are not well-maintained. Even if no rent increases are permitted, tenant benefits are likely to disappear as the unit is allowed to decay and its market value falls.

It should be noted that any benefits received by tenants are almost certain to be less than the costs incurred by landlords in the form of reduced rents. If a tenant pays $300 for a unit which would bring $500 on the free market, the landlord clearly loses $200. This does not imply that the tenant benefits by $200. The benefit he receives is the difference between the rent he pays for the unit and what he would be willing to pay if prices were not controlled. Since he would not be willing to pay more than the prevailing market price (he would be able to obtain a similar unit at that price), it is impossible for his benefit to exceed the landlord's cost. In the more likely event that he values the unit at less than its free market price, his benefit falls short of the cost to the landlord by that difference.

Another dilution of the benefits rent control confers on poor tenants results from the conversion of rental housing into condominiums.[3] Because rent control does not regulate the price at which buildings can be sold, owners may be able to avoid the resulting capital losses by selling these units out of the "clutches" of this legislation. Where such conversions occur, tenants must either arrange to buy their dwelling or move out. Because of difficulties in obtaining financing and making a downpayment, these conversions are likely to lead systematically to the displacement of the poorer tenants. Those who are displaced must bear the expense of moving, and their choice of rental housing is likely to be quite limited in a rent controlled environment.

Finally, although illegal, landlords may be able to recapture some of the tenants' benefits by accepting side payments for renting a unit to a particular tenant; or they may take advantage of this artificially created shortage by charging exorbitant fees for furnishing the unit. Taking all these influences into account, the benefits of rent control to the poor becomes less and less clear. Any gains they do receive will be inequitably distributed, rapidly diminished, largely confined to the few nonmobile poor, and very costly to provide.

Rent control is necessary to stop inflation

Historically, the introduction of rent control has coincided with periods of rapid inflation. Many cities with rent control ordinances presently in effect adopted them as more general price controls were phased out.[4] One can, of course, raise serious doubts about the ability of price controls to curb inflation.[5] But even if they are an effective tool in combating inflation, this does not imply that controlling only the price of rental housing will also succeed. Stopping or slowing the rate of price increases for one commodity will lower the overall rate of inflation only if it does not result in more rapid increases in the price of other commodities. But, to the extent that rent control holds down the price of housing, tenants have a larger portion of their income left over to spend on other things; and in spending this income on other goods, they will drive up their prices. Rent control, in other words, affects relative prices and relative price changes, but not the overall rate of inflation.

The view that high rents cause inflation is also incorrect in that it confuses high prices with rising prices. Even if one were to view landlords as self-interested monopolists, it does not follow that their "greedy" behavior would cause a continuous rise in rental prices. In such an environment these landlords would set rents at "high" levels, but they would find it unprofitable to further increase rents unless their costs or demand for their units were to increase. Since they have no control over either, it makes little sense to blame them for any ensuing rise in rental prices.

Inflation is largely the consequence of government policy concerning taxation, expenditure, and monetary affairs. If appropriate policies in these areas are adopted, inflation is not likely to be a problem. If they are not, nothing, including rent control, will succeed in halting it. The merits of this argument cannot account for its popularity. A more plausible explanation is that, during a period of concern about inflation, the public is more receptive to any program which can be put forth as an anti-inflation measure.[6]

Rent control is necessary to stabilize the economic characteristics of a city's population

Advocates of rent control frequently argue that in the absence of such enactments, the price of rental housing in central cities will rise very rapidly relative to tenants' incomes. Thus, these tenants will be unable to afford the price of housing and will be displaced by members of higher income groups.

It is true that certain aspects of rent control do have the effect of stabilizing a city's population and its economic characteristics. Particularly where new units are subject to control, the lack of vacant rental units will result in a reduction in the in-migration of new tenants and the mobility of the current ones. However, there are offsetting forces. To the extent that rent control leads to a deterioration of the existing housing stock, these units will be gradually vacated by current tenants and occupied by those from lower income groups. On the other hand, we would expect to see low-income tenants displaced by wealthier ones where rent control leads to the conversion of rental units to condominiums.

Considering all these forces, it is not clear how rent control will affect various income groups—it depends on each city's policy on vacated, newly constructed, and converted units. Also, it is not clear that the goal of preserving economic characteristics is a desirable one—to hold this view is to imply that the precontrol situation is the optimal one and that it remains optimal even though circumstances change.* Finally, if rent control is necessary to maintain an optimal situation with regard to economic characteristics, one may be excused for wondering how the situation developed in the first place in its absence.

Rent control benefits racial minorities

To the extent that racial groups differ systematically in their incomes, measures that succeed in preserving the economic characteristics of a city will tend as well to preserve the racial pattern. However, as we argued in the preceding section, there are no compelling reasons to believe that rent control will succeed in this. The truth of the matter is that, far from helping minorities, rent control promotes racial discrimination!

The main effect of rent control is to reduce rental prices below market clearing levels where the number of units of each type that tenants are willing to lease is just matched by the number of units that landlords are willing to offer for rent. At any lower price, the tenants will attempt to rent more housing, but landlords will gradually reduce the

---

*For a discussion of some disadvantages of reduced mobility, see the papers by Paish and Hayek.—Ed.

quantity of housing they make available for rent. In this situation landlords find a large number of prospective tenants eager to occupy their units at the maximum legal rent, and they have to devise some method for deciding which tenants to accept. This decision may be based on the willingness of tenants to make illegal side payments. Where the authorities succeed in preventing this, the landlord is likely to base his decision on the reliability of the tenant, on how much damage he is likely to inflict on the apartment unit, or on how many maintenance activities he is willing to undertake himself. Other things being equal, a landlord is likely to rent to tenants he personally likes; and to the extent that he has any racial prejudices, he will be inclined to select tenants in a racially discriminatory manner.

We are not suggesting that this criterion is never used in the absence of rent control. But landlords who engage in discriminatory practices will be faced with the necessity of accepting either lower rents or higher vacancy rates. They will thus pay for their discriminatory behavior in the form of reduced rental income. Under rent control the same practices will cost them nothing, so they will be more inclined to engage in them.

Tenant eviction

This type of discrimination is likely to occur as well in decisions concerning the eviction of tenants. Under rent control, where new tenants are easily obtained, a landlord will not be hesitant to evict for trivial reasons; and we should not be surprised to find racial considerations affecting eviction decisions. The New York City experience with rent control seems to confirm these developments. In no other city do tenant-landlord relationships appear to be so hostile or so intertwined with racial conflicts. Alleged abuses in selecting and evicting tenants became so widespread that city housing authorities were granted extensive authority to regulate these decisions—with the result that it is now extremely difficult to evict a tenant even for nonpayment of rent. In such an environment landlords have an even greater incentive to be very selective about tenants because they are likely to have them for a long time.

Rent control is necessary to prevent rent gouging

It is argued that price gouging is particularly likely to occur in rental housing because of that market's special nature: since housing is a necessity, it is impossible for tenants to protect themselves from rent increases by reducing the amount of space they choose to rent. This assertion is both incorrect and irrelevant. Even if tenants were to respond to increases by continuing to demand the same amount of housing, individual landlords could not raise rents with impunity. Just because a tenant is willing to pay a higher rent for his existing unit than he is currently paying does not imply that he will do so if he can obtain a similar unit from another landlord at a lower price. Even if all existing landlords simultaneously agreed to raise their rents—a development which would be very unlikely, given their large numbers in a typical city—they would soon be faced with competition from the owners of newly constructed units. At the higher rent, moreover, each member of the landlord cartel would have strong financial incentives to "cheat" and create more housing himself. In doing so the agreement would be undermined and market rents would fall.

In addition, it is simply not true that tenants will demand the same space in response to rent increases. Faced with this situation, they would find it advantageous to economize on housing—despite the fact that it is a "necessity"—and avoid substantial reductions in spending on other goods. Empirical evidence suggests that a 1 percent increase in the price of housing will result in a reduction in housing consumption of between 0.7 percent and 1.7 percent.[7]

Rent control is necessary to improve housing quality and reduce the number of slum dwellings

The basis for this argument is the idea that many tenants live in "slum" units only because they cannot afford the rental price of higher-quality housing. Therefore, it is implied that by reducing the rental price of housing, a rent control program will enable these tenants to abandon their "slum" units and move into better ones which they could then afford.

While it is true that at lower prices tenants on average would try to move to higher-quality units, their ability to do so is limited by the supply. It is simply impossible for everyone to occupy high-quality housing unless there is enough to go around. Currently, there is not, and rent control will not create any additions. On the contrary, this legislation makes the situation worse by discouraging both the construction of new dwellings (which tend to be of high-quality) and the maintenance of existing units.

There are two possible exceptions to the previous conclusion. If rent control leads to the rehabilitation and conversion of rental space to units for sale for owner-occupancy, average quality *may* be improved.[8] Also, it is possible that a rent control program which links rent increases to expenditures on maintenance and improvements will have the same result.[9]

Two types of housing improvements

However, those who argue that this type of rent control would lead to improved housing quality are implying that more improvements would be made under rent control than in its absence. To resolve this issue, it is useful to consider two types of housing improvements—those whose value to tenants exceeds their cost and those whose value is less than the cost.[10] It should be clear that in the absence of rent control, improvements of the first type will be made. Any profit seeking landlord will be happy to do so because he can recapture their cost in the form of higher rents and retain a unit with a higher market value. Assuming that there are minimal time delays and administrative costs associated with obtaining approval for the ensuing rent increase,[11] this kind of improvement would also be made under rent control. The second type of improvement would not be undertaken in the absence of rent control because landlords would be unable to recapture the cost. Under rent control, they might be. If we imagine a unit whose controlled rent is $50 less than the free market rent, a landlord can make repairs whose cost is up to $50 greater than the ensuing benefits to the tenant, raise the rent by the cost of the repairs, and still be able to benefit. The tenant will be made worse off by the amount by which the cost exceeds the benefit to him.[12] If this is the way that rent control leads to an improvement in housing quality, it is detrimental to the interests of the tenant.

SUMMARY

Because of the wide variations in rent control programs, it is difficult to make many generalizations about the impact of these programs. Nonetheless, it is our assessment that few of the alleged benefits of rent control are likely to be realized. Such programs do result in an income transfer from landlords to tenants, and that transfer may be viewed as desirable. However, we do not find this to be a compelling reason to support rent control programs, because there are much more certain, equitable, and efficient ways of affecting an income transfer from the rich to the poor.* It seems to us most unlikely that any of the remaining alleged benefits will be achieved through the imposition of rent control.

REAL DISADVANTAGES

Opponents of rent control have put forth several arguments which emphasize its detrimental impact. In reviewing these

*See in this regard "Questions and Some Answers about Rent Control" by Professor Edgar O. Olsen (especially pp. 110-115) in the present volume.—Ed.

arguments we emphasize the fact that the validity of each may depend upon the type of control program envisioned.

Rent control discourages the construction of rental housing

This argument is the one used most frequently to oppose rent control, and it is based on the simple notion that investors in rental housing are motivated by profit considerations.[13] This being the case, any legal change which has the effect of reducing the profitability of rental housing will result in a reduction in its construction.[14] Proponents of rent control usually deny that it has this effect by emphasizing the fact that most rent control ordinances exempt newly constructed units. The deterrent effect of rent control will, of course, be less under such a provision, but it will not vanish. In any community where old units are subject to rent control, it is quite likely that investors will view the extension of these controls to new units as a very real possibility.[15]

New construction regardless?

Advocates also rebut this argument by citing examples of new building that have occurred after the imposition of rent control. There are two reasons why this argument is not convincing. First, there is a necessary lag between the drawing board stage and the time when the units are made available for rent. Consequently, new units may come on to the market during the first few years of a rent control program simply because investors had committed themselves to these projects prior to the adoption of rent control.[16] In addition, it is entirely possible for a rent control program to have a negative impact on new building without completely ending it. Profitability depends on several factors—the existence of rent control is only one. Therefore, where other conditions are conducive to profitable construction, it should not be surprising to witness its continuance (but at a reduced rate) after the implementation of rent control. In fact, it is quite likely that the political pressures that often result in the adoption of rent control will be greatest in areas where rents are rising relatively rapidly because of low vacancy rates and high rates of population growth. For this reason, rent control is most likely to be implemented in areas which are otherwise very attractive for rental housing construction. The low rates of construction that finally emerge in such areas are perfectly consistent with the notion that rent control is a discouraging factor.

Some evidence

Data from rent control areas are fully consistent with the notion that this law discourages rental housing. In England, where strict rent controls have been in effect for over sixty years, the production of private rental housing has been at such a low level that the percentage of households living in this type of housing has fallen from 61 percent to below 15 percent.[17] New York City has also experienced a decline in the number and percentage of persons living in this type of housing.[18] Even in the District of Columbia, with its relatively short experience of controls, the number of units available for rent has fallen by 8,000 units,[19] and the number of multifamily building permits fell from 7,263 in the first four months of 1973 to 220 in the first four months of 1976.[20]

Rent control causes maintenance of rental housing to be reduced

A rigid system of rent control will result in a more rapid rate of depreciation of the rental housing stock; while a more flexible program which links rent increases to expenditures on repairs may lead to a less rapid rate of depreciation. But the idea that rent control is desirable if it leads to quality improvement, and detrimental if it results in a more rapid rate of housing depreciation must be rejected. Housing, like most durable goods, depreciates as a function of both age and of use. During this process, the flow of services from any housing unit decreases. Maintenance is a means of slowing or reversing this process.

Determining the optimal level can be made quite complicated, but, in general, it consists of weighing the increase in housing services which results from maintenance against its cost. Ideally, upkeep should be undertaken only to the point where the last dollar spent generates an increase in housing services of at least that amount. Expenditure beyond that is wasteful because cost exceeds benefit. Accordingly, maintenance should not be unambiguously viewed as desirable—too much can be just as bad as too little. What is important is whether rent control causes maintenance levels to move towards or away from the optimal—not whether it leads to more or less.

Optimal maintenance

In general, optimal maintenance will occur when rental units are privately owned and rented in uncontrolled markets. In that situation the owner must bear the cost himself, and he can determine the value in terms of the increased rent receipts which reflect its value to occupants. His failure to make repairs and improvements at optimal levels will result in a reduced flow of profits from his rental units, so it is in his self-interest to perform appropriately.[21] To the extent that rent control leads to either a higher or a lower level of maintenance, this should be viewed as one of its *disadvantages*.

In areas with rigid controls there is evidence of more rapid depreciation in the controlled housing sector. In New York City 29 percent of the rent controlled units are deteriorated as opposed to 8 percent of the uncontrolled units.[22] A similar relationship is found in both England and France.[23] On the other hand, rent controlled cities in Massachusetts and New Jersey, as well as from the District of Columbia, show little or no change.[24] This may reflect the fact that rent control programs in those areas have been in effect for such a short period of time that their impact is not yet apparent.

Rent control erodes the tax base and shifts a tax burden to homeowners

Although cities use a variety of definitions of real estate tax base, assessments are generally linked to the market value of the property in question. In the case of income producing property, the market value depends on the future stream of earnings which that property is expected to yield. To the extent that control leads potential buyers of rental units to anticipate reduced earnings in the future, the effect is to reduce the market value and, ultimately, the assessed value.

Rent control may also cause a further erosion in the tax base to the extent that it discourages new construction. In particular, it is likely to reduce the building of new rental units, but it may also have the effect of discouraging other types of construction on sites currently occupied by rental housing units. Any time a rental unit is to be razed to make way for a new building, opposition by its tenants is likely to arise. However, this opposition will be much stronger in the event that those being displaced are currently beneficiaries of rent control, because they have a stronger vested interest in their present rental unit. To the degree that this opposition results in costly delays and litigation, the effect can only be to discourage new construction in those cities.[25]

Severity and duration

The degree to which rent control leads to an erosion of the tax base depends upon its severity and duration. In New York City rent control is estimated to have caused a reduction in the tax base of nearly one-and-one-half billion dollars, and this reduction costs the city 115 million dollars annually in tax losses.[26] This is one of the reasons why the city has been skirting along the edge of bankruptcy.

Evidence from rent controlled communities in Massachusetts and New Jersey reflects no clear change in property
assessments, though this may change when rent control has
been in effect for a sufficient period of time to enable
reduced market values to be reflected in reduced assessed
values.[27]

The argument that any decline in the tax base resulting
from rent control causes a shift in the tax burden to
homeowners depends on certain assumptions concerning
local government expenditure and finance. Faced with a
declining tax base, local authorities can increase property
tax rates, they can cut spending, or they can utilize other
sources of tax revenue. Accordingly, the burden will fall on
property owners, on those who lose government services, or
on those who bear the burden of the alternate forms of
taxation. Which of these outcomes is most likely depends
upon the prevailing political climate of the area in
question.[28]

Rent control reduces mobility

There are two ways in which rent control is likely to reduce
mobility. First, to the extent that it reduces construction of
new rental housing and leads to lower vacancy rates,
residents will be deterred from moving by the increased
difficulty of locating a vacant rental unit. This will be the
case for residents of both controlled and uncontrolled units.
Also, residents of rent controlled units will be further
discouraged from moving because in so doing they must
forgo the subsidy associated with tenure. Because of the low
turnover of controlled units and the frequent practice of
decontrolling vacated units, it is most unlikely that these
families would be able to obtain another controlled unit
providing a similar subsidy.[29]

There are several disadvantages associated with this
reduced mobility. First, it tends to result in a misallocation
of the existing housing stock. Young, growing families will
be inclined to endure crowding rather than relinquish their
subsidy, while older neighbors hold on to larger units as
their family size declines with older children leaving home.[30]

Increased unemployment

A second problem that is likely to result from reduced mobility is an increase in unemployment. Most labor markets are characterized by rapidly changing job locations. As a result, many employees find it necessary to move frequently to keep their present job or to find a new one; and any obstacle to this mobility makes it more difficult to match job seekers with available positions. Those fortunate to have tenure in a rent controlled unit may find it advantageous to forgo employment opportunities at a distant location while continuing to search for a position which permits them to remain at their current address. Unemployment rates will be higher to the extent that workers behave in this fashion. Finally, reduced mobility may result in an increase in unnecessary commuting. Tenants of rent controlled units may choose to travel great distances to their job rather than relinquish a controlled unit. They would be much happier with a similar unit closer to their job, but, given the nature of rent control, they cannot obtain one without paying a much higher rent.

Rent control increases the cost of providing rental housing

This effect may come about in several ways. Rent enactments may lead to a substantial increase in the cost of financing housing construction and maintenance. The willingness of investors to commit their funds to any project depends upon the expected return from their investment as well as the risks associated with it. Both the existence of rent control and the threat of its adoption have the effect of increasing the risk associated with investing in rental housing, so investors will require the payment of higher interest rates as compensation. The importance of this aspect of housing costs should not be underestimated. For a typical apartment built in the United States in recent years, over 40 percent of rent revenues are used to pay debt charges.[31] A slight increase in the rate at which these buildings are financed can have a substantial impact on rent levels.

Expensive public housing

Rent control may also result in an increase in housing costs by causing private rental housing to be replaced with public housing units. Rent control inevitably results in a housing shortage and very low vacancy rates, and public officials may respond by erecting public housing units. Due to various inefficiencies, public housing is more costly to construct than private housing,[32] so any program which results in the displacement of the latter by the former will cause the cost of housing to rise.

Costs may rise because of additional expenses associated with dealing with the rent control bureaucracy.[33] Such costs can be substantial—particularly in a city where rent control rigidly restricts profits on rental housing to a fixed percentage of investment. There, landlords find it necessary to keep extensive records and to hire accountants and lawyers to represent them in applying for a rent increase.[34] Ultimately, these costs will be covered by rents or will increase the speed with which units are withdrawn from the rental stock.

Rent control is an unsatisfactory means of redistributing income

Advocates of rent control frequently present the issue in very simple terms: it is a means of preventing wealthy landlords from exploiting poor tenants. Strategically, this approach has much to be said for it. In today's political climate it is difficult for any elected official to oppose a program which is alleged to have this effect. However, when the facts of the situation are more closely examined, it becomes apparent that this description is quite misleading.[35] Even if we accept the assertion that landlords are wealthier, we should recognize that rent control programs have no mechanism for assuring that benefits are concentrated among poor tenants or that the greatest sacrifices are made by the wealthiest landlords. As a consequence, the benefits to tenants and the costs to landlords are likely to be distributed in a way that bears no close association with income.[36]

When we also consider families not living in rent controlled units, the futility of rent control as a comprehensive redistributive scheme becomes even more apparent. In New York City more than one-third of the families with below median incomes live in housing *not* subject to rent control, while over one-half of the families with above median incomes live in rent controlled units.[37]

Finally, if rent control is viewed as a means of assisting the poor, it is difficult to explain why such ordinances are consistently implemented in communities having high per capita incomes and, in most instances, an unusually low proportion of low-income residents.[38]

"Fair return" and the new rent control laws

Because of the high rates of inflation in recent years, newly adopted rent control ordinances have generally incorporated a method of determining rent ceilings which is more flexible than those found in earlier programs. Often, this flexibility is achieved by drafting these "modern" ordinances in such a way as to provide—at least in theory—a "fair return" to investors in rental property. These ordinances are often presented as a means of duplicating competitive housing markets under normal conditions—that is, when neither a housing shortage nor a housing surplus exists—in that they prevent landlords from exploiting their position during a housing shortage without denying them a reasonable return on their investment. On the surface, this approach to rent control seems quite reasonable—certainly much more so than an across-the-board freeze on rents or periodic but arbitrary increases in rent ceilings. However, there are serious difficulties involved in the implementation of this approach to rent control which should raise skepticism about the desirability of its adoption.

The operation of a "fair return" rent control program can be best explained in terms of the following equation:

(1) Ceiling Rent = Operating Costs + (Allowed Profit Rate) (Value of Rental Property)

Using this equation, ceiling rents are set in such a way as to generate adequate revenue to the landlord for him to cover all his operating costs (which are defined to include property taxes, utility charges, maintenance expenses, depreciation, insurance premiums, and the cost of management services) and have enough remaining to yield a reasonable return on his rental housing investment. For example, if the appropriate profit rate is determined to be 10 percent, and the value of a rental unit is set at $30,000, the ceiling rent will be set at $3,000 above the annual operating costs. Although the implementation of this approach seems quite simple, there are substantial difficulties involved in ascertaining each of the determinants of the ceiling rent, and the failure to do so properly can lead to serious difficulties.

In implementing this program, estimates of operating costs are generally based on the costs incurred during an earlier time period. However, during periods of inflation, the failure to provide for increases in these costs will result in the inability of landlords to achieve the stipulated rate of profit. Allowances can be made for anticipated increases in these costs, but it is unlikely that they can be predicted with a high degree of accuracy. While it is unfair to prevent unavoidable increases in costs from being reflected in higher ceiling rents, a program which allows all increases in cost to be passed on may also lead to difficulties. Under such a program unnecessary operating expenditures will be borne entirely by the tenants so long as the rent ceiling remains below the free market rent, and landlords will have no incentive to minimize these expenses. They may react by accepting kickbacks from contractors who overcharge for their services, by hiring friends and relatives at inflated salaries to perform management services, or by including fraudulent expenses in financial reports submitted to the rent authorities. These problems could be avoided by allowing landlords to pass on only unavoidable increases in costs, but the administrative expense of determining which costs are unavoidable may be prohibitive.[39] As they are currently constituted, rent control boards have neither the staff nor the expertise to perform this task properly.

Even greater problems arise in determining what profit

rate to allow landlords on their investment. Different groups have widely diverging ideas about what constitutes a fair rate of profit, with tenants often arguing that no profits should be permitted to those who sell necessities—like rental housing. However, if this type of control is to be viewed as an approximation of competitive markets, there appear to be at least two methods by which appropriate profit rates could be determined.

The first is to calculate the profit rate that is actually earned by owners of rental housing in a city where rents are not controlled, and then to set the allowed profit rate equal to it. In doing this, care should be taken to select a city where normal conditions exist in the rental housing market. Strictly speaking, it may be nearly impossible to do this because the real world is one of continuous disequilibrium,[40] so it would be very difficult to reach agreement on the city to be selected. Also, it would be very costly to gather the necesssary information before it became outdated as economic conditions changed.

Alternatively, the allowed rate of profit could be obtained by adopting the method used by public utility commissions in setting profit rates for regulated utilities. These commissions accept the notion that profit rates from various types of investment are related to the risks associated with those investments—the greater the risk, the greater the profit rate.[41] To determine what profit rate to allow, they observe profits on investments involving risks similar to those associated with investing in utilities and use these profit rates as a benchmark. But anyone familiar with the proceedings of these commissions is aware of the many difficulties involved in setting utility rates in this fashion, and the same problems occur in the case of rent ceilings. Risk is an elusive concept which is very difficult to quantify, so it is nearly impossible to identify with confidence which investments entail risks similar to those associated with investing in rental housing. It is not even clear that the risks involved in investing in different types of rental housing within the same city are the same, so a careful implementation of this approach may require that different profit rates be allowed on various types of rental property.

In practice, little attention is paid to these issues in

drafting rent control ordinances or in enforcing them. Often, a target rate of profit is selected largely on the basis of political considerations, and it is more-or-less ignored in the actual setting of rent ceilings.

The final step in implementing this type of rent control is to determine the value of the rental units subject to control.[42] But this poses a real dilemma, because the market price of an income generating asset depends on the stream of revenue it produces. Therefore, the value of a controlled apartment depends on the rents allowed, and it cannot properly be used as a guide for setting rents. For example, if investors become convinced that the rent control board is going to allow lower profits in the future, the market value of controlled units will fall. If the rent ceiling is based on current market value, its decline will result in a lower ceiling rent. The process will continue with each rent reduction leading to a lower market value, and the lower market value leading in turn to another rent reduction.

On the other hand, if the authorities allow higher profit rates, market values will rise and lead to another round of rent increases. The process will continue until the ceiling rent reaches the free market rent, and market values cease to rise. Therefore, if property is valued at current market value for rent control purposes, rents will either rise constantly or fall constantly unless the rent control authorities constantly succeed in setting the precisely correct profit rate. It is most unlikely that they will succeed in doing this, for profits, like all other economic phenomena in the real world, are in a continuous state of flux.

A second way of determining value is to base it on the price the current owner actually paid for the unit. One problem with this method is that identical units may have been purchased at different prices because they were bought several years apart. To the extent that this is the case, owners who have held their units for a long period of time will be limited to lower rents. The result will be to encourage the frequent sales of apartment buildings and to induce property transactions that are designed solely to achieve an increase in ceiling rents. For example, one can imagine two apartment owners who purchased similar apartment units for $20,000. If each of the two were to agree to buy the other's unit for $30,000, ceiling rents and profits would be increased for both. In this manner the rent control system could be rendered ineffective.

Even if all these difficulties could be circumvented, the "fair return" approach to rent control is flawed in that it destroys the signalling role that profits normally play in an economic system. Where demand for a particular product (like housing) rises, suppliers temporarily receive profits in excess of "fair" or "normal" levels. The existence of these high profits is what induces an increased supply. To the extent that modern rent control ordinances prevent these high profit rates from being realized, they have the effect of discouraging housing construction and perpetuating housing shortages.

NOTES

1 It should be noted that controlling the rental price of housing is not the same thing as controlling the price of housing services. If a landlord is able to reduce the level of housing services provided by his rental units by reducing maintenance without being forced to reduce the rent of the unit, he is able to increase the price of housing services. Because of the administrative difficulties involved in monitoring the level of housing services flowing from a particular housing unit, rent control programs nearly always focus on the price of housing units and ignore the rental price of housing services.

2 In his study of this issue, Johnson reports that the income of tenants tends to be slightly lower than that of landlords, the difference resulting from the fact that landlords are on average older and thus further advanced on an increasing lifetime earnings cycle. His major conclusion is that "...if one of the objectives of rent control is to aid low-income people...it does not achieve that objective." D. Gale Johnson, "Rent Control and the Distribution of Income," *American Economic Review* 41 (May 1951): 569-582.

3 The frequency of these conversions should not be underestimated. In the District of Columbia, approval to convert 5,000 units was granted during a six-month period following an extension of the rent control program. *Washington Post*, 12 July 1978, Section B, p. 3.

4 New York City's rent control laws are an extension of World War II price controls. In Washington and Boston controls were adopted as the nationwide price controls of the early 1970s were being phased out.

5 Michael Walker, ed., *The Illusion of Wage & Price Control* (Vancouver: The Fraser Institute, 1976).

6 The practice of linking a self-serving proposal to a noble cause is not unique to rent control proponents. We have seen airlines recommend fare hikes to conserve valuable fuel during an "energy crisis," and we observe numerous industries appealing for protective tariffs to "strengthen the nation's defence," where the relationship between the product they produce and national defence is most tenuous.

7 See Richard Muth, "The Demand for Non-Farm Housing," in *The Demand for Durable Goods*, ed. Arnold Harberger (Chicago: University of Chicago Press, 1960); Margaret Reid, *Housing and Income* (Chicago: University of Chicago Press, 1962); Tong Hun Lee, "The Demand Elasticities for Non-Farm Housing," *Review of Economics and Statistics* 46 (Feb., 1964): 82-89; and Frank de Leeuw, "The Demand for Housing: a Review of Cross-Section Evidence," *Review of Economics and Statistics* 53 (Feb. 1971): 1-10.

8 This depends on whether the additional improvements offset the effects of reduced maintenance on those units which remain in the controlled rental market. Also, these units will be occupied by different people, so it is not clear that the original tenants will attain better housing.

9 There is also the possibility that condominium conversions may hurt tenants, especially low-income tenants who cannot afford to acquire a newly converted condominium.

10 The statement that the value of these improvements to tenants exceeds their cost implies that after these repairs are made, tenants will be willing to accept a rent increase sufficient to cover the cost of the repairs.

11 We have little confidence in this assumption. In many rent control cities, approval for such increases occurs only after long delays and a lot of paperwork. In Washington, D.C. appeals of this nature generally take six to ten months to resolve, despite the fact that the rent control statute requires that decisions be made within ninety days. *Washington Post*, 16 January 1978, Section C, p. 1.

12 Evidence of this type of improvement is abundant in New York City. There, landlords found that having completed these repairs, tenants would rush to destroy them before approval to increase rents was received. To solve this problem a special team of inspectors was supplied with Polaroid cameras to quickly document completed repairs. *Barron's*, 15 April 1963, p. 1.

13 Even advocates of rent control seem to accept this notion, for they are not hesitant to condemn the greed of landlords.

14 Actually, any change which affects the expected profitability will have this effect. For this reason, construction is likely to decline in cities where the imposition of rent control is seriously threatened.

15 Such a belief seems entirely rational. A government simply has little credibility when it assures new investors that they will never be treated in the manner that old investors are currently being treated. Investors in rental housing in New York City can attest to this. There, units constructed after 1947 were exempt from rent control ordinances, and investors were assured that the city had no intention of changing that

policy. However, in 1969, when rent stabilization was introduced, owners of these new units were given the choice of either "voluntarily" signing up for that program or having their units subjected to the provisions of the old rent control law.

16 It is probably for this reason that Gilderbloom reaches the conclusion that there is no compelling evidence that a moderate rent control program affects construction. His data is from New Jersey, Massachusetts, and the District of Columbia during the years immediately following the adoption of rent control in those areas. John Gilderbloom, *The Impact of Moderate Rent Control in the United States: A Review and Critique of Existing Literature* (Sacramento: California Department of Housing and Community Development, 1977).

17 Joel F. Brenner and Herbert M. Franklin, *Rent Control in North America and Four European Countries* (Rockville: Council for International Urban Liaison, 1977), p. 4.

18 Paul L. Niebanck, *Rent Control and the Rental Housing Market in New York City* (New York: Housing and Development Administration, Department of Rent and Housing Maintenance, 1968), p. 29.

19 *Washington Post*, 12 December 1977, Section A, p. 1.

20 Bureau of the Census, US Department of Commerce, *Construction Reports,* Authorized Construction, Washington, D.C. Area, Series C41, 1976; figures preliminary by NAHB Economics Department, as reported in *Washington Star News*, 11 July 1976.

21 Strictly speaking, optimal levels of maintenance may not be attained in this situation. Because of "neighborhood effects," a reduction in maintenance by one owner may have the effect of lowering the value of neighboring homes or apartments which may be owned by someone else. Failure to account for this reduction in value may lead to too little maintenance. Also, some people may be concerned about the housing of others for various reasons. The best way of upgrading housing in response to these concerns may involve more maintenance of some units and less of others.

22 Niebanck, *Rent Control*, p. 120. Care must be taken not to accept these numbers blindly. In areas where new units are not controlled, the average age of controlled units is much greater than for uncontrolled units; and one would expect older units to be in worse condition. However, adjusting for age, the same relationship seems to hold. See Kristof, Table 5, in this volume.

23 Brenner and Franklin, *Rent Control in North America*, pp. 4, 27-28.

24 Gilderbloom, "Impact of Moderate Rent Control," p. 17.

25 Care should be taken not to overstate this point. Just because a rental unit is not built on a certain tract of land does not mean that that tract will sit vacant. Owner-occupied housing or commercial establishments may be built instead, in which case the tax base will be lower only to the extent that the assessed value of these buildings is lower. Even if the tract sits vacant, the loss in tax revenue will be partly offset by the city's avoiding the costs of providing services to those who would have resided in the unit. The really serious problems are most likely to occur where tax exempt public housing is constructed in an attempt to eliminate the housing shortage that

inevitably accompanies rent control.

26 Elizabeth Roistacher, *The Removal of Rent Regulation in New York City*, (New York: Department of Housing and Urban Development, 1977), p. 109.

27 Evidence suggests that this process is underway. There has been a dramatic increase in the number of assessment appeals filed by owners of controlled apartments in New Jersey. To the extent that these appeals succeed, assessed values will fall. See Gruen Gruen & Associates, *Rent Control in New Jersey: The Beginnings* (San Francisco: Gruen Gruen & Associates, 1977), pp. 66-74.

28 *Ibid.*, p. 63. Gruen and Gruen claim that in New Jersey the burden has been shifted to homeowners. The evidence they use to support this claim is the increase in the percentage of property taxes paid by owners of single family homes after the adoption of rent control. However, over the same time period many rental units were converted to units for owner-occupancy; so all that can be said with certainty is that a larger group of people is paying a larger proportion of property taxes.

29 Evidence from New York City confirms the notion that residents of controlled units will be especially immobile. There, less than 70 percent of the residents of controlled units have moved in the past ten years, while in the uncontrolled sector over 80 percent of the tenants have moved in the past five years. See Chester Rapkin, *The Private Rental Housing Market in New York City* (New York: Housing and Development Administration, Department of Rent and Housing Maintenance, 1965), Table 13, p. 57.

30 Studying New York City data for the year 1968, Niebanck reports that both overcrowding and underutilization occur more frequently in the controlled than in the uncontrolled sector. Niebanck, *Rent Control*, Table VI-6, pp. 159-160.

31 Emily Paradise Achtenberg, "The Social Utility of Rent Control," in *Housing Urban America*, ed. Jon Pynoos, Robert Schafer, and Chester W. Hartman (Chicago: Aldine, 1973), p. 437.

32 It has been estimated that public housing is about 10 percent more expensive to produce. See David M. Barton and Edgar O. Olsen, "The Benefits and Costs of Public Housing in New York City," Institute for Research on Poverty, Discussion Papers, no. 372 (Madison: University of Wisconsin, 1976), pp. 18-30.

33 A related cost which is absorbed by the taxpayer is the administrative cost of the program. In Boston this amounted to $15 per controlled unit per year. *Wall Street Journal*, 18 January 1974, p. 1.

34 A side effect of this procedure is that it may increase concentration in the housing market. The complexity of appeals may be such that only those landlords who deal with the rent control bureaucracy on a frequent basis are able to comply with the procedures necessary to obtain a rent increase approved. The nuisance factor alone may be sufficient to cause many small-scale landlords to leave the market. The result is apartment ownership increasingly dominated by a small number of owners.

35 See Note 2 above.

36 Roistacher has estimated the benefits to tenants in rent controlled

apartments and related these benefits to household income. Using New York City data for 1968, she found that white families earning more than $15,000 receive an average subsidy of $1081 per year from rent control. For white families earning less than $2000, the average subsidy is $825. For nonwhite families the subsidies are $1182 and $627, respectively. Elizabeth Roistacher, "The Distribution of Tenant Benefits Under Rent Control" (Ph.D. diss., University of Pennsylvania, 1972), Table VI-1, p. 237.

37 Niebanck, *Rent Control*, Table III-21, p. 94.

38 For a good discussion of this point, see Kenneth Baar, "Rent Control in the 1970's: The Case of the New Jersey Tenants' Movement," *Hastings Law Journal* 28, no. 3 (January 1977): 631-683. He attributes the "success" of the New Jersey Rent Control Movement to the fact that its beneficiaries were middle and upper class renters who had the time and know-how to organize into an effective political bloc.

39 This assumes that costs are objective; and measurable, in principle, by outsiders. But the basic economic understanding of costs is as opportunities forgone, or alternative costs. Only the individual decision maker, however, can know the next best choice given up (the cost). A body of literature has evolved which contends that costs are necessarily subjective, and not able to be determined by bureaucrats interested in establishing "fair return," for example. It includes: G.F. Thirlby, "The Subjective Theory of Value and Accounting 'Cost'," *Economica* (February 1946): 32-49; Ludwig von Mises, *Human Action* (Chicago: Regency, 1966), p. 97; *Epistemological Problems of Economics* (Princeton: Von Nostrand, 1960); James M. Buchanan, *Cost and Choice* (Chicago: Markham, 1969), pp. 21-34; J.M. Buchanan and G.F. Thirlby, L.S.E., *Essays on Cost* (London: Weidenfeld & Nicolson, 1973); "The Present State of the Debate," in *Collectivist Economic Planning*, ed. Friedrich A. Hayek, (Clifton: Augustus M. Kelley, 1975), pp. 226-227; Murray N. Rothbard, *Individualism and Economic Order* (Chicago: University of Chicago Press, 1948); Murray N. Rothbard, *The Counter Revolution of Science* (Glencoe, Ill.: The Free Press, 1952); *Man Economy and State*, (Princeton: Von Nostrand, 1962), pp. 290-294.

40 Cf. Israel Kirzner, *Competition & Entrepreneurship* (Chicago: University of Chicago Press, 1973).

41 Bond markets provide evidence which is consistent with this assumed relationship. Corporations with high bond ratings (which reflect low levels of risk) are able to borrow funds by paying a lower rate of interest than that paid by firms with lower bond ratings.

42 For convenience, the problems involved in determining appropriate profit rates are discussed separately from the problems involving the determination of the value of rental housing units. However, these issues are very intertwined. Allowing an inappropriate rate of profit creates no problem if the error is offset in establishing the value of the property in question. It makes little difference whether a landlord is permitted a 10 percent return on property valued at $20,000 or a 5 percent profit on the same property valued at $40,000.

Part Three
The Practice of
Rent Control

Chapter Four
Roofs or Ceilings?
The Current
Housing Problem

MILTON FRIEDMAN

GEORGE J. STIGLER

4. Bomb Damage or Rent Control? See page 321 for the answer.

THE AUTHORS

Winner of the 1976 Nobel Prize in Economics, MILTON FRIEDMAN was born in 1912 in New York City and graduated from Rutgers before taking his MA at Chicago and Ph.D. at Columbia. From 1935-1937 he worked for the US National Resources Committee and from 1941-1943 for the US Treasury. Since 1946 he has been Paul Snowden Russell Distinguished Service Professor at the University of Chicago. He has also taught at the Universities of Minnesota, Wisconsin, Columbia, and California, as well as lecturing at universities throughout the world from Cambridge to Tokyo.

He is the acknowledged leader of the 'Chicago School' which specializes in the empirical testing of policy propositions derived from market analysis.

Among his best known books are *Essays in Positive Economics* (Chicago, 1953), *Studies in the Quantity Theory of Money* (edited by Friedman, Chicago, 1956), *A Theory of the Consumption Function* (Princeton, 1957), *Capitalism and Freedom* (Chicago, 1962), and (with A. Schwartz) *A Monetary History of the United States* (Princeton, 1971).

GEORGE J. STIGLER is the Charles R. Walgreen Distinguished Service Professor of American Institutions, and Director of the Walgreen Foundation, in the Graduate School of Business at the University of Chicago. He has held these positions since 1958. Earlier Professor Stigler served on the faculties of Columbia University, Brown University, the University of Minnesota, and Iowa State College. In 1948 he lectured at the London School of Economics.

A member of the Research Staff of the National Bureau of Economic Research since 1941, Professor Stigler also belongs to the American Philosophical Society, the American Economic Association (President, 1964), the Royal Economics Society, and the Universities-National Bureau Committee for Economic Research.

Professor Stigler is the author of many articles on various aspects of economics, as well as of books, including *The Theory of Price*, which was first published in 1946, *The Organisation of Industry* (1968), and *Essays in the History of Economics* (1965).

Chapter Four
Roofs or Ceilings?
The Current
Housing Problem*

MILTON FRIEDMAN

*Paul Snowden Russell Distinguished Service Professor of
Economics, University of Chicago,
and Senior Research Fellow, Hoover Institution,
Stanford, California*

GEORGE J. STIGLER

*Charles R. Walgreen Distinguished Service Professor of
American Institutions, University of Chicago*

THE BACKGROUND

The San Francisco earthquake of 18 April 1906 was
followed by great fires which in three days utterly destroyed
3,400 acres of buildings in the heart of the city.

Maj. Gen. Greely, commander of the federal troops in
the area, described the situation in these terms: "Not a hotel
of note or importance was left standing. The great

*Reprinted with revisions from *Popular Essays on Current Problems*,
Vol. I, No. 2, (New York: The Foundation for Economic Education,
Inc., 1946).

apartment houses had vanished.... Two hundred-and-twenty-five thousand people were...homeless.'' In addition, the earthquake damaged or destroyed many other homes. Thus a city of about 400,000 lost more than half of its housing facilities in three days.

Various factors mitigated the acute shortage of housing. Many people temporarily left the city—one estimate is as high as 75,000. Temporary camps and shelters were established and at their peak, in the summer of 1906, cared for about 30,000 people. New construction proceeded rapidly.

However, after the disaster, it was necessary for many months for perhaps one-fifth of the city's former population to be absorbed into the remaining half of the housing facilities. In other words, each remaining house on average had to shelter 40 percent more people.

Yet when one turns to the *San Francisco Chronicle* of 24 May 1906—the first available issue after the earthquake—*there is not a single mention of a housing shortage!* The classified advertisements listed sixty-four offers (some for more than one dwelling) of flats and houses for rent, and nineteen of houses for sale, against five advertisements of flats or houses wanted. Then and thereafter a considerable number of all types of accommodation except hotel rooms were offered for rent.

Rationing by rents or chance?

Forty years later another housing shortage descended on San Francisco. This time the shortage was nationwide. The situation in San Francisco was not the worst in the nation, but because of the migration westward it was worse than average. In 1940, the population of 635,000 had no shortage of housing, in the sense that only 93 percent of the dwelling units were occupied. By 1946 the population had increased by at most a third—about 200,000. Meanwhile the number of dwelling units had increased by at least a fifth.

Therefore, the city was being asked to shelter 10 percent more people in each dwelling unit than before the war. One might say that the shortage in 1946 was one-quarter as acute as in 1906, when each remaining dwelling unit had to shelter 40 percent more people than before the earthquake.

In 1946, however, the housing shortage did not pass unnoticed by the *Chronicle* or by others. On 8 January the California state legislature was convened, and the Governor listed the housing shortage as "the most critical problem facing California." During the first five days of the year there were altogether only four advertisements offering houses or apartments for rent, as compared with sixty-four in one day in May 1906, and nine advertisements offering to exchange quarters in San Francisco for quarters elsewhere. But in 1946 there were thirty advertisements per day by persons wanting to rent houses or apartments, against only five in 1906 after the great disaster. During this same period in 1946, there were about sixty advertisements per day of houses for sale, as against nineteen in 1906.

In both 1906 and 1946, San Francisco was faced with the problem that now confronts the entire nation: how can a relatively fixed amount of housing be divided (that is, rationed) among people who wish much more until new construction can fill the gap? In 1906 the rationing was done by higher rents. In 1946, the use of higher rents to ration housing had been made illegal by the imposition of rent ceilings, and the rationing is by chance and favoritism. A third possibility would be for OPA* to undertake the rationing.

What are the comparative merits of these three methods?

THE 1906 METHOD: PRICE RATIONING

War experience has led many people to think of rationing as equivalent to OPA forms, coupons, and orders. But this is a superficial view; everything that is not as abundant as air or sunlight must, in a sense, be rationed. That is, whenever people want more of something than can be had for the asking, whether bread, theatre tickets, blankets, or haircuts,

---

*Office of Price Administration, the wage and price control rationing board used in the US during World War II.—Ed.

there must be some way of determining how it shall be distributed among those who want it.

Our normal peacetime basis of rationing has been the method of the auction sale. If demand for anything increases, competition among buyers tends to raise its price. The rise in price causes buyers to use the article more sparingly, carefully, and economically, and thereby reduces consumption to the supply. At the same time, the rise in price encourages producers to expand output. Similarly, if the demand for any article decreases, the price tends to fall, expanding consumption to the supply and discouraging output.

In 1906 San Francisco used this free market method to deal with its housing problems, with a consequent rise of rents. Yet, although rents were higher than before the earthquake, it is cruel to present-day house seekers to quote a 1906 postdisaster advertisement: "Six-room house and bath, with 2 additional rooms in basement having fire-places, nicely furnished; fine piano;...$45."

The advantages of rationing by higher rents are clear from our example:

- In a free market, there is always some housing immediately available for rent—at all rent levels.

- The bidding up of rents forces some people to economise on space. *Until there is sufficient new construction, this doubling up is the only solution.*

- The high rents act as a strong stimulus to new construction.

- No complex, expensive, and expansive machinery is necessary. The rationing is conducted quietly and impersonally through the price system.

The full significance of these advantages will be clearer when we have considered the alternatives.

Objections to price rationing

Against these merits, which before the war were scarcely

questioned in the United States, three offsetting objections are now raised:

(1)   The first objection is usually stated in this form: "The rich will get all the housing, and the poor none."

This objection is false: *At all times during the acute shortage in 1906 inexpensive flats and houses were available.* What is true is that, under free market conditions, the better quarters will go to those who pay more, either because they have larger incomes or more wealth, or because they prefer better housing to, say, better automobiles.

But this fact has no more relation to the housing problem of today than to that of 1940. In fact, if inequality of income and wealth among individuals justifies rent controls now, it provided an even stronger reason for such controls in 1940. The danger, if any, that the rich would get all the housing was even greater then than now.

Each person or family is now using at least as much housing space, on the average, as before the war. Furthermore, the total income of the nation is now distributed more equally among the nation's families than before the war. Therefore, *if rents were freed from legal control and left to seek their own levels, as much housing as was occupied before the war would be distributed more equally than it was then.*

That better quarters go under free market conditions to those who have larger incomes or more wealth is, if anything, simply a reason for taking long-term measures to reduce the inequality of income and wealth. For those, like us, who would like even more equality than there is at present, not just for housing but for all products, it is surely better to attack directly existing inequalities in income and wealth at their source than to ration each of the hundreds of commodities and services that compose our standard of living. It is the height of folly to permit individuals to receive unequal money incomes and then to take elaborate and costly measures to prevent them from using their incomes.

(2)   The second objection often raised to removing rent controls is that landlords would benefit. Rents would certainly rise, except in the so-called black market; and so would the incomes of landlords. But is this an objection? Some groups will gain under any system of rationing, and it is certainly true that urban residential landlords have benefited less than almost any other large group from the war expansion.

The ultimate solution of the housing shortage must come through new construction. Much of this new construction will be for owner-occupancy. But many persons prefer to or must live in rented properties. Increase or improvement of housing for such persons depends in large part on the construction of new properties to rent. It is an odd way to encourage new rental construction (that is, becoming a landlord) by grudging enterprising builders an attractive return.

(3)   The third current objection to a free market in housing is that a rise in rents means inflation, or leads to it.

But price inflation is a rise of many individual prices, and it is much simpler to attack the threat at its source, which is the increased family income and liquid resources that finance the increased spending on almost everything. Heavy taxation, governmental economies, and control of the stock of money are the fundamental weapons to fight inflation. Tinkering with millions of individual prices—the rent of house A in San Francisco, the price of steak B in Chicago, the price of suit C in New York—means dealing clumsily and ineffectively with the symptoms and results of inflation instead of its real causes.

Yet, it will be said, we are not invoking fiscal and monetary controls, and are not likely to do so, so the removal of rent ceilings *will*, in practice, incite wage and then price increases—the familiar inflationary spiral. We do not dispute that this position is tenable, but is it convincing? To answer, we must, on the one hand, appraise the costs of continued rent control, and, on the other, the probable additional contribution to inflation from a removal of rent controls. We shall discuss the costs of the present system next, and in the conclusion briefly appraise the inflationary threat of higher rents.

The present rationing of houses for sale

The absence of a ceiling on the selling price of housing means that, at present, homes occupied by their owners are being rationed by the 1906 method—to the highest bidder. The selling price of houses is rising as the large and increasing demand encounters the relatively fixed supply. Consequently, many a landlord is deciding that it is better to sell at the inflated market price than to rent at a fixed ceiling price.

The ceiling on rents, therefore, means that an increasing fraction of all housing is being put on the market for owner occupation, and that rentals are becoming almost impossible to find, at least at the legal rents. In 1906, when both rents and selling prices were free to rise, the *San Francisco Chronicle* listed 3 "houses for sale" for every 10 "houses or apartments for rent." In 1946, under rent control, about 730 "houses for sale" were listed for every 10 "houses or apartments for rent."

The free market in houses for sale therefore permits a man who has enough capital to make the downpayment on a house to solve his problem by purchase. Often this means that he must go heavily into debt, and that he puts into the downpayment what he would have preferred to spend in other ways.

Nevertheless, the man who has money will find plenty of houses—and attractive ones at that—to buy. The prices will be high—but that is the reason houses are available. He is likely to end up with less desirable housing, furnishing, and other things than he would like, or than his memories of prewar prices had led him to hope he might get, but at least he will have a roof over his family.

The methods of rent control used in 1946, therefore, do not avoid one of the chief criticisms directed against rationing by higher rents—that the rich have an advantage in satisfying their housing needs. Indeed, the 1946 methods make this condition worse. By encouraging existing renters to use space freely and compelling many to borrow and buy who would prefer to rent, present methods make the price rise in houses for sale larger than it would be if there were no rent controls.

One way to avoid giving persons with capital first claim to an increasing share of housing would be to impose a ceiling on the selling price of houses. This would reduce still further the area of price rationing and correspondingly extend present rent control methods of rationing rental property. This might be a wise move *if* the present method of rationing rented dwellings were satisfactory.

But what is the situation of the man who wishes to rent?

THE 1946 METHOD: RATIONING BY CHANCE AND FAVORITISM

The prospective renter is in a position very different from that of the man who is willing to buy. If he can find accommodation, he may pay a "reasonable," that is, prewar rent. But unless he is willing to pay a considerable sum on the side—for "furniture" or in some other devious manner —he is not likely to find anything to rent.

The legal ceilings on rents are the reason why there are so few places for rent. National money income has doubled, so that most individuals and families are receiving far higher money incomes than before the war. They are thus able to pay substantially higher rents than before the war, yet legally they need pay no more; they are therefore trying to get more and better housing.

But not all the millions of persons and families who have thus been trying to spread out since 1940 can succeed, since the supply of housing has increased only about as fast as population. Those who do succeed force others to go without housing. The attempt by the less fortunate and the newcomers to the housing market—returning service men, newlyweds, and people changing homes—to get more housing space than is available and more than they used before the war, leads to the familiar spectacle of a horde of applicants for each vacancy.

Advertisements in the *San Francisco Chronicle* again document the effect of rent ceilings. In 1906, after the earthquake, when rents were free to rise, there was 1 "wanted to rent" for every 10 "houses or apartments for rent;" in 1946, there were 375 "wanted to rent" for every 10 "for rent."

A "veteran" looks for a house

The *New York Times* for 28 January 1946 reported the experience of Charles Schwartzman, "a brisk young man in his early thirties," recently released from the army. Mr. Schwartzman hunted strenuously for three months,

> "riding around in his car looking for a place to live.... He had covered the city and its environs from Jamaica, Queens, to Larchmont and had registered with virtually every real estate agency. He had advertised in the newspapers and he had answered advertisements. He had visited the New York City Veterans Center at 500 Park Avenue and the American Veterans Committee housing sub-committee; he had spoken to friends, he had pleaded with relatives; he had written to Governor Dewey. The results?
>
> An offer of a sub-standard cold-water flat. An offer of four rooms at Central Park West and 101st Street at a rental of $300 a month provided he was prepared to pay $5,000 for the furniture in the apartment. An offer of one room in an old brownstone house, repainted but not renovated, at Eighty-eighth Street off Central Park West by a young woman (who was going to Havana) at a rental of $80 a month, provided he buy the furniture for $1,300 and reimburse her for the $100 she had to pay an agent to obtain the "apartment."
>
> And a sub-let offer of two commodious rooms in a West Side hotel at a rental of $75 a month only to find that the hotel owner had taken the suite off the monthly rental list and placed it on the transient list with daily (and higher) rates for each of the rooms."

Who gets the housing?

Rental property is now rationed by various forms of chance and favoritism. First priority goes to the family that rented before the housing shortage and is willing to remain in the same dwelling.

Second priority goes to two classes among recent arrivals: (1) persons willing and able to avoid or evade rent ceilings, either by some legal device or by paying a cash supplement to the OPA ceiling rent; (2) friends or relatives of landlords or other persons in charge of renting dwellings.

Prospective tenants not in these favored classes scramble for any remaining places. Success goes to those who are lucky, have the smallest families, can spend the most time in hunting, are most ingenious in devising schemes to find out about possible vacancies, and are the most desirable tenants.

Last priority is likely to go to the man who must work to support his family and whose wife must care for small children. He and his wife can spend little time looking for the needle in the haystack. And if he should find a place, it may well be refused him because a family with small children is a less desirable tenant than a childless family.

Socio-economic costs of present methods

Practically everyone who does not succeed in buying a house or renting a house or apartment is housed somehow. A few are housed in emergency dwellings—trailer camps, prefabricated emergency housing units, reconverted army camps. Most are housed by doubling-up with relatives or friends, a solution that has serious social disadvantages.

The location of relatives or friends willing and able to provide housing may bear little or no relation to the desired location. In order to live with his family, the husband must sacrifice mobility and take whatever position is available in the locality. If no position or only an inferior one is available there, he may have to separate himself from his family for an unpredictable period to take advantage of job opportunities elsewhere. Yet there is a great social need for mobility (especially at present). The best distribution of population after the war certainly differs from the wartime distribution, and rapid reconversion requires that men be willing and able to change their location.

The spectre of current methods of doubling-up restricts the movement not only of those who double up but also of those who do not. The man who is fortunate enough to have a house or apartment will think twice before moving to another city where he will be one of the disfavored recent arrivals. One of the most easily predictable costs of moving is likely to be an extended separation from his family while he hunts for housing and they stay where they are or move in on relatives.

The rent ceilings also have important effects in reducing the efficiency with which housing is now being used by those who do not double up. The incentives to economise space are much weaker than before the war, because rents are now lower relative to average money incomes. If it did not seem desirable to move to smaller quarters before the war, or to take in a lodger, there is no added reason to do so now, except patriotic and humanitarian impulses—or possibly the fear of relatives descending on the extra space!

Indeed, the scarcity resulting from rent ceilings imposes new impediments to the efficient use of housing: a tenant will not often abandon his overly large apartment to begin the dreary search for more appropriate quarters. And every time a vacancy does occur the landlord is likely to give preference in renting to smaller families or the single.

The removal of rent ceilings would bring about doubling-up in an entirely different manner. In a free rental market those people would yield up space who considered the sacrifice of space repaid by the rent received. Doubling-up would be by those who had space to spare and wanted extra income, not, as now, by those who act from a sense of family duty or obligation, regardless of space available or other circumstances. Those who rented space from others would be engaging in a strictly business transaction and would not feel that they were intruding, accumulating personal obligations, or imposing unfair or unwelcome burdens on benefactors. They would be better able to find rentals in places related to their job opportunities. Workers would regain their mobility, and owners of rental properties their incentive to take in more persons.

THE METHOD OF PUBLIC RATIONING

The defects in our present method of rationing by landlords are obvious and weighty. They are to be expected under private, personal rationing, which is, of course, why OPA assumed the task of rationing meats, fats, canned goods, and sugar during the war instead of letting grocers ration them. Should OPA undertake the task of rationing housing? Those who advocate the rationing of housing by a public agency argue that this would eliminate the discrimination against new arrivals, against families with children, and in favor of families with well-placed friends.

Problems of "political" rationing

To be fair between owners and renters, however, OPA would have to be able to tell owners that they had excessive space and must either yield up a portion or shift to smaller quarters. One's ear need not be close to the ground to know that it is utterly impracticable from a political viewpoint to order an American family owning its home either to take in a strange family (for free choice would defeat the purpose of rationing) or to move out.

Even if this basic difficulty were surmountable, how could the amount of space that a particular family deserves be determined? At what age do children of different sex require separate rooms? Do invalids need ground floor dwellings, and who is an invalid? Do persons who work in their own homes (physicians, writers, musicians) require more space? What occupations should be favored by handy locations, and what families by large gardens? Must a mother-in-law live with the family, or is she entitled to a separate dwelling? How long would it take an OPA board to answer these questions and to decide what tenants or owners must "move over" to make room for those who, in the board's opinion, should have it?

The duration of the housing shortage would also be affected. In fairness to both tenants and existing landlords, new construction would also have to be rationed and subjected to rent control. If rents on new dwellings were set considerably higher than on comparable existing dwellings, in order to stimulate new construction, one of the main objectives of rent control and rationing—equal treatment for all—would be sacrificed. On the other hand, if rents on new dwellings were kept the same as rents on existing dwellings, private construction of properties for rent would be small or nonexistent.

We may conclude that rationing by a public agency is unlikely to be accepted on a thoroughgoing basis. Even if applied only to rented dwellings, it would raise stupendous administrative and ethical problems.

Sources and probable duration of the present shortage

The present housing shortage appears so acute, in the light of the moderate increase in population and the real increase in housing since 1940, that most people are at a loss for a general explanation. Rather they refer to the rapid growth of some cities—but all cities have serious shortages. Or they refer to the rise in marriage and birth rates—but these numbers are rarely measured, or compared with housing facilities.

Actually, the supply of housing has about kept pace with the growth of civilian nonfarm population, as the estimates based on government data show (Table 1).

TABLE 1
RISE IN HOUSING AND NONFARM
POPULATION (USA 1940-1946)

	Nonfarm		
	Occupied dwelling-units (million)	Civilian population (million)	Persons per occupied dwelling-unit (No.)
30 June 1940	27.9	101	3.6
30 June 1944	30.6	101	3.3
End of Demobili-zation (Spring 1946)	More than 31.3	About 111	Less than 3.6

Certain areas will be more crowded in a physical sense than in 1940, and others less crowded, but the broad fact stands out that the number of people to be housed and the number of families have increased by about 10 percent, and the number of dwelling units has also increased by about 10 percent.

Two factors explain why the housing shortage seems so much more desperate now than in 1940, even though the amount of housing per person or family is about the same.

- The aggregate money income of the American public has doubled since 1940, so that the average family could afford larger and better living quarters even if rents had risen substantially.

- Rents have risen very little. They rose by less than 4 percent from June 1940 to September 1945, while all other items in the cost of living rose by 33 percent.

Thus, both the price structure and the increase in income encourage the average family to secure better living quarters than before the war. *The very success of OPA in regulating rents has therefore contributed largely to the demand for housing and hence to the shortage, for housing is cheap relative to other things.*

Future housing problems

Rent ceilings do nothing to alleviate this shortage. Indeed, they are far more likely to perpetuate it: the implications of the rent ceilings for new construction are ominous. Rent is the only important item in the cost of living that has not risen rapidly. Unless there is a violent deflation, which no one wants and no administration can permit, rents are out of line with all other significant prices and costs, including building costs. New construction must therefore be disappointingly small in volume *unless*

- an industrial revolution reduces building costs dramatically, or

- the government subsidizes the construction industry.

The industrial revolution in building methods is devoutly to be wished. But if it comes, it will come much faster if rents are higher. If it does not come, existing construction methods will, for the most part, deliver houses only to those who can afford and wish to own their homes. Homes to rent will become harder and harder to find.

Subsidies for building, in the midst of our high money incomes and urgent demand for housing, would be an unnecessary paradox. Now, if ever, people are able to pay for their housing. If subsidies were successful in stimulating building, rent ceilings could gradually be removed without a rise in rents. But building costs would still be high (higher than if there had been no subsidy) and so housing construction would slump to low levels and remain there for a long period. Gradually, the supply of housing would fall and the population would rise sufficiently to raise rents to remunerative levels. A subsidy thus promises a depression of unprecedented severity in residential construction; it would be irresponsible optimism to hope for a prosperous economy when this great industry was sick.

Unless, therefore, we are lucky (a revolutionary reduction in the cost of building apartments and houses), or unlucky (a violent deflation), or especially unwise (the use of subsidies), the "housing shortage" will remain as long as rents are held down by legal controls. *As long as the shortage created by rent ceilings remains, there will be a clamor for continued rent controls.* This is perhaps the strongest indictment of ceilings on rents. They, and the accompanying shortage of dwellings to rent, perpetuate themselves, and the progeny are even less attractive than the parents.

An incomplete and largely subconscious realization of this uncomfortable dilemma explains the frequent proposal that no rent ceilings or that more generous ceilings be imposed on new construction. This proposal involves a partial abandonment of rent ceilings. The retention of the rest can then be defended only on the ground that the present method of rationing existing housing by chance and favoritism is more equitable than rationing by higher rents, but that rationing the future supply of housing by higher rents is more equitable than rationing by present methods.

CONCLUSIONS

Rent ceilings, therefore, cause haphazard and arbitrary allocation of space, inefficient use of space, retardation of new construction and indefinite continuance of rent ceilings, or subsidization of new construction and a future depression in residential building. Formal rationing by public authority would probably make matters worse.

Unless removal of rent ceilings would be a powerful new stimulus to inflation, therefore, there is no important defence for them. In practice, higher rents would have little *direct* inflationary pressure on other goods and services. The extra income received by landlords would be offset by the decrease in the funds available to tenants for the purchase of other goods and services.

The additional inflationary pressure from higher rents would arise *indirectly*; the higher rents would raise the cost of living and thereby provide an excuse for wage rises. In an era of direct governmental intervention in wage fixing, the existence of this excuse might lead to some wage rises that would not otherwise occur and therefore to some further price rises.

How important would this indirect effect be? Immediately after the removal of ceilings, rents charged to new tenants and some existing tenants without leases would rise substantially. Most existing tenants would experience moderate rises, or, if protected by leases, none at all. Since dwellings enter the rental market only slowly, average rents on all dwellings would rise far less than rents charged to new tenants and the cost of living would rise even less.

As more dwellings entered the rental market, the initial rise in rents charged to new tenants would, in the absence of general inflation, be moderated, although average rents on all dwellings would continue to rise.

After a year or so, average rents might be up by as much as 30 percent.* But even this would mean a rise of only

---

*The actual increases that followed decontrol in 1949 averaged only about 12 percent. See US Congress, House Committee on Banking and Currency, *Extension of Rent Control 1950*, Hearings on H.R. 8276, 81st Cong., 2d. sess., 1950, pp. 483-98.—Ed.

about 5 percent in the cost of living, since rents account for less than one-fifth of the cost of living. A rise of this magnitude—less than one-half of 1 percent per month in the cost of living—is hardly likely to start a general inflation.

The problem of preventing general inflation should be attacked directly; it cannot be solved by special controls in special areas which may for a time bottle up the basic inflationary pressures but do not remove them. We do not believe, therefore, that rent ceilings are a sufficient defence against inflation to merit even a fraction of the huge social costs they entail.

No solution of the housing problem can benefit everyone; some must be hurt. The essence of the problem is that some people must be compelled or induced to use less housing than they are willing to pay for at present legal rents. Existing methods of rationing housing are forcing a small minority—primarily released veterans and migrating war workers, along with their families, friends, and relatives— to bear the chief sacrifice.

Rationing by higher rents would aid this group by inducing many others to use less housing and would, therefore, have the merit of spreading the burden more evenly among the population as a whole. It would hurt more people immediately, *but less severely*, than the existing methods. This is, at one and the same time, the justification for using high rents to ration housing and the chief political obstacle to the removal of rent ceilings.

A final note to the reader: we should like to emphasize as strongly as possible that our objectives are the same as yours—*the most equitable possible distribution of the available supply of housing* and *the speediest possible resumption of new construction*. The rise in rents that would follow the removal of rent control is not a virtue in itself. We have no desire to pay higher rents, to see others forced to pay them, or to see landlords reap windfall profits. Yet we urge the removal of rent ceilings because, in our view, any other solution of the housing problem involves still worse evils.

Chapter Five
Questions and Some Answers
about Rent Control
An Empirical Analysis of
New York's Experience

EDGAR O. OLSEN

5. Bomb Damage or Rent Control? See page 321 for the answer.

THE AUTHOR

EDGAR O. OLSEN, Ph.D., is currently Visiting Scholar at the US Department of Housing and Urban Development. Professor Olsen is a native of New Orleans, Louisiana, and received his undergraduate training at Tulane University. In 1968 he received his Ph.D. in Economics from Rice University. He was a post-doctoral fellow at Indiana University in 1967-1968 and an economist at the RAND Corporation from 1968 to 1970. Since 1970 he has been on the faculty of the University of Virginia.

Professor Olsen has written extensively on the theory and practice of housing economics—in particular about housing subsidies and rent control. His publications in scholarly journals include: "A Competitive Theory of the Housing Market," "Some Theorems in the Theory of Efficient Transfers," and "An Econometric Analysis of Rent Control."

Chapter Five
Questions and Some Answers about Rent Control An Empirical Analysis of New York's Experience

EDGAR O. OLSEN

Associate Professor of Economics,
University of Virginia;
Visiting Scholar,
US Department of Housing and Urban Development

On 30 January 1942, President Roosevelt signed into law the Emergency Price Control Act. The rent control provisions of this law were implemented in New York City (NYC) in November 1943 setting the maximum rents for all rental dwelling units at their levels of March of that year. The responsibility for rent control in NYC was transferred from the federal to the state government in 1950 and from the state to the city government in 1962. Almost everywhere else in the United States, rent control ended early in the 1950s.

To know the effects of any government program is to know the difference between what did happen in the presence of the program and what would have happened in its absence. Obviously it is no easy matter to know what would have happened in the absence of rent control.

Unfortunately, there is no other way to learn about its effects.

This paper summarizes what is known about the effects of rent control in NYC. Although there has been extensive experience with rent control throughout the world, much of the reliable knowledge about its effects refers to NYC. There are several reasons for this. First, good methods for learning about rent control were not developed until the late 1960s, and NYC was one of the few cities in the United States having rent control at this time. Secondly, good data for analyzing rent control is available for NYC, and thirdly, at least some members of the city government wanted to know the effects of the program.

In a sense it is misleading to talk about *the effects* of rent control since different rent control ordinances have different provisions, and these differences can lead to different results; furthermore, the effects in the first year may be different from the effects in later years. The major provisions of NYC's rent control ordinance are presented in the appendix to this chapter. Most of the results reported here refer to the effects of the ordinance twenty-five years after its imposition. These caveats should be kept in mind by anyone interested in predicting the effects of a proposed rent control ordinance.

EFFECTS OF RENT CONTROL IN NEW YORK CITY

This section will answer several important questions about rent control based on empirical evidence from NYC. It is essentially a summary of the technical work done by myself and others and represents a fairly exhaustive treatment of relevant information.

Is rent control a solution to a housing shortage?

Rent control is almost always proposed initially as a solution to a housing shortage, the manifestations of which are rapidly rising rents and a low vacancy rate. (Rapidly rising prices of owner-occupied houses are strangely

ignored.) There is little doubt that in the short run rent
control can slow the rate of increase in rents. However, this
does not mean that it is a solution to the problem of
inflation. Money that tenants would have spent on housing
is spent on other goods and services, driving up their prices.
There is no reason to expect the overall rate of inflation to
be affected by rent control. Perhaps because this argument
is obvious once said, no one has attempted to provide
empirical evidence to support it.

In the case of the vacancy rate we are more fortunate.
Rent control in NYC must be terminated if the vacancy rate
in the controlled sector exceeds 5 percent. That is, a low
vacancy rate in the controlled sector is the official rationale
for the continuation of rent control. Obviously, this
rationale would make no sense if decontrol would lead to a
higher vacancy rate. Table 1 suggests that this is exactly
what would happen. In 1940, when neither NYC nor other
U.S. cities had rent control ordinances, the vacancy rate in

TABLE 1
COMBINED RENTER AND OWNER
VACANCY RATES

	New York City	Other Cities
1940	7.3	4.7
1950	1.1	1.4
1960	2.0	4.0

Notes: In 1940 other cities consisted of all cities of 50,000 inhabitants or
more; in 1950 all cities of 100,000 inhabitants or more; in 1960 central
cities of all SMSAs.

Sources: Sixteenth Census of the United States: 1940, Table 73. US
Census of Housing: 1950, Table 27. US Census of Housing: 1960, Tables
9 and 15.

NYC was greater than the vacancy rate in other cities. In
1950, when almost all of these cities were covered by federal

rent controls, the vacancy rates were much lower than in 1940 and about the same in NYC as in other cities. By 1960 almost all other cities had long since decontrolled rents, but NYC still had a rent control ordinance. The vacancy rate in NYC was half of that in other cities, and the disparity in the rental vacancy rate (2.2 percent versus 6.2 percent) was even greater. Furthermore, Table 2 indicates that the vacancy rate

TABLE 2
RENTAL VACANCY RATES BY CONTROL STATUS IN NEW YORK CITY

	1960-1962	1965	1968
Controlled	0.8	2.0	1.0
Single Room Occupancy	7.6	13.0	6.3
Decontrolled	4.3	5.9	2.1
Never Controlled	3.9	4.4	0.7

Note: The vacancy rates for 1960-62 were obtained by dividing the number of vacancies in 1962 by the number of available units in 1960.

Sources: Kristof, pp. 1 and 110; Niebanck, p. 185.

in uncontrolled housing in NYC is typically greater than in controlled housing. Therefore, *the evidence from NYC strongly suggests that rent control exacerbates rather than solves a housing shortage.*

Should rent control be supported by people who support housing subsidies?

Since many people continue to support rent control decades after it was imposed in response to a temporary shortage, there must be other reasons for their support. I think that many supporters view it as a way of providing housing subsidies.

The purpose of a housing subsidy is to induce recipients to live in better housing than they would occupy were they given unrestricted cash grants with the same costs to whomever bears the costs. An unrestricted cash grant is a cash transfer with no strings attached. Housing subsidies come in many forms. For example, the amount of the subsidy may be a certain percentage of the recipient's rent, or the recipient may receive a cash payment provided that he occupies housing meeting certain standards. An unrestricted cash grant will ultimately lead a family to occupy better housing. The purpose of a housing subsidy is to produce an even greater improvement in housing conditions without providing a larger subsidy.

The evidence from NYC suggests that rent control does not produce this result and hence does not attain the primary goal of a housing subsidy program. In separate studies using slightly different samples and assumptions, Joseph DeSalvo and I found that, on average, occupants of controlled housing in 1968[1] lived in apartments about as good as the ones that they would have occupied in the absence of rent control.

In our studies, we used market rent as our measure of the desirability of an apartment. That is, if one apartment would rent for twice as much as another on the uncontrolled market, then we considered the former to be twice as desirable as the latter.

The studies essentially posed two empirical questions. First, what would be the market rent of the apartment that each family would have occupied in the absence of rent control? Second, how much would a given controlled apartment rent for in the uncontrolled market? By comparing the answers to these questions we are able to say whether persons living in rent controlled apartments would have occupied a more desirable or a less desirable apartment in an uncontrolled market.

The market rent of the apartment that the family would have occupied in the absence of rent control is the same as the amount that it would have spent on housing if controls had been absent. We predicted this amount for each family in controlled housing by using data on the housing expenditures of families who had the same characteristics and lived in uncontrolled housing. Similarly, we predicted the market rent of each family's controlled apartment by using data on the rents of uncontrolled apartments with similar characteristics.

DeSalvo found that the sum of the predicted market rents of controlled units exceeded the sum of the predicted housing expenditures of their occupants in the absence of controls by only 1.6 percent; I found that the latter exceeded the former by 4.4 percent. *For the typical family, the benefit of rent control stems from its effect on consumption of nonhousing goods and services.* I estimated that, in aggregate, occupants of controlled housing spend 9.9 percent more on nonhousing goods and services than they would have spent in the absence of rent control. DeSalvo did not make this comparison.

The only other estimates of these magnitudes, calculated by Elizabeth Roistacher in her doctoral thesis, present a different picture.[2]   Roistacher concludes that the aggregate market rent of controlled units in New York in 1968 was 19.7 percent greater than the aggregate market rent of the apartments that these families would occupy in the absence of rent control and that they spent 8.6 percent more on nonhousing goods and services. Unfortunately, her study contains a statistical bias which can be expected to result in an overestimate of the improvement in housing. Specifically, she was able to identify certain controlled units for which it was reasonable to believe that market rents had been underestimated. She adjusted these predictions upward by a reasonable amount. However, she failed to realize that there were certainly other apartments where market rents had been overestimated. Correcting some underestimates, while doing nothing about overestimates, results in an overestimate of the aggregate market rent of controlled units. Therefore, we can only conclude from her study that the improvement in housing is likely to be less than 19.7 percent while the increase in nonhousing consumption is in the neighborhood of 8.6 percent.

In short, the evidence from New York City suggests that rent control causes tenants in the controlled sector to spend most of their resulting increase in disposable income on items other than housing. Consequently, little improvement in their housing condition occurs. Therefore, surprising though it might seem, *no one who favors housing subsidies should support rent controls.*

Should people who favor unrestricted cash grants to low-income families favor rent control?

It is often argued that rent control is simply a way of redistributing income from the rich to the poor because landlords are richer than tenants. For this reason rent control is supported by many people who favor unrestricted cash grants to low-income families. Of course, it is not true that every tenant is poorer than his landlord, but even if this were the case, rent control would be a very poor redistributive device.

One important reason is that it distorts consumption patterns substantially. Many occupants of controlled housing live in apartments much less desirable than they would choose if they were given unrestricted cash grants each month, equal to the difference between the market rent and the controlled rent of their apartment, and required to live in uncontrolled housing. Other occupants of controlled housing live in much more desirable apartments.

DeSalvo, Roistacher, and I could have predicted the housing expenditures of families in controlled housing had rent control been replaced by unrestricted cash grants in these amounts. We could then have calculated the difference between this predicted housing expenditure and the predicted market rent of the controlled apartment occupied by each family. The size of this difference indicates the extent of the distortion in a family's consumption pattern. Unfortunately, this comparison did not occur to us. However, I did make another comparison which shows the extent of the distortion.

For each occupant of a controlled apartment, I estimated the annual unrestricted cash grant which, if given to the family in place of the benefits of rent control, would make the family neither better nor worse off than it was under rent control. My estimate of the average cash grant for 1968 is $213. The cost to landlords in this year (that is the difference between the market and actual rents) was $406 per controlled apartment. In other words, the cost of rent control to landlords is about twice its value to tenants, due to its distortion of their consumption patterns. Some tenants occupy much better housing than they would with unconditional cash grants; others much worse. Rent control is, therefore, a very inefficient redistributive device.

Rent control is not only an inefficient redistributive device but also a grossly inequitable one. There is undoubtedly a great variance in the cost borne by equally wealthy families. Rent control is not limited to low-income families and does not serve all such families. Among families who occupy controlled housing and are similar in many respects, there is an enormous variance in benefits. In short, there is nothing approaching equal treatment of equals under rent control. While there is no evidence on the distribution of the cost of rent control in NYC, the following propositions are almost certainly true:

- The majority of families at each income level do not own rental housing.

- The cost of rent control is borne overwhelmingly by people who own rental housing.

- Equally wealthy owners of rental property do not bear the same cost because they hold different proportions of their assets in this form.

Two important questions flow from these propositions:

- Why should rent control, which allegedly serves a public purpose, be financed by an implicit tax on such a small proportion of the population?

- Why should the magnitude of this tax on equally wealthy people depend upon the proportion of their assets held in the form of rental housing?

Table 3 presents the distribution of income in controlled and uncontrolled housing in NYC in 1968. Clearly, rent control is not limited to low-income families and does not serve all such families.

TABLE 3
DISTRIBUTION OF RENTER HOUSEHOLDS IN
CONTROLLED AND UNCONTROLLED
HOUSING BY INCOME:
NEW YORK CITY, 1968

Income of Head and Related Persons	Controlled	Uncontrolled
Under $2,000	12.2%	4.1%
2,000-3,999	21.6	9.0
4,000-5,999	22.5	14.8
6,000-7,999	17.3	16.9
8,000-9,999	10.7	15.1
10,000-14,999	10.7	24.6
15,000-24,999	3.8	11.7
25,000 or more	1.0	3.9
TOTAL	100.0*	100.0*

*Totals may not add due to rounding error.

Source: Lowry, DeSalvo, and Woodfill, p. 249.

Even among families who occupy controlled housing and are the same with respect to income, family size and the age, sex and race of the head of the household, there is an enormous variation in benefits, because the excess of market rent over controlled rent is different for different controlled units, and because some families experience greater distortions in their consumption patterns than other families. I have estimated that the mean benefit for families with average characteristics was $213 during 1968 and that the standard deviation in benefits is $261.

CONCLUSIONS

Rent control is a cause of, rather than a solution to, a housing shortage. Unlike housing subsidies it does not result in better housing for its beneficiaries. It is an inefficient and inequitable redistributive device. Even though New York City has had more experience with rent control than any other place in the United States, there are still many unanswered questions concerning its effects in New York. My conclusion from the experience of New York City is that no area should adopt a rent control ordinance unless there is compelling evidence that it will have different effects than the New York City ordinance. This ordinance appears to have no redeeming social value.

APPENDIX

Major Provisions of NYC's Rent Control Ordinance

This appendix provides a summary of the major provisions of NYC's rent control ordinance as of 1968, the year for which major data sources are available. Recently, there have been important changes in the law. However, most of the studies of the effects of rent control in NYC rely on data for 1968 or earlier.

In 1943, virtually all private rental housing in NYC was covered by rent control. By 1968, only 69 percent of such units were covered and the percentage of all units that were owner-occupied had risen from about 16 to 24. The next few paragraphs will describe provisions which influenced this change in the composition of the stock.

When the war ended, dwellings built after 1 February 1947 were exempted from controls, presumably in order to stimulate new construction. By 1968, 20 percent of all private rental units had never been covered by rent control.

Between 1943 and 1968, about 460,000 units were removed from the controlled inventory. About half of these units are now rented in the uncontrolled sector. The numbers of units decontrolled for various reasons are presented in Table A1.

Some of the other half removed have been converted from renter- to owner-occupancy. The number of such units is not known but is probably small because there were only 93,000 cooperative and condominium apartments in NYC in 1968, and many of these were undoubtedly never a part of the rental inventory. It appears that no one has sought an explanation for the surprisingly small number of changes in tenure. Certainly, one reason is that occupants of controlled apartments cannot be evicted in order to allow an owner to convert his building into a cooperative or condominium. The rent control ordinance severely limits the grounds on which a tenant may be evicted, and for all but a few of these grounds (nonpayment of rent—for example) the procedures for evicting a tenant are costly and the probability of success is low. Of course, the owner could wait until his units were vacated. However, it is probably difficult to convert some but not all of the apartments in a building to owner-occupancy and, if the owner waited until all tenants voluntarily vacated their units, the forgone rental revenues might be substantial.

TABLE A1
1965 DECONTROLLED DWELLINGS IN NYC
BY REASON FOR DECONTROL

	Number	Percentage
Total Decontrolled	199,000	100.0
Apartments in 1 and 2 family houses without businesses that became vacant after May, 1953 and automatically decontrolled	135,000	67.8
Dwellings once part of a larger apartment which was subdivided into smaller units	31,000	15.6
Dwellings occupied by landlord for at least one year and subsequently rented to a tenant	22,000	11.1
High rent decontrol (monthly rent greater than $250)	7,000	3.5
Reason unspecified	4,000	2.0

Source: Rapkin, p. 17.

The other units covered by rent control and not a part of the rental inventory in 1968 were demolished to make way for new residential buildings and nonresidential uses. The number of such units is not known. The rate at which this demolition occurred was undoubtedly slowed by the restrictions on evicting tenants.

As a result of new construction, decontrol, demolition, and changes from renter- to owner-occupancy, the composition of the stock by tenure and control status has changed substantially. Table A2 displays these changes for the 1960s.

The provisions mentioned in the preceding paragraphs concern which units are covered by rent control. Other provisions concern the conditions under which the controlled rent may be changed. Petitions for increases and decreases in maximum rents are handled in the offices of the District Rent Directors. Their decisions may be appealed to the office of the City Rent Administrator and then through the court system. In 1965 the District Rent Offices handled

TABLE A2
AVAILABLE HOUSING UNITS IN NYC BY TENURE AND CONTROL STATUS: 1960, 1965 and 1968
(Numbers in Thousands)

Tenure and Control Status	1960		1965		1968	
	No.	%	No.	%	No.	%
Total	2699	100.0	2792	100.0	2798	100.0
Renter	2115	78.4	2145	76.8	2122	75.8
Controlled	1628	60.3	1476	52.8	1359	48.6
Decontrolled	170	6.3	199	7.1	224	8.0
Never Controlled	207	7.7	333	11.9	395	14.1
Public Housing	111	4.1	138	4.9	144	5.2
Owner	583	21.6	647	23.2	676	24.2
Homeowner	n.a.	n.a.	570	20.4	583	20.8
Cooperative	n.a.	n.a.	77	2.7	93	3.3

Note: n.a. refers to data which are not available.

Source: Niebanck, p. 28.

about 660,000 cases. About 1 percent of these cases were appealed to the City Rent Administrator and 600 of these cases were brought up for court review.

The major provision accounting for increases in controlled rents allows tenants to voluntarily agree to a two-year lease calling for a rent increase of up to 15 percent. Almost all such agreements occur when a family is trying to obtain occupancy of a vacant controlled apartment. Even with an increase in rent, most of these apartments are bargains for many families compared with the alternative of

TABLE A3
SELECTED NYC RENT CHANGES GRANTED FROM
1 MAY 1962, THROUGH 31 DECEMBER 1968

	Number of Units with Rent Changes	Average Monthly Dollar Payment	Average Percent Adjust- ment
Selected Increases Granted			
Total for improvements	1,350,823	4.83	6.5
Increased Services or Facilities	955,246	5.22	7.1
Major Capital Improvements	168,070	4.13	5.6
Substantial Rehabilitation	227,500	3.84	4.8
Other	7	2.00	3.3
Total for Costs	84,263	10.26	10.1
Net Annual Return	82,413	10.23	10.2
Increased Costs: Small Structures, Hotels, etc.	1,850	11.48	7.4
Selected Decreases Granted			
Total, Painting and other Services	1,005,731	10.53	17.4

Source: Niebanck, p. 124.

renting in the uncontrolled sector. Since the landlord is free to choose his tenants, he is able to get these families to agree to an increase in the controlled rent. In the 1960s, about half of the dollar value of the increases in controlled rents was attributable to this provision. The numbers and average amounts of rent increases for other reasons are shown in Table A3.

A tenant is entitled to a rent reduction if there is any decrease in essential services (such as refrigerators, stoves, and heating), if equipment is not maintained, or if the building seriously deteriorates. There are detailed provisions concerning how often the landlord must paint. Table A3 contains the number and average amount of rent decreases granted. About half of the tenant applications for rent decreases are settled by the landlord restoring services. One-fourth are denied.

Finally, as a condition for renting an apartment, it is illegal for a landlord or superintendent to (1) accept a cash bonus, (2) accept any gift of value, rental fee, or commission, (3) require a new tenant to buy furniture, (4) charge the rate for a furnished apartment if the tenant has been permitted to bring in his own furniture, or (5) require more than one month's rent as a security deposit.

NOTES

1 The information for these studies was derived from the special New York City Housing and Vacancy Survey undertaken in 1968. This survey collected many pieces of information for about 35,000 housing units.

2 Although Roistacher's results on this particular issue are different from Olsen's and DeSalvo's, her conclusions are that New York's "rent control has undesirable redistributional effects among tenants of the controlled sector," and that "discrimination against minorities is likely to be more prevalent in a controlled market." She further concludes that "given the social goals of income redistribution, increased housing consumption for lower income households, and the removal of urban decay and related social problems, it is clear that rent control is not an ideal policy for protecting tenants from inflationary rents" (p. 284, Reference 10).

Chapter Six
The Effects of
Rent Control and
Rent Stabilization
in New York City

FRANK S. KRISTOF

6. Bomb Damage or Rent Control? See page 321 for the answer.

THE AUTHOR

FRANK S. KRISTOF received his Ph.D. in economics from Columbia University in 1952. Since that time he has been engaged continuously in the field of housing and urban problems, beginning as a Housing Market Analyst with the Federal Housing Administration (FHA) (1952-1955). He next spent eighteen months with the New York State Temporary Rent Commission in 1955-1956, completing four monographs on the economics of rent control based upon special survey data provided by the Census Bureau. This work led to his appointment as Assistant Chief of the newly created Housing Division at the US Bureau of the Census (1956-1960). He returned to New York City as Deputy Director (1961), then Director (1963) of the Bureau of Planning and Program Research of the City's Housing and Redevelopment Board. In 1967 he was appointed by the Mayor as Assistant Administrator for Programs and Policy of the newly created New York City Housing and Development Administration. In 1968, Dr. Kristof became Chief Economist for another new organization, the New York State Urban Development Corporation (UDC), and in 1977 he was appointed Vice President for Planning and Program Development. In 1968 Dr. Kristof resigned from UDC to become President of the Rent Stabilization Association of N.Y.C., Inc., where he is now located.

Dr. Kristof also taught at Columbia University from 1965 to 1976 as Adjunct Professor of Urban Planning in the School of Architecture and Planning. He has intermittently carried out studies and completed reports on international problems of housing and urban development on a consulting basis.

Chapter Six
The Effects of
Rent Control and
Rent Stabilization
in New York City*

FRANK S. KRISTOF

President,
The Rent Stabilization Association
of N.Y.C., Inc.

SUMMARY

The Fifteenth Interim Report of the Temporary Commission on City Finances addresses a subject of critical importance to New York City; that is, the future of rent control and rent stabilization. Recently, the State legislature approved a four-year extension of the Emergency Tenant Protection Act, which, in effect, authorizes the continuance of a widespread rent stabilization program in New York City. This action had strong political support, but is inconsistent with New York City's attempt to solve its financial and housing problems.

Rent control and rent stabilization reflect a succession of trade-offs made among political, economic, and social variables, the inevitable consequences of which public officials fail to perceive. Calculations of the costs versus the benefits of these policies, with regard to the city's housing, finances, and economy, clearly demonstrate the net adverse effect of rent control and rent stabilization.

*This article is based on the author's Fifteenth Interim Report to the Mayor by the Temporary Commission on City Finances.

The effect, if not the purpose, of rent control and rent stabilization is the subsidization of renters by owners. Cumulatively, this subsidy has exceeded $20 billion. Wholly aside from the question of fairness involved in a governmentally imposed requirement that one segment of the private sector subsidize another, there is no doubt that the imposition of controls on rent increases, without similar imposition of controls on the expenses incurred in the operation of apartment buildings, has caused and continues to contribute markedly to the deterioration of New York City's housing stock. Rent control and rent stabilization have already facilitated the destruction, beyond repair, of a significant portion of the housing inventory in New York City, and until rents are permitted to reflect the true costs of operating urban housing the premature decay of rental structures will persist.

Continuance of rent control and rent stabilization as permanent features of the New York City real estate market has also meant: (1) a loss of investments for countless New Yorkers whose savings went into producing the city's housing stock; (2) the destruction of the concept of owner-management; (3) the withdrawal of mortgage finance institutions from most of the rental market; and (4) the avoidance of new construction by responsible investors.

Moreover, rent control and rent stabilization programs have a severe, adverse impact on the finances of the City of New York. By depressing property tax assessments and promoting real estate tax delinquency and the abandonment of rental properties, rent control and rent stabilization diminish receipts from the single most important source of city revenues, the real property tax. This report concludes that elimination of rent control and rent stabilization, as recommended, would increase real property tax receipts by $100 million or more annually. Maintaining, and perhaps even reducing, real property taxes in order to stimulate economic development is highly desirable. The prospect of this happening would be greatly increased by eliminating rent control and rent stabilization and, thereby, expanding the real property tax base.

Precisely because the elimination of rent control and rent stabilization programs is so long overdue, the attendant political problem has been exacerbated, and it is hardly likely that many New Yorkers will readily accept the conclusion that it is in their best interests to rescind laws that have artificially maintained the cost of rental housing at below-market levels. Nonetheless, with due consideration to the human problems involved in the elimination of a major subsidy program that has been in effect for thirty-three years, the Temporary Commission on City Finances has concluded that this is in the best interests of the city as a whole.

HISTORICAL PERSPECTIVE ON HOUSING POLICIES IN NEW YORK CITY

Introduction

The present existence of rent control in New York City dates back to its Federal initiation in 1943 as a wartime anti-inflationary device. When Federal controls lapsed in 1950, a State rent control program was enacted by the State of New York to prevent "speculative, unwarranted and abnormal" increases in rents and evictions of tenants during a period of housing "emergency" (shortage).[1]

During the years 1950-1961, the detrimental effects of rent control did not impinge upon public consciousness. Complaints of owners that they could not maintain their properties with the existing rent restrictions largely fell on deaf ears. It was a period of only slowly rising operating costs that were partially offset by the curtailment of services by owners to the extent feasible.[2]

Rent control politics

It must be remembered that the concept of rent control in New York State at its inception in 1950 was that it was a temporary measure to protect tenants from "excessive" rent increases during an undefined "wartime" transition period to more normal housing market conditions. The name of the administering agency was the Temporary State Housing Rent Commission, and it was substantially in this spirit that the program was administered. In January 1955, incoming Governor Averell Harriman discussed the subject as follows in his message to the Legislature:

> "In the administration of such a law, however, we can seek to hold injustices to a minimum . . . by drawing upon factual rather than emotional or political considerations, by moving ahead from a controlled to an uncontrolled housing market as fairly and speedily as possible; by administering the law so as to maintain dwellings in good repair and preserve the health and safety of the occupants.
>
> Rent ceilings do not bring roofs overhead. Rent control must be viewed as only a single aspect of a broader housing program and as an interim device until such time as an adequate housing supply makes it no longer necessary."[3]

Curiously enough, it was in this legislative session that an attempt to liberalize the basis for approval of "hardship" rent increases processed through the rent agency was defeated as a result of public reaction generated largely by the governor's rent commissioner. For the first time, suspicions among observers were stirred that the temporary life of rent control might prove much more extended than earlier had been expected. These suspicions proved to be well-grounded, certainly with respect to the future of rent control in New York City.

During the city's 1961 mayoral election, what was seen to be the state's relatively liberal administration of the rent law became a political issue. As a result of the political imbroglio, the state transferred to the city the authority to administer rent control in February 1962.

Two facts lay behind the political popularity of rent control in New York City. First, over three-quarters of the city's population lived in rental quarters; second, as originally conceived and operated in New York State, rent control was extended to the bulk of the rental population, rich and poor, totally without discrimination.

A consequence of this situation is that the city's renters have been divided into two classes—the "haves" and the "have-nots." The "haves" are families who retained occupancy of their controlled apartments or who were lucky enough to acquire one. The "have-nots" are the low- or moderate-income families who, unable to acquire controlled apartments, had to rent uncontrolled apartments at a median rent approaching twice (1.67 times) that for controlled apartments.

Neither the need for space nor the ability to pay for housing has had any part in determining who would be fortunate enough to acquire (or retain) a controlled apartment. The ludicrous results that follow can be seen by comparing the rent control experience of a high-income and a low-income group in 1968:

TABLE 1
PERCENTAGE OF INCOME REQUIRED FOR RENT IN CONTROLLED AND UNCONTROLLED HOUSING—NEW YORK CITY, 1968

Item	Rent Controlled Occupancy	Uncontrolled Occupancy
Income Group	$10,000-$14,000	$4,000-$5,000
Number of Households	135,000	103,373
Median Monthly Gross Rent	$108	$123
Gross Rent as a Percentage of Income (Median)	10%	28%

Source: Unpublished data supplied by US Bureau of the Census, 1968 Housing and Vacancy Survey, New York City.

Given the figures illustrated in Table 1, it becomes clear why the political backbone of rent control comprises not only low-income families, but also the city's politically potent and middle-income affluent classes, who, on this issue, ignore political affiliation.[4] Had the reformers of rent control ever succeeded in establishing a needs test (such as the 25 percent rent-income ratio mandated for federally assisted housing), as a qualification for rent control protection, its middle-class political support would have largely eroded, and a dismantling of the system would have become infinitely easier.

The statutory basis for rent control

The extension of wartime rent controls in New York State was essentially regarded as a temporary measure. For this reason, a vacancy rate of 5 percent was established in the legislation as the criterion of the restoration of a normal supply-demand relationship in the housing market. Anything short of a 5 percent vacancy rate would be *prima facie* evidence of a continued "housing shortage." Given the limited experience with this type of legislation, few persons, except a handful of theoretical economists, raised questions about such a determination. The basis for the establishment of rent control in 1950, and its ultimate perpetuation in New York City, was the "desperate housing shortage." The claim of a housing shortage, in New York City particularly, has been both politically and statutorily sustained by the persistent and abnormally low vacancy rate experienced in the city since the end of World War II, even while other major rental cities, whose wartime controls were ended, realized substantial increases in vacancies since 1950, see Table 2 below.

TABLE 2
RENTAL VACANCY RATES IN
SIX U.S. CITIES—1950-1970

Year	New York	Boston	Chicago	St. Louis	San Francisco	Washington
			Rental Vacancy Rate			
1950	1.2	1.0	1.0	0.7	2.0	1.3
1960	2.2	5.1	5.2	5.4	6.6	3.8
1970	2.0	6.0	6.7	12.3	4.7	5.3

Source: U.S. Census of Housing, 1950, 1960, 1970.

A fundamental defect of the vacancy rate as a measure of housing shortage is the linkage between the price of and the demand for housing. This point was made in the city rent agency's official report in 1964: "Although its influence is not readily separated from other factors, the relatively low supply price for controlled units has increased the demand for rental housing in New York City."[5] It is a basic economic fact that any time the price of a commodity artificially is depressed below its market price, the demand for that commodity will increase. The demand for rental housing is not exempt from this principle. The fact that the median gross rent of uncontrolled apartments in 1960 was 54 percent higher than that of controlled units largely explains the persistence of a low vacancy rate and a tight housing market in New York City at a time when vacancies had become plentiful in major rental cities without controls.[6] We can see that the city's precontrol rental housing supply was in no significant way different from other major rental cities in terms of the amount of available housing relative to the population served.

Demographic trends

A number of disparate factors operative during the 1960s combined to create a crisis in the rent controlled housing inventory by 1969. Aside from the political necessity of maintaining rent control, the city's administrations had pursued vigorous programs of publicly assisted low- and middle-income housing construction which, during the late 1960s, had begun to have a perceptible effect upon the city's housing situation in conjunction with the demographic trends of the postwar period.

There were adverse demographic trends, notably an exodus of predominantly white middle-class families from the city and, within the city, to its outer rings. During the decade of the 1950s the city experienced a net loss of 1.2 million white persons: an additional 825,000 white persons were lost by out-migration during the 1960s. These losses were offset only by the combined effect of black and Hispanic in-migration and the high birth rate among these groups.

The enormous exchange of minority populations for white ones accelerated the racial changeover of many of the city's neighborhoods, particularly in the boroughs of the Bronx and Brooklyn. Thus the normal pull of the suburbs for middle-class white families was accentuated by the push on white families created by prejudices and fears of new neighborhood conditions with which they did not know how to cope. The problem was both social and economic, since the existing population in changing neighborhoods found the mores and behavior patterns of many of the incoming lower-income minority families alien and threatening.

Both the conventionally financed as well as the subsidized middle-income housing programs carried out in the city contributed to the reshuffling of white and minority residential patterns. Public housing, both the new and the old, increasingly became tenanted by black and Hispanic minorities at the same time as subsidized middle-income and privately financed full taxpaying housing was tenanted predominantly by white middle-class families, most of them fleeing older changing neighborhoods. Public policy efforts to avoid these results only temporarily retarded the developing patterns.

As fast as white families evacuated older rent controlled neighborhoods they were replaced by minority families, almost invariably of lower incomes. By 1969, a new phenomenon in the city became clearly observable. This was the widespread abandonment of apartment structures in racially changing neighborhoods. Estimates at that time indicated that, between 1965 and 1968, 100,000 rental apartments in the city's changing neighborhoods had been lost through abandonment.[7] This stunning discovery, revealed by periodic census housing surveys required under the city's rent law, led to cumulative pressures for a re-examination of the entire rent control system.

Rent stabilization in 1969

One outcome of the changing residential patterns was that market pressures of the white middle-class population upon the new high-rent housing in the city created sharply rising rents, violent complaints, and a political reaction that in 1969 led to new municipality imposed controls over all post-1947 rental construction previously free of controls.[8] *This was regarded by rental property owners and their mortgage lenders as a shabby betrayal of trust and led to virtual cessation of private new rental construction.* Three years later, the city again lured some investors into the market with a ten-year modified tax exemption program for new conventionally financed rental housing.[9] The new controls placed upon post-1947 residential construction were not as onerous as the city's rent control system. Termed rent stabilization, it is an industry policed system that provides for voluntary self-regulation of the formerly free market buildings through a Rent Guidelines Board, an industry run Rent Stabilization Association which is required to provide a code for the stabilization of rents, and a Conciliation and Appeals Board designed to handle landlord-tenant complaints.

Maximum base rent in 1970

Cumulative evidence of deterioration, disinvestment, and abandonment in the controlled housing inventory in 1970 led to the first major reform of rent control since 1950. New local legislation created a "maximum base rent (MBR)" which represents an approximation of the rent required to operate controlled buildings under current costs, including an 8 percent return on equalized assessed value. The MBR is required to be adjusted biannually. Rents are permitted to rise by 7.5 percent annually until the MBR is reached. When apartments are vacated, the next renter could be charged the full MBR then prevailing, irrespective of the percentage increase it represented over the previous rent.

The MBR was designed to be a computerized system. The input data forms proved far too complex to be completed accurately by most owners, while the short time allotted to collect and "clean up" the data overwhelmed an inadequate staff. The whole system finally collapsed and reverted to a hand tooled operation that never met its statutory time deadlines. More important, a last-minute city council amendment of the law destroyed its usefulness to building owners. This arose from the provision that denied rent increases to owners who could not certify that their buildings either were free of building code violations or that such violations were being removed. An estimated 30 percent of the controlled inventory never obtained MBR rent increases because owners were unable or unwilling to make the expenditures required to remove violations.[10]

Vacancy decontrol in 1971

In 1971, the State intervened in New York City's housing situation by legislating a Vacancy Decontrol Law which permitted all apartments, stabilized or controlled, that were voluntarily vacated by tenants to be rented at a free market rent. This law became effective on 1 July 1971 and survived only until 1 July 1974 when, after a bitter political struggle, it was replaced. New state legislation terminated the concept of vacancy decontrol for stabilized properties but retained the substance of the concept for rent controlled properties, except that, after a negotiated market rent was agreed upon for a vacated unit, it thereafter came under the rent stabilization system.[11]

RENT CONTROL AND RENT STABILIZATION IN 1977

The current rental market

With the exception of 90 percent of one- or two-family rental units and all post-1947 rental units in less than six-unit structures, virtually all unsubsidized rental housing today is under rent control or rent stabilization. Most of the pre-1947 structures contain both stabilized and controlled units, and they are thus subject to two separate administrative entities. Rents under both systems now move up regularly—7.5 percent annually for qualified rent controlled units (to the extent that the market permits) and about 5 percent annually for post-1947 stabilized buildings. The difference is less than it appears, since stabilized structures were much nearer market rents at the time they were initially placed under controls in 1969 than are their rent controlled counterparts. On the other hand, more controlled units each year approach their market price through vacancy turnover. In 1975, about one-half (642,000) of the city's 1,265,000 rent controlled housing inventory of 1970 remained under rent control.[12] As of January 1977, it is estimated that about 500,000 units remain under the rent control, while the number under rent stabilization amounts to some 900,000 units.

The disruption of the rental housing market caused by the twists and turns of rent legislation has had devastating effects. Except for savings and loan institutions, which have only limited financing alternatives such as one- and two-family owner-occupied houses, the financial community has largely abandoned both the financing of new rental housing and the refinancing of existing rental housing in New York City. However, financing for cooperative and superluxury rental apartments is still generally available.

Demographic impact

Coupled with the disastrous economic effects of the 1974-1975 recession, which for New York City began as far back as 1971, both economic and demographic trends have turned sharply negative for the rental housing industry. For the first time in its history, between 1970 and 1975 the city lost both population and households. The decrease in population numbered 413,000 persons, and there were 72,000 fewer households in 1975 than in 1970. After taking into account natural increase in population, the foregoing figures mean that net population out-migration (predominantly white) numbered nearly 600,000 persons.[13] These outflows equal or exceed the city's out-migration of the 1950s and 1960s.

During the years 1970-1975, the city also lost 500,000 jobs, more than wiping out the gain accumulated over the years 1950-1970. On the housing side, losses through abandonment in the ten years 1965-1975 numbered approximately 200,000 (mostly rental) housing units. And finally, for six perilous months during 1975-1976, the city hovered on the brink of fiscal bankruptcy.

What do these events foretell for the future of rental housing in New York City? The answer is necessarily a complex one and can more efficiently be addressed by examining a number of individual components.

Housing deterioration

The City's 1975 housing and rental survey for the first time permitted a glimpse of the extent of deterioration in rent controlled apartments compared with decontrolled apartments of similar age groups.[14] The data show that in every maintenance category except one (rodent infestation) the proportion of deficiencies in the controlled sector exceed those in the uncontrolled sector by up to 100 percent or more. The deficiencies in the decontrolled sector, meanwhile, are reasonably comparable to those for rental housing in all central cities of the Northeast Region as shown in Table 3.

TABLE 3
PERCENTAGE OF RENTER-OCCUPIED
HOUSEHOLDS BY INDICATORS OF QUALITY
OF HOUSING MAINTENANCE

Item	New York City		Central Cities Northeast Region
	Controlled Units	Decontrolled Units	
Dilapidated or Lacking Plumbing Facilities	9	5	n.a.
Breakdown of Toilet	6	3	3
Breakdown in Heating System	34	13	20
Broken Plaster, Peeling Paint	23	10	18
Holes in Walls, Ceiling	30	16	19
Holes in Floor	12	7	6
Rodent Infestation	28	31	n.a.

Note: n.a.: not available.

Sources: U.S. Bureau of the Census: *1975 New York City Housing and Vacancy Survey; Annual Housing Survey,* 1975, Part B, "U.S. and Regions, Indicators of Housing and Neighborhood Quality."

Housing abandonment

The city's rising tide of rental housing abandonment over the past ten years has focused attention upon rent control as a contributory factor. There is little dispute about the contribution of rent control in accelerating undermaintenance—with its consequent deterioration and disinvestment in rental housing—as well as influencing the withdrawal of institutional investment from this sector.[15]

Abandonment can also be traced, in part, to the complex of economic, demographic, and social factors affecting cities across the nation that led to a weakening and collapse of the market for older rental housing. The maturation of the automotive age caused unprecedented scattering of people. Decentralized industry, in efficient single storey plants designed to accommodate the automobile, taps widely dispersed labor market areas. The loss of population and jobs from obsolete and noncompetitive residential and industrial facilities in cities inevitably follows. But with rent control, the phenomenon of housing abandonment has been exacerbated in New York City.

Without rent control, the abandonment of older, obsolete housing would not have occurred on the massive scale that has been experienced by the city over the past ten years, nor with the same extent of neighborhood deterioration. The tempering factor in moderating the rate of deterioration and abandonment would have been the existence of market rentals that could sustain better maintenance and the economic viability of existing housing in neighborhoods where demand remained strong. As occurred in all other areas of the nation, the rearrangement of the population under a market rent system would have led to many adjustments in the usage of housing space relative to household decisions about rental expenditures.

Population migration

It is a matter of speculation whether New York City's out-migration would have been hastened or slowed by a phasing out of rent control in the immediate postwar period. Much would have depended upon the extent of in-migration by rural black and Hispanic persons in the early 1950s. Certainly there might have been substantial dislocation of families lodged in bargain housing they never could have afforded in the absence of rent control. On the other hand, such displacement would not necessarily have driven these families out of the city. They would have had to face up to the prospect of paying the market price for their housing or move to housing in locations that they more readily could afford. Clothing the market discipline that families must occupy the housing they can afford with terms such as "speculative, unwarranted and abnormal" increases in rents (as defined by whom?) only results in distortions of the market. Families in controlled housing frequently pay a fraction of the rent paid by higher-income families, but often do so for poorer housing— a common result of rent control. The ethics of such a set of conditions have not yet been explained by rent control adherents. As much as a 50-percent rent increase for a family at the city's median rent-income ratio of 19 percent in 1950 would have increased its rent-income ratio to 28.5 percent which, although financially inconvenient, would not necessarily have resulted in unbearable budgetary hardship. It may be noted that young families who bought new homes in the suburbs at that time frequently undertook housing expense-to-income ratios of 30 percent or more.

Given the speculative character of any discussion about what would have happened had the city shifted to a free market in 1950, the ultimate impact of a shift to market rents would have depended upon the short-term match between jobs and the number of persons in the labor market and upon the ensuing population flows arising from these relationships in conjunction with the impact of higher housing costs. It is difficult to conjecture to what extent the migration of rural black population into the city would have been deflected, given the displacement of some 3.5 million black persons from rural farm areas of the South between 1950 and 1970.[16] Had rent controls been lifted, conventional new construction would have tended to moderate the overall rise of rents, a feat that clearly was achieved in uncontrolled

Washington, D.C., where median rents between 1950 and 1970 increased no more than did New York City's controlled rents as is shown in Table 4 below:

TABLE 4
MEDIAN GROSS RENT FOR NEW YORK CITY
AND FIVE MAJOR RENTAL CITIES:
1950, 1960, 1970

City	Median Gross Rent			Change, 1950-1960		Change, 1960-1970	
	1950	1960	1970	$	%	$	%
New York City	$49	$73	$109	$24	40%	$36	49%
Five Major Rental Cities*	48	82	118	36	71	40	44
Boston	49	82	126	33	67	44	54
Chicago	48	88	121	40	83	33	38
San Francisco	42	73	135	31	74	62	85
St. Louis	37	66	90	29	78	24	36
Washington, D.C.	57	81	119	24	42	38	47

*Five largest cities, other than New York City, with 60 percent or more of their housing occupied as rental units; data show average of the medians.

Source: US Bureau of the Census, *Census of Housing, 1950, 1960,* and *1970,* Vol. 1, Part 1.

COSTS OF RENT CONTROL AND RENT STABILIZATION

Property valuations and real estate taxes

For twenty-three years of its thirty-three year history, the magnitude of the cost of rent control has effectively been concealed. Its contribution to housing abandonment has become evident over the past ten years. But only in recent years has rent control's contribution to the city's diminishing real estate tax base and reduced tax collections become apparent. In the thirteen years prior to fiscal year 1974-1975, aggregate real property assessed values in New York City increased at an average of $1 billion annually. Although the dollar amount remained fairly constant, the percentage increase gradually decreased over time. In fiscal years 1973-1974 and 1974-1975, the increases were $0.6 and $0.7 billion, respectively; in fiscal year 1975-1976, it fell to $0.3 billion. In fiscal year 1976-1977, total assessed values recorded the first loss since the depression of the 1930s—a decrease of $0.8 billion.

Another new phenomenon is the rise in outstanding unpaid real estate taxes. This figure has crept up from relatively modest figures of $150 million-$200 million in the late 1960s to new peaks in recent years. The City Record of 2 September 1976 shows the following:

TABLE 5
UNPAID NEW YORK CITY TAXES

1975-1976 Unpaid Real Estate Taxes	$ 242,569,502
1974-1975 and Earlier	328,388,719
Unpaid Water and Sewer Taxes	
Through 1975-1976	119,281,669
Cancellations and Remissions 1971-1975	440,100,000
	$1,130,339,890

Aside from the cancellations and remissions which are already written off, it is not known how much of the remaining $690 million will be collected, given the precarious state of the private real estate market today, even though some or all of these obligations represent the ostensible support for $1.45 billion of currently outstanding tax anticipation notes.[17] This kind of financial accounting is part of the reason for the existence of the Emergency Financial Control Board (EFCB) chaired by the governor. As City Comptroller Harrison J. Goldin commented in discussing the tax deficiency account in a recent report, "This deficiency becomes a part of the City's accumulated deficit as exposed by the new accounting and budgeting reforms which will bring an end to the spending of phantom revenues."[18]

A major contributor to this state of affairs, both the cessation of growth in assessed values as well as the cumulating real estate tax deficiencies, is rent control. It is directly responsible for the drop in average market values of controlled buildings from five and six times the annual rent roll in the early 1960s to a multiple of one or less today. This drop in turn forms the basis for reductions in assessed valuations as well as the inability of owners to pay taxes on their occupied buildings due to inadequate controlled rents. Chronic tax delinquency inevitably leads to loss of the building either through *in rem* proceedings (tax delinquent three or more years) or by abandonment.

A graphic picture of the interwoven effects of poverty, rent control, tax assessment, and tax collections has become available from a 1974 property-by-property study of sixteen blocks in a poverty area of the Bronx containing 393 parcels. The study found that over 40 percent of the 393 parcels have been taken by the city in *in rem* proceedings; an additional 25 percent of the parcels were seriously behind in taxes. Over one-quarter, 28 percent, of the parcels were vacant in 1974 (structures demolished) compared with 14 percent in 1972. After eliminating tax exempt parcels, the study showed that tax collections were current on only 29 percent of the parcels in the area in 1974.[19] This example makes clear why tax assessments in the Bronx have declined in five of the past six years. More important, it illustrates the devastating impact of the poverty culture on normal economic parameters of a middle-class society.

A $20 billion subsidy

It is worth repeating some observations made elsewhere of

the costs and benefits of rent control in New York City.[20] The Rand Corporation in 1969 estimated that the difference between the economic rents and controlled rents of some 1,240,000 housing units under rent control aggregated about $807 million or $650 per family for the year 1968.[21] Using this analytical approach, the present writer estimates that, over the thirty-three year life of rent control, an estimated income transfer to tenants of some $20 billion has been made from controlled apartment owners and their mortgage lenders. At the inception of rent control in 1943, 80 percent of the city's families (all tenants) were recipients of this beneficence, whether millionaire or welfare recipient. Over the years, this proportion has declined somewhat, but not greatly, given today's combination of rent control and rent guidelines.

The elimination or diminution of owner's operating profits is a result of rental revenues depressed below market values. A side consequence of this has been the destruction of the life savings of small investors, for whom real estate investment has been a classic method of ensuring an income in the retirement stage of life. This is reflected by the decline in value of rent controlled properties from five and six times the annual rent roll in the early 1960s to one times the rent roll or less today. Nearly half (46 percent) of all rent controlled apartments in the city in 1968 were in the hands of small investors who owned one to three buildings.[22] This type of owner, who tended to pay close attention to the operations of his building(s), has largely been replaced by owners today who, in the investment climate to which the controlled rental market has degenerated, can profit on such investments only by "milking" the buildings and abandoning them when the tenants move or refuse to pay the rent.

The reduction or minimization of services to tenants follows as a result of rental revenues that do not keep pace with the increasing costs of operating urban housing. Minimal maintenance, deferral of repairs, and deterioration of the building reflect the disincentive for owners to make capital improvements based on expectations of declining revenues relative to increasing costs.

Probably the most damaging costs of long-term rent control in a community are the psychological attitudes it engenders. The rent control syndrome among New York City's tenants is that of the tenant's right to enjoy possession of his apartment without being disturbed by periodic rent increases, irrespective of rising costs that create the need for them. Since 1970, this attitude has been disrupted by the 7.5 percent annual increase required under the Maximum Base Rent (MBR) system. Nevertheless, the truculence about rent increases among long-term, rent controlled tenants has spilled over into the city's publicly assisted middle-income housing programs, where tenants have taken the position that the rent burdens caused by increased interest rates, operating, and fuel costs should be shouldered by the city treasury, not by the tenants.[23]

Mortgage chaos

Widespread withdrawal of mortgage finance institutions from the financing of multifamily rental housing in New York City for many years is a direct consequence of the city's restrictive rent laws. Despite the fact that a free flow of mortgage lending funds to the multifamily housing sector is essential for its survival, the gravity of the problem has only recently become manifest. The problem has been addressed by the public sector in terms of the "redlining" of neighborhoods—the unwillingness of financial institutions to make mortgage loans in certain areas. Although this situation was basically created by rent control, it has been exacerbated by the social and economic deterioration of "redlined" neighborhoods, a rising tide of abandonment, and the increasing incidence of violence and crime to the point where these neighborhoods are avoided by apartment seekers who have any locational choices. Legislative proposals to proscribe "redlining" practices deal with the effects of the problem, not with their causes. Furthermore, private financial institutions have a fiduciary responsibility to their depositors. These institutions have no responsibility, or even right, to invest funds under social, economic, or public policy conditions that create high risks of loan defaults. Until public policy addresses this basic impediment to private investment, the life blood of mortgage financing for multifamily housing will not be available to property owners from most lending institutions. Public sector attempts to circumscribe the ability of lending institutions to reject high-risk loans must be accompanied by steps to ensure the safety of such loans. Otherwise such efforts will either be struck down by the courts or force lending institutions out of business.

CONCLUSIONS

Since the late 1950s and up to the present time, rent control has been a political football between the state legislature and the City of New York, to a degree that the original intent of "moving ahead from a controlled to an uncontrolled housing market as fairly and speedily as possible,"[24] not only has vanished from sight but has been qualified markedly in the legislation authorizing rent control. Introduced in 1943, rent restrictions have become perpetuated as a permanent institution on legal grounds that appear increasingly dubious.

Within the context of this background, the experience of thirty-three years of rent control in New York City may be summarized in a single phrase—"unmitigated disaster." As a housing tool it is a blunderbuss dispensing unnecessary and never-intended benefits to more than one-half of its beneficiaries initially, and to 15 percent of the families under controls today. It is contributing to the deterioration of the sound housing stock of the city and of its good neighborhoods. It is a major contributor to the city's real estate tax delinquency problem. Hundreds of millions of dollars are lost annually through reduced tax assessments on rent controlled properties or through building abandonment and demolition. Finally, rent control and rent stabilization have gone far toward bankrupting or demoralizing the real estate industry and undermining the financial status of institutions that have substantial mortgage investments in rent controlled properties.

The concept of owner-management has been largely destroyed; experienced owners and managers have withdrawn steadily from the rent controlled sector. The city's mortgage finance institutions basically have withdrawn from new commitments to the rent controlled stock, while few are willing to finance new rental construction. In summation, it may fairly be posited that few efforts of public policy have caused as much economic and fiscal chaos to a community as this example of legislative mismanagement has achieved in New York.

The necessity to liquidate rent controls and rent stabilization in New York City today is more urgent than ever before.

NOTES

1 Emergency Housing Rent Control Law, N.Y. Session Laws 1950, Ch. 250, Section 3.
2 Although illegal under the rent law, the practice of curtailing services nevertheless was widespread.
3 State of New York, Temporary State Housing Rent Commission, *People, Housing and Rent Control in Buffalo*, 1956, p. iii.
4 For example, some of the classic constitutional tests of the law fought through the highest courts were cases between wealthy landlords and their equally wealthy tenants.
5 The City of New York, City Rent and Rehabilitation Administration, *People, Housing and Rent Control in New York City*, 1964, p. 39.
6 "Major rental cities" are defined here as the six largest cities (New York City, Boston, Chicago, St. Louis, San Francisco, and Washington, D.C.) with 60 percent or more of their housing occupied as rental units.
7 F.S. Kristof, "Housing: The Economic Facets of New York City's Problems," in *Agenda for a City: Issues Confronting New York* (New York: Institute of Public Administration, Sage Publications, 1970), p. 365.
8 Apartment structures with six or fewer rental units were excepted.
9 The building of conventionally financed new rental housing had violent ups and downs in New York City since the end of World War II. The adoption of a new zoning ordinance in 1961 led to an enormous burst of conventional rental construction during the years 1961-1965 under the more liberal provisions of the old zoning ordinance that permitted more intensive use of building parcels. By

1966, completions under the old zoning ordinance had petered out, but developers had so flooded the market and depressed new construction rents during the years 1963-1965 that a combination of caution and resentment with the strictures of the new zoning ordinance caused a sharp drop in new conventional starts after 1965. Thus the market was unprepared for the strong rental demand of 1967-1968 that caused free market rents to jump vigorously, climaxed by city council imposition of rent stabilization in 1969.

10 The unwillingness arose from previous experience that many owners had of the inventiveness of tenants in creating code violations to prevent restoration of rent cuts imposed under "rent-impairing" violation provisions of the city rent law.

11 Rent stabilized units that had been decontrolled during the period that the vacancy decontrol law was in effect were, meanwhile, returned to the rent stabilization system.

12 Lawrence M. Bloomberg, *The Rental Housing Situation in New York City 1975*, New York: City of New York Housing and Development Administration, Department of Rent and Housing Maintenance, 1976. (About 125,000 of this decrease in controlled units is due to demolitions and abandonments.)

13 F.S. Kristof, "Housing and People in New York City," *City Almanac*, Vol. 10, no. 5 (New York: The New School for Social Research, 1976), p. 5.

14 There is one major physical difference—the decontrolled apartments are in structures of one to five units compared with controlled units in structures of six or more apartments. The city's 1960 rent study, however, in comparing the characteristics of three- to nine-unit structures with those containing ten or more units (all under control) concluded that "little in the foregoing description of the housing...of small versus large structures indicates fundamental differences between these two types of housing (except for) the better quality of units in large structures..." (p. 124).

15 For a comparison, see Ira S. Lowry, *Rental Housing in New York City*, Vol. 1. *Confronting the Crisis* (New York: The Rand Institute, 1970), and George Sternlieb, *The Urban Housing Dilemma* (Rutgers University: Center for Urban Policy Research, 1972).

16 This occurred as the nation's farm population dropped from 23 million to 10 million over the two decades.

17 Between December 1975 and March 1976 the city defaulted on $280 million of these notes. Emergency state legislation classified these nonpayments as a "moratorium," which since has been struck down by the courts.

18 "Communication from the Comptroller...Feb. 14, 1976," minutes of The City Council, 24 February 1976, City Record, 5 March 1976.

19 Monte Radock, Preliminary Staff report: Real Property Abandonment in New York City, (Savings Bank Association of New York State, 1974).

20 The following is an updating of findings made in F.S. Kristof, "Rent Control within the Rental Housing Parameters of 1975," *American*

Real Estate and Urban Economics Association Journal Vol. III, no. 3 (Winter 1975): 55, 57.

21 Ira S. Lowry, Joseph S. DeSalvo, and Barbara M. Woodfill, *Rental Housing in New York City* Vol. II (New York: The Rand Institute, 1971), p. 92.

22 George Sternlieb, *The Urban Housing Dilemma* (The City of New York, Department of Rent and Housing Maintenance, 1972), Exhibit 12-1, p. 454, provided the basis for this estimate.

23 For a comparison, see F.S. Kristof, "Rent Control Within the Rental Housing Parameters of 1975," *American Real Estate and Urban Economics Association Journal* 3, no. 3 (Winter 1975) :56.

24 Governor Averell Harriman, Message to the Legislature, 20 January 1955.

Chapter Seven
The Economics of Rent Restriction

F.W. PAISH

7. Bomb Damage or Rent Control? See page 321 for the answer.

THE AUTHOR

FRANK PAISH was born in January 1898. Eldest son of Sir George Paish, he was educated at Winchester College and Trinity College, Cambridge. Employed by Standard Bank of South Africa, 1921-1932. Lecturer at London School of Economics, 1932-1938; Reader 1938-1949; Professor of Economics with special reference to Business Finance from 1949 to 1965. Deputy-Director of Programs, Ministry of Aircraft Production, 1941-1945. Author (with G.L. Schwartz) of *Insurance Funds and their Investment* (1934), *The Postwar Financial Problem and Other Essays* (1950), *Business Finance* (1953), *Studies in an Inflationary Economy* (1962), *How the Economy Works, and Other Essays* (1970).

Chapter Seven
The Economics of Rent Restriction*

F.W. PAISH

Emeritus Professor of Economics,
University of London

In view of the important part rent restriction now plays in the economic systems of many countries, it is remarkable how little attention its economic aspects have attracted. Apart from the brief though admirable discussion in Mr. Roy Harrod's *Are These Hardships Necessary?* there is very little reference to the subject in recent British economic literature. It is quite understandable that politicians should have avoided the subject, for the emotions it arouses are too deep and too widespread to allow it to be discussed in public with both frankness and safety; but it is a little surprising that British economists, in the security of their studies, should have shown so little inclination to follow up the many interesting questions which the subject raises.

In the following article, after an outline of the history of rent restriction and a glance at the legal difficulties of its enforcement, I approach the subject mainly from two points of view: the inequity of its results as between individual tenants and individual landlords, and even more as between those with houses and those without; and its economic effects in discouraging the adequate maintenance of house property and in reducing the mobility of labor.

*Reprinted by permission of the author and publishers from *Lloyds Bank Review*.

151

THE HISTORY OF RENT RESTRICTION

Old control

The history of rent restriction in England begins very nearly thirty-five years ago, with the passage of the Increase of Rent and Mortgage Interest (War Restrictions) Act in December 1915. This Act made it generally illegal for landlords of unfurnished houses, or parts of houses let as separate dwellings, of which either the rent charged in August 1914, or the net rateable value did not exceed £ 35 in London or £ 26 elsewhere, to charge rents higher than those charged in August 1914, except insofar as improvements had been made or the rates increased. It also prohibited the calling-in of mortgages on rent restricted property or the raising of interest rates on them. The general principles of this Act have been maintained in all subsequent legislation.

After the 1914-1918 War, some concessions were made to help the landlord to meet the greatly increased cost of maintenance and repair. In 1919, increases of 10 percent and in 1920, of 40 percent, were permitted in the 1914 "standard rent," provided that the premises were kept "in a reasonable state of repair." On the other hand, the scope of the Act was extended in 1919 to cover all houses of which neither the standard rent nor the net rateable value exceeded £ 70 in London and £ 52 elsewhere, in 1920 increased to £ 105 in London and £ 78 elsewhere. Thus, all except the largest houses were made subject to control. At the same time, the protection of the Act was extended, not only to the "statutory tenant," but also to his widow or any relative who had been resident in his house for six months or more at the time of his death, though these in turn could not pass on their rights to yet another generation.

In 1923, after the short but violent depression which ended the postwar boom, the first steps were taken towards the withdrawal of rent control. Under the Act of that year, any house of which the landlord obtained vacant possession, or of which the sitting tenant accepted a lease of two years or more, became automatically decontrolled. When, ten years later, the results of the 1923 Act were reviewed, it was considered that, whereas the release of the larger houses had been proceeding too slowly, that of the smaller houses had been too fast. Under the Act of 1933, therefore, controlled houses were divided into three groups. Those of which both the recoverable rent (standard rent plus permitted increase) and the net rateable value were above £ 45 in London and £ 35 elsewhere were decontrolled immediately; those below these rates, but with a new rateable value of £ 20 in London and £ 13 elsewhere, continued to become decontrolled as they fell vacant; and those with still lower rateable values ceased to be decontrollable. In 1938, the second of these groups was in turn subdivided. The upper section, consisting of houses with net rateable values above £ 35 in London and £ 20 elsewhere, was decontrolled at once, while the lower section became permanently controlled.

Thus, in August 1939, all pre-1914 houses with net rateable values above £ 35 in London and £ 20 elsewhere had been excluded from control, together with a substantial though unknown number of smaller houses. The number of these decontrolled houses was estimated by the Ridley Committee in 1945 at 4.5 million. Also outside the control were some 4.5 million houses built since 1919, of which some 3 million were in private ownership and were mainly owner occupied and 1.5 million were owned by local authorities. Thus, out of a total of about 13 million houses and flats, only about 4 million, all with net rateable values not exceeding £ 35 in London and £ 20 elsewhere, and almost entirely owned by private landlords, were still subject to control. The recoverable rents of these houses were usually from 20 percent to 30 percent lower than the uncontrolled rents of similar houses.

New control

On 1 September 1939, all dwelling houses not subject to the old control and with net rateable values of not more than £ 100 in London and £ 75 elsewhere were made subject to a new control, with standard rents fixed at the rents which were being paid on the date of the Act, or, if not let on that day, at the last previous rent paid. All new houses, or those never let before, were to have as their standard rents whatever was charged at their first *bona fide* unfurnished letting. This Act is still in force, though it has been supplemented by the Furnished Houses (Rent Control) Act of 1946, which established rent tribunals to review rents of furnished accommodation, and by the Landlord and Tenant (Rent Control) Act of 1949, which gave to these same tribunals power to fix the rents of unfurnished houses let for the first time. The recommendation of the Ridley Committee, that rent tribunals should have the power to adjust in either direction anomalies in the existing standard rents of controlled houses, has never been adopted. No attempt has so far been made to control the prices at which houses may be sold.

LEGAL DIFFICULTIES AND INJUSTICES

The results of this long series of rent restriction Acts cannot be regarded with satisfaction from any point of view. It has long been realized that they have serious legal difficulties. Apart altogether from the question of evasion, and even after the immense case law developed by thirty years of litigation, the legal position in any particular case is often still obscure.

What exactly is part of a house let as a separate dwelling? Just how many acres of land must go with a house to make it a farm and therefore outside the scope of the Acts? Just how much furniture is needed to constitute a furnished house? Does a man automatically convert his office into a dwelling house by keeping a camp bed in it, and if not, how frequently must he sleep there to bring it within the Acts? Would an owner, with an invalid wife and three young children, who wishes to obtain occupation of his own house, suffer more hardship if his request were refused than the tenant, with only one child but a bedridden mother-in-law, would suffer if it were granted?

These are a very small sample of the thousands of cases decided yearly in the courts. Apart from such questions, it is often a matter of great difficulty to discover what is the standard rent of any particular house, especially if it has been owner occupied for any considerable time. If a house was last let in 1815, then the rent paid at the time of the battle of Waterloo is the standard rent today.

Tenants and landlords

If the rent restriction Acts are a lawyer's nightmare, they offend at least as much against the ordinary standards of equity. Of three identical houses in the same road, one may be let at 10 shillings a week under the old control, the second at 15 under the new control, while the rent of the third, let for the first time since the war, may be 25 shillings or more. There is no guarantee that the poorest tenant rents the cheapest house, or that the poorest landlord owns the dearest one. Indeed, the landlord of the cheapest house may well be poorer than his tenant, for before 1914 small house property was a favorite medium for the investment of small savings.

Those without houses

But the inequity of the present system as between tenant and tenant, or between tenant and landlord, fades into insignificance compared with the inequity as between those who are lucky enough to have rent restricted houses and those who have no houses at all. It is an economic truism that the fixing of maximum prices without the imposition of rationing normally results in part of the demand at the fixed price going unsatisfied. Even if the maximum rents fixed were completely consistent as between themselves this difficulty would remain. Since 1939, money earnings and most prices have approximately doubled; controlled rents (apart from increases in rates) have not risen at all. Thus, in real terms, the rents of some 8.5 million out of the 13 million prewar houses have been approximately halved. Is it to be wondered that the demand for houses to let at controlled rents is enormously in excess of the supply? Is it surprising that rent restricted houses are used less economically than they would have been if rents had risen in proportion with other prices and incomes, and that an unsatisfied demand is squeezed out, to be concentrated on the other sectors of the market—local authorities' houses, furnished accommodation, and houses available for purchase with vacant possession?

Of the sectors not covered by the rent restriction Acts, rents of local authorities' prewar houses, though frequently higher than before the war, are in general held at a level far below that necessary to equate supply and demand; while rents of their new houses, though higher than those of their older ones, even allowing for their improved amenities, are held by subsidies at a level far below current market values. Thus, a great unsatisfied demand is concentrated on the two remaining sectors, pushing prices there far above what they would have been if prices in all sectors had been allowed to find their market level. Sometimes tenants of furnished rooms (often in rent restricted houses) will venture to bring cases of unusually high rents to the notice of the rent tribunals set up under the Furnished Houses Act, even though the tribunals cannot give security of tenure for more than a few months at a time. But such controls, even if successful, cannot provide accommodation where it does not exist; and even if they could be universally enforced, their only result would be to reduce the supply and expand the demand for furnished rooms until there remained, for those left over who were unable to provide the deposit on a purchased house, the choice only between the hospitality of relatives and the hardly warmer welcome of a public institution.

Houses for sale

There remains only one sector of the market where no attempt has yet been made to control prices—the market in houses for sale. In spite of the fact that the demand here is limited to those able to provide at least the minimum deposit, prices for houses with vacant possession, especially for the smaller houses, have been forced up to a level far above that of most other prices. It is difficult to generalize the increase in house prices since 1939, but perhaps it would not be far from the truth to say that in many parts of the country small houses are costing from three to four times, and larger houses from two to three times, what they would have cost before the war. Only for the largest houses, unsuitable for conversion into commercial premises and requiring more service to run than is within the power of most post-tax incomes to command, is the rise in prices not abnormal.

The rise in the price of small houses cannot, however, be taken as an indication of the rise in rents which would follow the withdrawal of rent restriction; for much of it is due to the concentration upon the only completely free sector of the market of the excess demand created by the artificially low rents ruling in at least two of the other sectors. The repeal of rent restriction would almost certainly be followed by a sharp drop in the prices of at least the smaller houses offered for sale with vacant possession.

ECONOMIC EFFECTS

Inadequate maintenance

The economic aspects of rent restriction reveal disadvantages at least comparable with those of its legal and equitable aspects. They are mainly two: the impairment of the landlord's ability and incentive to maintain premises in good condition, and the impediments which the Acts place in the way of the mobility of labor.

As regards the first of these, it is common ground that the cost of maintaining and repairing houses has risen markedly since before the war, probably more than twice everywhere, and in some areas three times or more. At these prices, many landlords are unable to pay for adequate repairs out of the controlled rents and leave themselves any income at all, while others, especially owners of older property unsuitable for owner occupancy, find that it pays them better to collect what income they can until their property becomes actually uninhabitable than to spend money on repairs which will never yield a reasonable return on the expenditure. The probability that property will be treated in this way is increased by the tendency of the better landlords, faced with the choice between running their property at a loss and allowing it to decay, to sell it for what it will fetch to those who are less scrupulous in their methods of management. Thus, much property is being allowed to degenerate into slums, or at best maintained at a level much below that which is economically desirable and which it would have paid landlords to achieve if rents had been allowed to find their market level. For the ultimate results of this policy we have only to look across the English Channel, where inflation has gone considerably further than here, and the gap between controlled rents and those which would enable property to be kept in good repair is, therefore, even wider.*

Reduction in mobility

The second of the economic disadvantages of rent restriction, at least in the short run, is probably even more serious than the first. Rent restriction involves what is in effect a tax on the landlord and a subsidy to the tenant. But it is a subsidy which the tenant receives only so long as he stays in his existing house. Should he leave it for any reason, he is deprived, not only of his subsidy, but also of his right to rent another house even at the full market price. If he happens to live in a council house, it may be possible for him, by arrangement with the local authority, to exchange houses with someone else in the same district, or even to be allotted a new house on surrendering his old one. But if he lives in a privately owned house, or if he wishes to move outside his district, his chance of renting another within a reasonable time is small, unless he either has access to some special favor or is prepared to break the law by offering some consideration in addition to the controlled

*Illustrations of this phenomenon can be found in Bertrand de Jouvenel's essay in this volume on France's experience of rent restriction.—Ed.

rent. Otherwise, he will have to make do with furnished lodgings until first he qualifies to be regarded as a resident and then his name has slowly climbed to the top of the local authority's housing list. It is little wonder that the much needed increase in the mobility of labor is so difficult to achieve.

Expedients to restore mobility

If, however, a tenant inhabits a privately owned house suitable for owner occupancy, there are ways in which he may be able to retain at least part of the benefit of his rent subsidy after leaving his present house. So long as he remains a statutory tenant, the selling value of his present house is probably a good many hundred pounds less than it would be if the landlord were able to offer it with vacant possession. It may sometimes be possible for the tenant to obtain a share of this margin between the "sitting-tenant" and the "vacant-possession" values of his house, either by agreeing to leave in exchange for a cash payment, or by buying his house for something more than its "sitting-tenant" value and subsequently reselling it for its full market value with vacant possession. How much of the margin he will be able to secure for himself, and how much he will have to leave for this landlord, will depend on their relative bargaining powers; the tenant will no doubt do his best to conceal his desire to leave until the bargain has been completed. If in either of these ways he can make a substantial profit, he can use this to pay part of the purchase price of a house in the district to which he wishes to move, borrowing the remainder from a building society or other source.

Fewer houses to let

It should be noted that every time this sort of transaction occurs a house is permanently transferred from the letting market to the selling market. The same is true whenever a house falls vacant on the death of a tenant; for it will usually pay the landlord to sell it to an owner occupier rather than relet it at the controlled rent. Thus, despite the delay due to the right of a resident wife or relative to succeed to the tenancy for one further lifetime, it seems probable that the indefinite continuation of the present system will result in the gradual withdrawal from the letting market of all privately owned houses suitable for owner occupancy.

The demand for houses to let will therefore become increasingly concentrated on the new houses built by public authorities. The satisfaction of this demand, at subsidized rents, would require not only a long continued diversion to housing of resources urgently needed in other fields but also a continually mounting annual charge on the Exchequer and local governments for subsidies. This cost, for prewar and postwar houses, is already in the neighborhood of £ 40 million a year (in addition to the subsidies on temporary houses) and is rising by something like £ 5 million a year.

Chapter Eight
Recent British Experience
A Postscript from 1975

F.G. PENNANCE

8. Bomb Damage or Rent Control? See page 321 for the answer.

THE AUTHOR

The late FRED PENNANCE was McRobert Professor of Land Economy, University of Aberdeen. Educated at the London School of Economics, graduating in 1950, he spent a year there in the Economic Research Division, before joining the College of Estate Management, University of Reading, where he subsequently became Head of the Economics Department. Immediately prior to his move to the University of Aberdeen in 1974, Professor Pennance was a Visiting Professor at the University of British Columbia.

With Arthur Seldon, he compiled *Everyman's Dictionary of Economics* (1965), and has written many scholarly works on the theory and practice of urban land economics.

Chapter Eight
Recent British Experience
A Postscript from 1975*

F.G. PENNANCE

McRobert Professor of Land Economy,
University of Aberdeen

The purpose of this essay is to provide an up-to-date perspective on the state of British rent control legislation. The earlier history of British rent restriction is set out in Professor Paish's essay which preceded this one.

Postwar decontrol—and recontrol

The main change during the 1950s was the Rent Act of 1957 which freed the more expensive properties from control. This experiment in decontrol "from the top" was not repeated. Instead the Rent Act of 1965[1] effectively reversed the process. Practically all tenancies of uncontrolled dwellings with a rateable value of £ 400 or less (in London) or £ 200 (elsewhere) were given security of tenure similar to that afforded by the old rent control system. The 1965 system introduced a new concept—rent regulation—

---

*An earlier version of some of the material in this essay appeared in *Verdict on Rent Control* (Institute of Economic Affairs, 1972).

under which machinery was established for fixing "fair rents" for regulated dwellings. Application for a "fair" rent to be determined and registered could be made by a landlord, tenant, or both to the local rent officer or, on appeal from his decision, to rent assessment committees. Until such a "fair" rent had been registered for a dwelling, its rent was effectively pegged at the level obtaining when the Act came into force. A registered "fair" rent might raise, lower, or simply confirm the rent formerly payable; but once fixed it held for three years unless either a new "fair" rent was applied for jointly by both landlord and tenant or a change in circumstances occurred.

The Housing Finance Act, July 1972, sought to extend this system by converting both (private) rent controlled tenancies and local government council tenancies into regulated tenancies at fair rents.[2] Virtually all rented property was thus placed under the umbrella of rent regulation. The parallel changes in the 1972 Act were a rent allowance payable to private tenants in need (to be financed, initially at least, by the government) and rent rebates for council tenants in need. Housing subsidies to local authorities, formerly used largely to reduce council rents indiscriminately, were reformed to support the grant of rent rebates according to need and to stimulate slum clearance.

The explanatory white paper accompanying the Housing Finance Bill[3] recognized the failings of rent control in promoting disrepair and reduction of the available stock of rentable dwellings by accelerated obsolescence and the transfer of homes to the more lucrative sale market. It agreed that, "rent legislation cannot cure a housing shortage. It can only mitigate the effects of the shortage by giving comfort to sitting tenants at the expense of prospective tenants." Yet it evidently saw no dissonance between these observations and the statement that, "so long as there is a shortage of dwellings to let, tenants will need to be protected by rent restriction and given security of tenure."[4]

It saw the "fair rent" system as the lifting mechanism designed to remove the logical *impasse*. This belief was based on the 1971 report of the Francis Committee established in 1969 to examine rent regulation, which had offered "the general view that the system is working well."[5]

The rent allowance system would mitigate hardship to needy tenants arising from higher rents.

"Fair" rent for Buckingham Palace?

The implication was clearly that the "fair rent" system, if generalized, was capable of producing investment returns to landlords sufficient to maintain and encourage expansion of the stock of private rentable homes. But no evidence was produced to support this article of faith. Certainly the "general view that it was working well" cannot count as evidence. It is no surprise to find that it "works." Rent officers are no doubt sensible, hardworking and conscientious. They have a national association, write papers, hold conferences: in short, they behave much like other responsible public officers required to produce valuations according to statutory rules. They would probably have no difficulty at all in fixing a "fair" rent for Buckingham Palace if need be. But this proves nothing except that operational rules can be invented for any situation as long as the operators are under no compulsion to consider the economic facts of life or the effects of their decision.

Confusing the causes

The report of the Francis Committee was painstaking and thorough; with its appendices it runs to over five hundred pages; yet only four of them are devoted to the effect of rent regulation on the availability of homes for renting! Even then, the views expressed were elliptic, to put it mildly:

> "...there can be little doubt that the broad picture is a gloomy one. The supply of private unfurnished accommodation for renting is continuing to diminish. It would be wrong to attribute this solely or even mainly to rent regulation. The trend was there before the Rent Act 1965 did anything to halt it. The inference seems to be that this trend is largely due to the advantages of, and the widespread desire for, owner-occupation."[6]

It is of course true that continuing inflation, rising money (and real) incomes, and the substantial tax advantages to mortgagor homeowners would be likely to produce a marked shift to home ownership from rented homes. But this is a far cry from concluding that rent regulation can be whitewashed. It was responsible for the continuing shrinkage in rentable accommodation. The Francis Committee concluded its four-page review of this crucial issue with a significant table comparing vacancies advertised in the *London Weekly Advertiser* during March 1963 and March 1970. Unfurnished vacancies numbered 767 in 1963 and 66 in 1970. Furnished vacancies increased from 855 to 1,290. Since at that time furnished homes represented virtually the only free sector of the rental market, there were obviously forces at work other than an autonomous shift in consumer preferences towards owner-occupation. It is strange that the Francis Committee forebore to draw the obvious conclusion —that rent regulation had affected supply.

The economic fallacy—and economic incest

A "fair rent," as defined by the statutory rules for determining it, is in effect what the market rent would be if supply and demand for homes in an area were broadly in balance, and taking into account age, character, quality, and location. It thus specifically excludes from the reckoning the one economic factor likely to produce any easing of a situation of shortage. A "fair" rent is therefore by definition a *restricted* rent, except in the peculiar circumstances where it is presumably unnecessary to bother with a fair rent! Unfortunately, there is also an inevitable tendency for "fair" rents to be determined by the "fair" rents already established for comparable properties in the area. This form of economic incest is common to most forms of valuation based on statutory rules. What it means in effect is that situations of shortage are not only perpetuated but also likely to be exacerabated unless further compensatory "rules" are established.

In these circumstances there is little comfort to be drawn from the observed result that many applications to rent officers have produced increases in rent. What matters for investment incentives is the return achieved: not whether rent has been increased but by *how much*. A reduction in a rate of a slide downhill does nothing much for morale if everyone else is climbing.

Control continues to creep

The Rent Act 1974 hastily introduced by the Labour government in taking over from the Conservatives, began the process of dismantling the 1972 Act which Labour's election manifesto had promised. It halted even the weak moves to rationalize council rents which the 1972 Act had implemented and with impeccable logic extended the range of private rental regulation to include (effectively for the first time ever) furnished accommodation.

The results have been predictable and swift. Tenants occupying furnished accommodation have gained by obtaining greater security of tenure but at the expense of a significant erosion in existing and an almost total freeze-up of new supplies of furnished accommodation on the market. The recent correspondence columns of newspapers in Britain have been thick with recrimination and counter-recrimination on this score.

The overall picture has been further complicated by the one-year total freeze on all rents imposed as an anti-(?) inflationary measure in March 1974. This was lifted in March 1975, but regulated rents have since then been screwed down relative to other prices in the economy by restrictions on the rate at which rents may be increased. The provisions of the Housing Finance Act 1972, which envisaged the gradual decontrol of all properties still held in the vise of the older rent control, have been scrapped by the Housing Rents and Subsidies Act 1975. As a sop, landlords of rent controlled accommodation are now permitted to increase the controlled rent by a proportion of the cost of any repairs.

Rent regulation has been further amended by the 1975 Act. Rent officers are now required to disregard, in fixing "fair" rents, any improvements (or deterioration) in the amenities of an area since the last rent registration. In tune with other instructions to rent officers, "amenity" is left undefined by the Act. Rent companies complain that registered "fair" rents average only a half to three-quarters what an open market rent would be. Taken in conjunction with the March 1975 rules relating to the phasing of any rent increases (increases of over 80 p. (roughly $2) a week must be phased over two years), this means in effect that rent regulation is failing to provide landlords with gross incomes sufficient to warrant adequate maintenance expenditure.

Even if the 1972 Act generated misgivings, it also offered qualified hope that things might in the end be changed for the better. Possibly there is still hope in the fact that more recent legislation has still retained the idea of housing allowances for needy renters in the private sector. Therein lies the seed of a restoration of a free market in rental housing. But presently it lies on stony ground and the private landlord in Britain is a threatened species, more so than ever before.

NOTES

1 Both the 1957 and 1965 Acts are now consolidated, for England and Wales, in the Rent Act 1968.
2 The Rent Act, 1968 and the Housing Act, 1969 contained provisions for a form of "creeping decontrol" by transfer of tenancies from control to regulation on change of tenancy, improvement of the property to minimum standards, death of two successive statutory tenants, or by ministerial order.
3 Fair Deal for Housing, Cmnd. 4728, HMSO, July 1971.
4 *Ibid.*, p. 6.
5 Report of the Committee on the Rent Acts, Cmnd. 4609, HMSO, 1971, p. 8.
6 *Ibid.*, p. 82.

Chapter Nine
The Repercussions
of Rent Restrictions

F.A. HAYEK

9. Bomb Damage or Rent Control? See page 321 for the answer.

THE AUTHOR

FRIEDRICH AUGUST HAYEK, Dr. Jur., Dr. Sc. Pol. (Vienna), Dr. Sc. (Econ.) (London). Educated at the University of Vienna, he was Director of the Austrian Institute for Economic Research, 1927-1931, and Lecturer in Economics at the University of Vienna, 1929-1931. From 1931 to 1950 he was Tooke Professor of Economic Science and Statistics, University of London; 1950-1962 Professor of Social and Moral Science, University of Chicago; 1962-1968 Professor of Economics, University of Freiburg i. Brg., West Germany.

Professor Hayek's most important publications include *Prices and Production* (1931), *Monetary Theory and the Trade Cycle* (1933), *The Pure Theory of Capital* (1941), *The Road to Serfdom* (1944), *Individualism and Economic Order* (1948), *The Counter-Revolution of Science* (1952), *The Constitution of Liberty* (1960), *Studies in Philosophy, Politics and Economics* (1967), *Law, Legislation and Liberty* (3 vols., 1973, 1976, 1979), and *New Studies in Philosophy, Politics, Economics and the History of Ideas* (1978).

In 1974 Professor Hayek was awarded the Nobel Prize in Economics.

Chapter Nine
The Repercussions
of Rent Restrictions*

F.A. Hayek

Nobel Laureate 1974

The problem of rent control is still frequently judged only in terms of its impact on landlord and tenant, so that other far-reaching repercussions on the whole economic system are largely ignored or underrated. Even when some notice is taken of them, a distorted and sometimes totally false view spills over from popular misconceptions even into learned debates. It is here that some drastic rethinking is needed.

What I shall try to do, therefore, is to deal in turn with the major consequences of statutory rent restrictions and the reduction of rents below market prices through the government financing of building construction. I shall start with their impact on the general supply of accommodation

*This essay was adapted with the author's permission by the Institute of Economic Affairs from a lecture delivered at Königsberg in 1930 and was originally published in *Schriften des Vereins für Sozialpolitik* 182 (Munich, 1930). This version was first published in *Verdict on Rent Control* (Institute of Economic Affairs, 1972), and is reprinted with the permission of the publisher.

It was freely translated from German and simplified by several hands, and the final result is a less elegant prose style than the author used later in writing in English.

to rent and on the main types of dwellings, then go on to consider their effects on how the supply is distributed among people in search of a home, on income distribution, and on the pattern of production in general, with particular reference to the supply of capital. My terms of reference require me to concentrate entirely on the control of domestic rents, without going into the closely related and most important question of the impact of rent regulation on business premises, which I have previously discussed in a similar context.[1]

If my account of the impact of rent restrictions seems exaggerated in any particular, I would emphasize that my thoughts are attuned to the Viennese scene. The ways in which these conditions differ from those in Germany are well-known. The best way to dramatize this contrast is by pointing out that it will be another two years before the average Viennese rent reaches a temporary peak equivalent to 30 percent of prewar rents, despite there being at present no government powers to allocate or assign accommodation, in brief, no thoroughgoing state control.

Even so, I believe my principal reflections to be equally valid in a German context. Basically, deductions which can more easily be drawn from Vienna than elsewhere must also hold good where less severe forms of rent restriction are practiced. The theory can be worked out by pure reason; all that Vienna provides is a convenient source of illustration. Far from exaggerating the consequences, they would be still more striking were it not for the decline in Vienna's population.

THE UNIQUE CHARACTERISTIC OF HOUSING

A unique feature of price control in housing compared with that in other goods and services is that wartime housing regulations have been retained and enforced ever since. The reason is not that housing is more "necessary" than, say, food, nor that it has become harder or more costly to supply than other necessaries, but simply that, unlike almost all other consumer goods, it is a *durable* commodity which, once produced, remains available for many decades and is therefore in some ways more vulnerable to state control than, say, bacon or potatoes.

It is precisely because of this unique feature of housing that the most unwelcome of all the effects of price pegging, its effect on supply, is neither generally felt nor even generally recognized. We are faced with the problem of evaluating the significance of rent controls not merely as temporary but as permanent expedients. On a shorter view we could allow ourselves to assess their effects on the distribution and enlargement of the existing housing *stock*. Instead we must tackle the underlying problem, that of meeting *indefinitely* an emergent demand for homes at repressed rents.

Elasticities of demand and supply

We pay too little attention to the phenomenal rise in demand for homes which must occur every time rents fall below the level at which they would settle in an unfettered market. It is not merely a matter of the undoubted elasticity of demand in the housing market, reacting as it does every time lower building costs enable rents to be reduced with a corresponding rise in demand. The housing shortage which inevitably follows every statutory limitation of rent levels is directly related to the difficulty of finding new accommodation. It turns the occupation of a dwelling into a capital asset and encourages a tenant to hang on to his home even when he would surrender it at the reduced price provided he could be sure of finding another home when he wanted one.

In these circumstances a large unsatisfied demand for housing was obviously bound to emerge, even without an increase in population, and the only way to bridge this gap was by the government financing of house-building. When, as in Vienna and Austria generally, there is in addition a big difference between statutory rents and rents which would prevail in the open market, the prospect of fully satisfying the demand for homes at depressed rents seems totally illusory. Despite a decline in population of one-seventh and an increase in housing stock of something like one-tenth (there are no reliable figures), no one can pretend that the

demand for housing is less than it was. That depressed rents
are largely responsible for the increased demand for homes
in Germany as well, and that the current housing shortage is
to that extent a product of rent restriction, can also be seen
from the decline in population density in almost every city
in the country since the war. I shall return to the changing
contemporary significance of such estimates of average
population density.

Government supply in long run

Over and above this supply gap, which can be met only by
government (or municipal) building schemes, we have to
take into account the demands generated by population
expansion, and further—and here are the basic problems of
housing controls as a permanent institution—the whole
range of demand created by the misallocation of the available stock of rentable accommodation. State control as an
emergency measure could jog along contentedly enough
with new building intended to supplement the housing stock
built by private enterprise. In the *long term*, however, if
public finance is being used to build homes, the demand for
which has increased due to a lowering of rents, it will
ultimately have to be applied to *all* new building of houses
to let. Hence—and the literature on the subject shows that
this is worth emphasizing—it is not enough to build publicly
financed homes in the hope that they will constitute an
additional supply; if the aim is to keep rents *permanently*
depressed, then for as long as rents are held below market
rates it will be necessary to use public money to provide
total supply.

This development not only raises complex financial
questions. Very few government authorities will want to
assume responsibility in this way for all types of housing. In
general, it will prove necessary to limit government building
to the more modest types of dwelling, with the natural
corollary that they will be the only types to enjoy rent
protection. Limiting the applicability of rent regulations
in this way to particular classes of dwellings, however,
gives rise to other difficulties too often overlooked.

For if public building operations and the supply of below-cost homes are to be confined, as they must be, to the classes of dwelling for which society is prepared to shoulder full responsibility indefinitely, they must also inevitably cater for the social class whose lot society wishes to ease, and not for the better-off. Hence it is futile to think that resources currently deemed appropriate to public expenditure on building can be used both to make up the shortfall of homes for the poorest sections of the community and *at the same time* to erect homes of better than average quality for the majority of the population. Better standards can be achieved with public funds (where there is sufficient surplus finance) to put up a number of model homes. But every attempt to depress rents even in this latter category below the levels required to pay off capital and interest will founder, unless there is available enough public money to meet the demand for all housing in this class indefinitely.

It is worth noting an unfortunate side effect of some significance which will occur even when government finance is confined to building homes for the poorest sections, that is, those whose needs alone it can hope to satisfy. I refer to the relatively large gap that will emerge between rents for the best housing that government money can build and for the privately constructed alternative. A large number of people will therefore inevitably settle for a home of poorer quality than they would have occupied if rents had shown a smooth progression instead of such a disproportionate variation.

EFFECTS ON DISTRIBUTION

So much for the ways in which rent restrictions affect the quantity and composition of available housing. How do they affect its distribution? Most experts have gone no further than to repeat and briefly illustrate the *cliche* that housing conditions are "fossilised" by rent controls. An associated phenomenon seems to account for most of the "far-reaching effects" I have mentioned.

The assumption of this further argument is that rent regulations will continue as at present for homes of all classes, and that the housing shortage created by rent restriction will inevitably persist. While this situation continues, the attitude to changing circumstances of anyone with a low-rental home will be governed by the conditions before rent regulation came into force. Clearly, such a distribution of available homes to rent, understandable though it may be on historical grounds, must conform less and less to diverse changing needs the longer the controls have been in force. Clearly, also, the implications of such a limitation for the mobility of manpower must be harmful.

Extent of "fossilisation"

Before I examine these implications, however, I should first like to consider the true extent of this "fossilisation," and where we should look for a thaw, if any. Some adjustment is made, for example, when the occupier of a controlled tenancy sublets or "sells" his tenancy (in fact if not in law); in other words, when he transmits his controlled tenancy in exchange for money, and in cases—and these are in the majority—where an exchange takes place between two homes of different standards. For reasons explained, by no means all the tenants who would take smaller homes, given the chance under free market rents, will sublet the corresponding portion of their existing dwellings or welcome an exchange. The only possible result is that a proportionately smaller share of the housing stock becomes available to those who must depend on satisfying their requirements by subrenting, buying, or exchanging property than if they were competing freely for their share with all the other home seekers on the open market.

Thus the interplay between supply and demand must be weighted against the tenant in those partial markets where prices are free, and here, too, rents demanded will be higher than in an open market. The growing section of the community which neither enjoys controlled tenancies nor is catered for by government financed building is thus worse off than if there were no protective legislation at all. In practice this means that many younger people pay a form of tribute to their elders still living in their prewar homes; and this subsidy may amount to more than the rent they would be paying a landlord if there were no controlled tenancies.

In practice very few can avail themselves of this means of restoring mobility, and it therefore plays only a minor role. For the majority, it is a harsh and rigid fact of life that tenants cling to their dwellings, thereby preventing the adaptation of housing on offer to changing requirements in terms of size, position, and standards. As a result, while there are isolated instances of population densities so divergent as to make a mockery of statistical averages, there are disproportionately more acute housing shortages where average densities are truly comparable, that is, where the number of homes on offer is comparable, than there would be in the open market.

Immobilizing labor

The restrictions on the mobility of manpower caused by rent controls mean not only that available accommodation is badly used to satisfy diverse housing requirements. They also have implications for the deployment and recruitment of labor to which too little attention is paid.

In normal times regional switches in industrial manpower requirements entail considerable labor migration, and, despite the unusually large changes in industry in the past decade, migrations have been blocked by rent controls. Left to itself, and given an unfettered wage structure, this immobility would prevent wages in different regions from evening themselves out, and cause marked variations between the regions.

As things stand, however, collectively negotiated wage settlements largely rule out such variations, and two other results therefore follow. First, the wage-earner will choose to commute rather than move whenever his new place of work is within reach of his home, either on a daily or a weekly basis, even though he may find this mode of living by no means satisfactory. The wage-earner who is prevented from moving will have to spend extra time and money, which represent a cut in pay, further aggravated because regional differences have been eliminated. From the economic standpoint, this and all other expenditures incurred by people because they are "wedded" to their homes are downright wasteful. B. Kautsky[2] points out that the cause of Vienna's increased tram traffic, which doubled between 1913 and 1928 at a time of diminishing population, can only have been this inhibited mobility. P. Vas,[3] admittedly with some exaggeration, estimates that "the additional fares squeezed out of the Viennese public by rent control alone" amounted to at least two-thirds of the annual outlay on new building in the city.

Commuting or unemployment?

Commuting, however, is not always a feasible alternative to moving house, and if it is not, the result is unemployment. Joseph Schumpeter, writing in *Deutsche Volkswirt*, once gave forceful expression to the importance of the correlation between lack of mobility of labor and unemployment, an importance which cannot be rated too highly. I shall merely mention one example of it which came to my notice recently.

A manufacturer of my acquaintance, with a factory in a small town some five hours from Vienna and an office in Vienna itself, went to the labor exchange in Vienna to ask for an electrical fitter for his provincial factory. Twenty or so fitters, some of whom had been out of work for a long time, applied for the vacancy, but every one of them withdrew rather than give up a protected tenancy in Vienna for unprotected works accommodation. Weeks later the industrialist had still not found his fitter. Every manufacturer in Austria with a factory outside the main industrial centres can tell you countless similar stories.

I would almost go as far as to say that when the reduced rents policy succeeds in providing low-cost homes for *all comers* the repercussions will be even more disastrous. We should not forget that city dwellers, who form the bulk of those living in rented accommodation, are not the only ones who move. Every successful attempt to provide low-cost rented accommodation in an urban area must also accentuate the drift from the countryside to the towns. No one would wish, whether for economic or for social reasons, artificially to encourage the growth of mammoth cities. Yet such is the inevitable consequence of inhibiting rent increases which act as a useful brake on this drift to the towns. The greatest harm must come from aiding it in boom periods, as unemployment must inevitably shoot up in any subsequent recession. In practice, even when rents have been buoyed up by a flourishing economy, this has also had its good side.

Incidentally, it is questionable, to put it no stronger, whether one should set out to make it easier for the poorer sections of the community to have children at the expense of the more prosperous, or to improve the lot of the urban population at the expense of the rural. Yet this is the inevitable outcome of a policy of federal or provincial subsidies which aid city growth and prevent the size of households from adjusting naturally to incomes.

(There is one last aspect closely connected with the wasteful distribution of available accommodation: the way it obscures genuine trends in demand both for location and quality. I deal with it below.)

EFFECT ON SUPPLY OF CAPITAL FOR INVESTMENT

Current housing policies affect the supply of investment capital to the economy in two ways. First, the supply of new capital is reduced because income from housing is insufficient to repay existing loans. This is of much importance to industry, since in present circumstances a good deal of this amortization would not have been ploughed back into housing but would have become available to the rest of the economy, at least for a transitional period. Second, and more important, as a result of public building schemes immense sums were used at one time for purposes other than those best designed to increase human productivity, that is, those which would have been served in the normal course of events but for the housing policies followed.

Public building investment distorts resource allocation

The importance of the absorption of resources by public building is best shown by comparing the amount spent in Vienna alone on domestic building (at least 700 million schillings) with the market value of Austria's entire share capital as quoted on the Vienna Stock Exchange which, the Austrian Institute for Market Research has calculated, amounted to 961 million schillings in 1929. Given the subsequent 25 percent drop in share prices, the total value cannot now be much over 700 million schillings.

Even so we are very far from having bridged the housing "gap." Can one doubt that, allowing for federal and provincial expenditure on domestic housing and for all the administrative expenses of operating the present policy, an outlay which exceeds the total value of Austria's industrial investment capital must have major repercussions? Even assuming that, after taxation, only part of this capital would have gone to industry, this state of affairs cannot fail to affect human productivity, and hence wage levels.

When we try to assess this deployment of capital, or indeed to assess housing policies as a whole, our attitude to one question is crucial. Anyone who believes that the economic difficulties, especially the heavy unemployment, of the postwar period can successfully be combatted by stimulating consumption—that there is no shortage of the means of consumption but that the obstacle to the fullest use of available resources is that consumers' incomes are too low—and who consequently looks to public works of every kind to tone up the economy in the long term, takes a more benign view than I do of the present outlay on housing and the tendency inherent in present-day housing policies to push up consumption at the expense of capital formation.

There is unfortunately no space for a criticism of this most dangerous of the prevalent errors of economic theory which, originating in America, is steadily gaining more ground.

Homes not provided for the right people

Quite apart from the repercussions of draining off capital

from other sectors of the economy, a further question is whether the present outlay on housing succeeds in satisfying housing requirements as well under the present restrictive system as would an identical outlay under a free market system.

This brings me to the question postponed earlier, and by the same token to one of the gravest problems of present housing policies. For what we saw earlier of the uneconomic distribution of existing accommodation applies with equal force to building operations with no free market prices to guide them. My argument is in no way affected should rent restrictions not be applied to new building. It is rather that the needs of those who happen not to have any accommodation at present and who accordingly head the queue for new construction do not coincide with the needs which would come to light if existing accommodation were distributed rationally. It would make sounder sense to apportion some of the available accommodation among the homeless, and to build new homes on a completely different pattern and in different areas, that is, homes for which real demand exceeds supply.

At present we really have no idea how much housing is required, of what size, or where. So instead of building with a view to supplementing the existing range of homes, we carry on as if new home seekers had no interest whatever in existing accommodation, and as if the housing needs of tenants in controlled dwellings were immutably fixed for all time. For example, suppose that quite fortuitously a rural or urban district has a number of young couples looking for homes; in present circumstances homes will be built even though far more people are already living there than want to do so and even though the homes required would soon become available if mobility were restored. Alternatively, homes may be built for families with children simply because there are many such families without suitable accommodation; but at the same time there may be many older couples occupying homes which no longer correspond to their needs and which would be suitable for families.

The tremendous waste entailed in such arbitrary building must call seriously in doubt the proposition, partly supported by C. Kruschwitz,[4] that rent restrictions should only be abolished when supply and demand have balanced themselves out; indeed it leads us to question the very idea that this balance can ever be achieved in such conditions. Before the war, that is, independently of restrictive legislation, Adolf Weber noted that "the basic cause of housing difficulties is...the variance between the extreme flexibility of present-day economic relationships and the rigidity of the housing market."[5]

Do we really stand a chance of eliminating our present housing shortage while we persist in denying even to new building the possibility of responding to changing needs?

Value of theoretical analysis

The specific object of my paper was to give a systematic picture of the repercussions of restrictive rent legislation. If this account seems to boil down to a catalogue of iniquities to be laid at the door of rent control, that is no mere coincidence, but inevitable because it stems from both a theoretical and a liberal treatment of the problem, which are one and the same. For I doubt very much whether theoretical research into the same problems carried out by someone of a different politico-economic persuasion than myself could lead to different conclusions. Therefore, if theory brings to light nothing but unfavorable conclusions, it must indicate that though the immediate benefits of rent control, for which it was introduced in the first place, are obvious to everyone, theory is needed to uncover the unintentional consequences which intervention brings in its wake.

That these unlooked-for consequences are incidentally unwelcome should surprise no one. Everyone is naturally at liberty to weigh for himself the benign against the damaging consequences of rent control. Nor is recognition of the damaging consequences in itself tantamount to opposition to rent control. What *is* necessary is to know them for what they are before venturing an opinion for or against.

However, if in my concluding remarks I am to draw any lessons for future policy from our investigations, then I am bound to say that, having weighed the advantages against the drawbacks, I have come to the conclusion that the indispensable condition for an escape from our present troubles is a speedy return to an open market in housing.

TRANSITION TO AN OPEN MARKET

Even so, given agreement on that ultimate goal, we are still left with the question of how best to use our knowledge of present conditions to regulate the transitional period. A conviction that an open market is *per se* the most desirable condition is of course far from an assertion that the immediate abolition of rent control as things are is the most effective method of achieving it.

Dangers of sudden lifting of controls

Indeed, precisely because rent control means so much more than that tenants pay less rent than they would do otherwise, because it means that available accommodation is distributed quite differently from the way it would be in an open market, it follows that the freeing of the market would not only bring an extra charge on the tenant but also cause changes in the pattern of distribution.

Were controls to be lifted suddenly, these changes would inevitably take place on such a scale that the market would be utterly disorganized, with all the resulting dangers. It would suddenly become apparent not only that there was a serious imbalance between supply and demand, but also that prices for a particular kind of home in particular localities had risen out of all proportion to their value. The worst of the pressure would doubtless fall on small dwellings, as the demand for them by people obliged to leave their larger homes owing to rent increases would be considerably higher than the demand from those with the means to move into the relatively cheaper larger homes thus vacated. This pressure would be aggravated by the absence of a ceiling on rents. Attempts would undoubtedly be made to push rents up to grotesque levels, and in the initial confusion they would probably succeed.*

In my view, the remedy is not to raise rents gradually, as is generally suggested, up to the critical point, by which I mean the point which would establish prices on the open market, and thus harmonize supply and demand, which would provide freedom of movement, and which would be reached virtually instantaneously. For the transition to go through smoothly, some prior correction of existing distribution patterns is called for.

The only solution I can envisage is to try to create as large an open market as possible alongside a temporary retention of controls in specific cases. In other words, the proposal is progressively to enlarge as far as possible the existing free market sector catering for noncontrolled tenancies, subletting and home buying. A basis for this already exists since, as explained earlier, an ever-increasing proportion of the population no longer enjoys the benefits of rent control. What is now needed is to block the transfer of protection, so that new home seekers start off on the right footing, thus avoiding misdirection of future demand and also putting the maximum number of existing dwellings on the free market, but without creating a new demand by the eviction of tenants.

I hope this basic outline of the subject will be found adequate. It leaves me free to indicate in "verbal shorthand" those measures which I think offer the best hope of achieving this end.

Practical measures

Plainly the first step must be to detach tenancy protection from *property* and attach it to *persons*, by which I mean to an occupier or his *bona fide* dependents. The inheritance or transmission of a protected *tenancy* would then cease. The next stage would be to remove controls from the largest

---

*For an analysis of an actual decontrol situation that does not support this view, see the essays "Decontrol" and "Postscript" in this volume.—Ed.

size, and lastly from homes previously sublet or subdivided, when a landlord chooses to divide up a building rather than to let it as a self-contained unit. The conversion into flats of existing large dwellings ought to be especially encouraged, although probably little encouragement would be needed to persuade landlords to let freely part of a building formerly wholly subject to rent control. The supply of homes could be speeded up by the imposition of a tax or similar levy on the rental income not only of occupied but also of unoccupied property. Another move designed to ease the tenant's position transitionally *vis-à-vis* the market in the face of legislation weighted in favor of the landlord would be to require landlords to give long notice periods, while allowing tenants to give shorter ones.

What is of supreme importance, however, is that all subsequent building operations should align their prices with the rents which emerge from these partial markets. With this in view some public aid might need to be given to building merely to stop rents in particular areas and for certain types of housing from rising above the levels to which private enterprise building could ultimately be expected to bring them.

Even so, money from whatever source should be applied only where at least a market return on investment is to be expected, and, when public money is used, the rents asked should be no lower than foreseeable average rents after the abolition of rent control. And if, in order to keep rents down, public money is to be used at all, the lesson we must draw is that it should be used exclusively to build the very smallest and cheapest of homes.

NOTES

1 F.A. Hayek, "Das Mieterschutzproblem: Nationalökonomische Betrachtungen," *Bibliothek für Volkswirtschaft und Politik*, No. 2 (Vienna, 1929). To a large extent the paper which follows is based on the earlier, more detailed study.
2 B. Kautsky, *Schriften des Vereins für Sozialpolitik*, 177 III (1930), p. 70 ff.

3 P. Vas, *Die Wiener Wohnungszwangswirtschaft von 1917-1927* (Jena, 1928), p. 35.

4 Carl Kruschwitz, *Schriften des Vereins für Sozialpolitik*, 177, I (1930), p. 48.

5 Adolf Weber, *Die Wohnungsproduktion* (Tübingen, 1914), p. 354.

Chapter Ten
No Vacancies

BERTRAND DE JOUVENEL

10. Bomb Damage or Rent Control? See page 321 for the answer.

THE AUTHOR

BERTRAND DE JOUVENEL was born in Paris in 1903. M. de Jouvenel is the descendent of a famous family which gave France noted statesmen and writers. He studied mathematics and law. After graduating he entered French politics, but later went into journalism, becoming an active reporter on international affairs. In the latter part of World War II he took refuge in Switzerland, where he completed his great work, *Du Pouvoir*, an analysis of present-day totalitarianism. In 1947 he was appointed to the University of Manchester, where he lectured on society and sovereignty. He is now president of a bureau of economic research in Paris (SEDEIS), and editor of *Analyse et Prevision*.

Among his many writings are: *The Crisis of American Capitalism* (1933); *Problems of Socialist England* (1946); *Du Pouvoir* (1945), published in English; *On Power* (1948); *Ethics of Redistribution* (1951); *The Political Good* (1955); *The Art of Conjecture* (1971). More recently, he has written: *Arcadie, Un Civilization de Purisance* and *François*.

Chapter Ten
No Vacancies*

BERTRAND DE JOUVENEL

President,
SEDEIS, Paris

A DOLLAR A MONTH

A dollar a month will pay a wage-earner's rent in Paris. Our authority for this assertion is the Communist-dominated Federation of Labor Unions, the CGT. In setting forth its demands for a minimum wage to ensure a decent living, it produced a worker's budget in which the expenditure on rent was put at 316 francs. (In this analysis, all figures will be stated in dollars at the rough valuation of 300 francs to the dollar).

Against this figure one may set the estimate of the conservative Union of Family Associations. Thinking in terms of families, this source sets the expenditure on rent, providing adequate space, at a dollar and a half for a man and wife with two children; for a family of six the expenditure on rent should go up to a little less than two dollars.

Artificially low rents

Such cheapness is amazing. In the CGT budget, rent is reckoned as equal in cost to transport to and from work. To put it another way, a month's rent for an individual worker

*First published in the US by the Foundation for Economic Education, Inc., Irvington-on-Hudson, New York, October 1948.—Ed.

costs little more than six packets of the cheapest cigarettes. For a large family of six it costs as much as eleven packets of cigarettes (cigarettes, now unrationed in France, cost 15 cents a packet).

Even in a worker's very modest budget such an expenditure absorbs but a small part of his income, 2.7 percent of the minimum income demanded by the CGT; as little as 1.2 percent of the income of a six-member family as calculated by the Union of Family Associations.

Against such estimated blueprint budgets we can resort to actual declarations of wage-earners canvassed by the French statistical services. It appears from their budgets that, on average, rent makes up 1.4 percent of wage-earners' expenditures; for white collar workers rent goes up to 1.7 percent of total expenditures.

In practice there are many rents lower than a dollar a month; rents of half-a-dollar are not uncommon. Nor should it be assumed that the lodgings are necessarily worse, for price and comfort, as we shall see, are unrelated.

Such low rents are not a privilege confined to wage-earners. Middle class apartments of three or four main rooms will frequently cost from $1.50 to $2.50 per month. Rents paid by important officials or executives range from $3.50 to $8 or $10 a month. There is no close correlation between income and rent. Rent seldom rises above 4 percent of any income; frequently it is less than 1 percent.

It is not then surprising that Parisians spend on entertainment every month far more than they pay for three months' rent.

Here lies an apartment

This may seem a very desirable state of affairs. It has, of course, its drawbacks.

While, on the one hand, you pay no more than these quite ridiculous prices if you are lucky enough to be in possession of a flat, on the other, if you are searching for lodgings you cannot find them at any price. There are no vacant lodgings, nor is anyone going to vacate lodgings which cost so little, nor can the owners expel anyone. Deaths are the only opportunity.

Young couples must live with in-laws, and the wife's major activity consists in watching out for deaths. Tottering old people out to sun themselves in public gardens will be shadowed back to their flat by an eager young wife who will strike a bargain with the janitor, the *concierge*, so as to be first warned when the demise occurs and to be first in at the death. Other apartment chasers have an understanding with undertakers.

"BOOTLEG" HOUSING

There are two ways of obtaining an apartment which death has made available. Legally, if you fulfil certain conditions which give you a priority, you may obtain from a public authority a requisition order; you will usually find that the same order for the same apartment has been given to possibly two or three other candidates. The illegal method is the surest. It is to deal with the heir, and with his complicity immediately to carry in some pieces of your furniture. As soon as you are in, you are king of the castle.

Buying one's way into an apartment will cost anything from $500 to $1,500 per room. At such prices you may also share flats which the tenants will agree to divide. As for wage-earners, they may as well give up hope of setting up house; they will have to stay with their families or live in very miserable hotels by the month.

In short, rents are very low but there are no lodgings available. Nor are any being built. And practically none have been built for the last twelve years.

There are some 84,000 buildings for habitation in Paris: 27.2 percent of them were built before 1850, 56.9 percent before 1880. Almost 90 percent of the total were built before World War I. Most of the additional new building was carried out immediately after that war; then it slackened, and by 1936 had practically stopped.

Parisian plight

Even a very lenient officialdom estimates that there are about 16,000 buildings which are in such a state of disrepair that there is nothing that can be done but to pull them down. Nor are the remainder altogether satisfactory. To go into sordid details, 82 percent of Parisians have no bath or shower, more than half must go out of their lodgings to find a lavatory, and a fifth do not even have running water in the lodgings. Little more than one in six of existing buildings is pronounced satisfactory and in good condition by the public inspectors. Lack of repair is ruining even these.

Owners can hardly be blamed. They are not in a financial position to keep up their buildings, let alone improve them. The condition of the owners can hardly be believed. To take an example of a very common situation, here is a lady who owns three buildings containing thirty-four apartments, all inhabited by middle class families. Her net loss from the apartments, after taxes and repairs, is $80 a year. Not only must her son put her up and take care of her, but he must also pay out the $80. She cannot sell; there are no buyers.

When the owner tries to milk a little net income from his property by cutting down the repairs, he runs great risks. Another person postponed repairs on his roofs; rain filtering into an apartment spoiled a couple of armchairs. He was sued for damages and condemned to pay a sum amounting to three years of the tenant's paltry rent.

The miserable condition of owners is easily explained. While rents since 1914 have at the outside multiplied 6.8 times, taxes have grown 13.2 times, and the cost of repairs has increased from 120 to 150 times the 1914 price!

RENT CONTROL TAKES ROOT

The position is, of course, as absurd as it is disastrous. An outsider might be tempted to think that only an incredible amount of folly could have led us to this. But it is not so. We got there by easy, almost unnoticed stages, slipping down on the gentle slope of rent control. And this was not only the work of socialist regimes but of successive parliaments and governments, most of which were considered to be rather conservative.

Legacy of World War I

The story starts with World War I. It then seemed both humane and reasonable to preserve the interests of the families while the boys were in the army or working for victory. So existing situations were frozen. It was also reasonable to avoid disturbances at the end of the war. The veterans' homecoming should not be spoiled by evictions and rent increases. Thus prewar situations were hardened into rights. The owner lost—"temporarily," of course—the disposition of his property, and the stipulations of law superseded agreement between the parties. This was only for a time.

But by the time the situation was reviewed in 1922, retail prices had trebled with rents still at their prewar level. It was then plain that a return to a free market would imply huge increases, an index to them being provided by rents in the smallish free sector, which hovered around two and one-half times the 1914 rents. The legislators shrank from this crisis. Wages were by then three and one-half times what they had been in 1914, and the expenditure on rent in the worker's budget had shrunk from something like 16 percent before the war to around 5 percent. In our times habits become quickly ingrained. Instead of regarding rent as constituting normally one-sixth of one's expenditures, one took it now as being normally one-twentieth. Also, a "right" had developed, the right to dig in. Always very sedentary, the French now had struck roots in their rented lodgings.

The legislators decided to deal with this matter in a prudent, statesmanlike manner. So the tenant's right to retain possession was confirmed but the rent was raised slightly. Successive increases were granted in further laws, all hotly debated. A new owner-tenant relationship thus took shape. The owner was powerless either to evict the tenant or debate the price of rent with him, because the state took care of that. The price rose but slowly, while in the meantime the field of regulation was progressively enlarged to bring in such flats as had not been previously regulated. New buildings put up since 1915 were alone left unregulated to stimulate construction. This exception was not to endure for long.

The fear of liberty

No systematic view inspired this policy. It just grew from the fear of a sudden return to liberty which seemed ever more dangerous as prices rose. And, of course, if one had to control the price of rent, one could not allow the owner to dispossess tenants, because in that case he might easily have made an agreement secretly with the new tenant; so rent control implied necessarily the denial of the owner's right to evict.

What then happened to rents under this regime? In 1929, with retail prices more than six times what they had been in 1914, rents had not even doubled; real rents, that is, rents in terms of buying power, were less than a third of what they had been before the war.

Lawmaking on rent control continued; indeed no single subject has taken up so much of the time and energy of parliament. But the improvement in the condition of the owners, when it came, was not the work of the legislators. It was brought about by the economic crisis which lowered retail prices. Thus, by 1935, rents then being almost three times their prewar level, retail prices were down and owners obtained almost two-thirds of their prewar real income. Or rather they would have obtained it had not the Laval government then decided on a cut of 10 percent in rents as one of the measures designed to bring down the cost of living and implement a policy of deflation.

When the Popular Front came to power in 1936, the process of devaluations started again, retail prices soared, and real income from buildings crumbled from year to year.

Then came World War II. The return to liberty which had been devised for 1943 was, of course, shelved, and all rents were frozen, including this time those of recent buildings which had until then escaped.

THE BUSY LAWMAKERS

Since the Liberation, an order in council of 1945 and two laws in 1947 have intervened, bringing up to 119 the number of laws or quasi-laws on the subject since 1918. The new laws have provided for increases jacking up rents. Apartments built before 1914 can now be rented at prices 70 percent above the 1939 price. But while rents increased 1.7 times retail prices rose more than 14 times. In other words, the buying power of rents was set at 12 percent of its 1939 level, already greatly depressed as we have seen. The buildings put up since 1914 were more severely treated on the assumption that the ruling rents in 1939 had been more adequate. The permissible increase over 1939 levels was set at 30 percent, thus keeping the buying power of these rents at 9 percent of what it was before World War II. It was further specified, for buildings dating back to 1914 or earlier, which comprise as we have noted nine out of ten of the total stock, that their rents should in no case be more than 6.8 times the 1914 rent. This in spite of the fact that retail prices were then 99.8 times as high as in 1914.

In short, owners of new buildings have been allowed to get in terms of real income less than a tenth of what they got before World War II.

Owners of old buildings, that is, nine-tenths of all buildings, have been allowed to get in terms of real income either 12 percent of what they got in 1939 or a little less than 7 percent of what they got in 1914—whichever is the lesser, the law took care to specify!

The price predicament

If on the other hand a builder were now to put up flats similar to those in existence, these new apartments would have to be let for prices representing from ten to thirteen times present rent ceilings, in order to reward the costs of construction and the capital invested. According to an official source, a report of the Economic Council, a wage-earner's apartment of three small rooms and a kitchen now renting for $13 to $16 a year(!) would have to be rented for $166 to $200 a year; and a luxury apartment of 1,600 square feet floor space would have to be rented for $55 to $70 a month, compared with the current price of $14 to $17 a month. Obviously, as long as the rents of existing buildings are held down artificially far below costs, it will be psychologically impossible to find customers at prices ten or twelve times higher, and hence construction will not be undertaken.

Such is the differential between the *legal* and the *economic* price of lodgings that even the most fervent advocates of freedom are scared at the prospect of a return to it; they shudder at the thought of a brutal return to reality. They feel that if the right to dismiss tenants were restored together with the right to bargain and contract with them, evictions could not be executed—the whole nation of tenants sitting down to nullify the decision. The thing, they say, has not gone too far, the price of rent is too far removed from the cost.

Hence the strange plans which are now being considered by the French parliament. It is proposed to maintain a right of occupation, a right to retain one's lodgings, and it is proposed to arrive at a "fair price fixing." That is, the true service value of every flat would be fixed according to floor space, the value per square metre being multiplied by a coefficient according to the amenities, situation, and so forth. Thus the "fair rent" would be ascertained. But it would not be wholly paid by the tenant. He would benefit by a special subsidy, an inflationary measure of course, as are all subsidies. Nor would the larger part of this fair rent be paid to the owner. It would be divided in slices. A slice to correspond with the cost of upkeep would be paid to the owner, not directly but to a blocked account to make sure it was spent on repairs. A much bigger slice for the reconstitution of the capital investment would not go to the owner at all, but to a National Fund for Building. Thus the dispossession of the owners would be finally sanctioned. They would be legally turned into the janitors of their own buildings, while on the basis of their dispossession a new state ownership of future buildings would rear its proud head.

Road to ruin

Possibly the French example may prove of some interest and use to our friends across the sea. It goes to show that rent control is self-perpetuating and culminates in both the physical ruin of housing and the legal dispossession of the owners. It is enough to visit the houses in Paris to reach conclusions. The havoc wrought here is not the work of the enemy but of our own measures.

Chapter Eleven
The Rise, Fall, and Revival of Swedish Rent Control

SVEN RYDENFELT

11. Bomb Damage or Rent Control? See page 321 for the answer.

THE AUTHOR

Sᴠᴇɴ Rʏᴅᴇɴꜰᴇʟᴛ was born in 1911; at university 1934-1936; teacher's training college 1936-1938. He was a secondary school teacher, 1938-1945, returning to university after the war to study and teach, becoming a Doctor of Economics in 1954. Since 1961 he has been a lecturer in economics with tenure for life at the University of Lund.

His publications include his doctoral dissertation, *Communism in Sweden* (1954), books and articles on rent control and housing policy, as well as on other socio-economic subjects.

Chapter Eleven
The Rise, Fall, and Revival of Swedish Rent Control

Sven Rydenfelt

*Lecturer in Economics,
University of Lund,
Sweden*

"Economics does not say that isolated government interference with the prices of only one commodity or a few commodities is unfair, bad, or unfeasible. It says that such interference produces results contrary to its purpose, that it makes conditions worse, not better, *from the point of view of the government and those backing its interference*." Ludwig von Mises[1]

A "TEMPORARY" EMERGENCY REGULATION MADE PERMANENT

When rent control was introduced in Sweden in 1942 in accordance with almost unanimous support in parliament, the decision was founded on a conviction that it was an emergency regulation that would be abolished as fast as possible after World War II. It was believed that wartime inflation would be followed by a deflation with sharp declines in prices, as happened after World War I.

However, the strong deflation which followed World War I did not recur after World War II. For this reason rents in Sweden after 1945 remained at a level far below the prices of other commodities. And while rental costs of apartment houses remained for a long time almost unchanged, salaries and wages rose rapidly, as Table 1 demonstrates.

TABLE 1
RENTAL COSTS AND WAGES
(Sweden 1939-1975)

	1939	1942	1945	1950	1960	1970	1975	Average Annual Rate of Growth
Rental Costs (1942 = 100)	83	100	103	104	166	253	370	4.2%
Wages (1942 = 100)	80	100	108	162	391	917	1600	8.7%

Sources: "Rental costs": rents, fuel and light based on the cost-of-living index of the Board of Social Welfare. "Wages": paid to workers in industry, communications, public services, etc., based on the statistics of the Board of Social Welfare. The 1975 figures are preliminary.

In spite of all the good intentions to abolish rent control soon after the war, it succeeded in surviving until 1975, when its last remnants were finally removed (350,000 out of 2,000,000 housing units in apartment houses). The moral is that rent control is easy to introduce but hard to abolish.

A housing shortage develops

To the economist, it seems self-evident that a price control like the Swedish rent control must lead to a demand surplus, that is, a housing shortage. For a long period the general public was more inclined to believe that the shortage was a result of the abnormal situation created by the war, and this even in a nonparticipating country like Sweden. The defenders of rent control were quick to adopt the opinion held by the general public. All attempts by critics to point to rent control as the villain in the housing drama were firmly rejected.

The foremost defender of rent control in Sweden was for many years Alf Johansson, Director-General of the Royal Board of Housing, who has been called "the father of the Swedish housing policy." In an article in 1948 he described the development of the housing shortage thus:

"An acute shortage of housing units developed as early as 1941. In the following year the shortage was general and reached approximately 50,000 units in the urban communities, i.e., somewhat more than the house construction during a boom year."[2]

In a lecture he described the situation in 1948 as follows: "We have the same shortage as at the end of the war, but the situation has not deteriorated in spite of a very great increase in demand."[3] According to Mr. Johansson's rough sketch, the housing shortage in Sweden reached its peak as early as 1942—50,000 dwellings—and remained practically unchanged in the following years.

The actual development was quite different, as was revealed in the reports of the Public Dwelling Exchange offices. Only Malmö—the third largest city—had an exchange of this kind during the early war years; its reports provide a detailed account of the development (Table 2).

Stockholm, the capital of Sweden, opened a dwelling exchange office for the first time in 1947. Its reports give an illuminating picture of a rapidly deteriorating situation in the housing market. Families with two children, which in 1950 obtained a housing unit through the exchange office, experienced an average waiting time of nine months. The development during the following years is shown in Table 3.

Conclusion

Thus, the "popular opinion" encouraged by defenders of

TABLE 2
DEVELOPMENT OF HOUSING SHORTAGE
IN MALMÖ, 1940-1977

| Year | Vacancies | APPLICANTS | |
		Total	Without a Dwelling
1940	1,144	—	58
1941	1,047	—	129
1942	593	—	138
1943	165	—	205
1944	44	301	247
1945	41	390	288
1946	22	323	221*
1947	8	539	418
1948	—	2,409	1,698
1949	—	6,693	3,472
1950	—	9,939	4,803
1960	—	24,901	4,254
1970	—	34,478	10,660
1975	3,802	23,902	8,590
1977	4,200**	30,225	12,682

*In 1946 all "old" applications were deleted from the records and a new "purge" is going on in 1975.
**Preliminary
Source: Reports of the Dwelling Exchange Office.

TABLE 3
AVERAGE WAITING PERIOD FOR
DWELLINGS IN STOCKHOLM

Year	Months	Year	Months
1950	9	1954	26
1951	15	1955	23
1952	21	1956	30
1953	24	1957	35
		1958	40

Source: Reports of the Dwelling Exchange Office. The series was not continued after 1958.

rent control, that the Swedish housing shortage was a product of the war, does not accord with the evidence demonstrated either by the Malmö data or the Stockholm data. In fact, all of the data indicate that the shortage during the war years was insignificant compared with that after the war. It was only in the postwar rent control era that the housing shortage assumed such proportions that it became Sweden's most serious social problem.

HOUSING AND POPULATION

The rapidly increasing housing shortage after 1945 soon ripened into a situation which could no longer be attributed to the supply dislocations that were supposedly created by the war. New explanations were needed. That most commonly adopted by the general public was the assumption that the shortage was a consequence of insufficient construction activity. If population increased at a faster rate than the number of housing units, there was bound to be a shortage, people thought; and they therefore adopted the untested assumption that construction was lagging behind. Among the defenders of rent control this population growth explanation became for a long time the most fashionable.

Fallacy of the population growth explanation

The defenders of rent control were anxious to emphasize that special consideration must be given to the rise in the marriage rate after 1940, since most housing units are occupied by married couples. The following quotation from an article by Mr. Johansson is significant:

> "During 1945-46 the number of marriages in the cities was 50 percent higher than the average for the 1930s. Under such conditions it is not difficult to explain why the addition of new housing units, even though large, has been absorbed and the shortage left unaltered."[4]

Let us confront this "model" with statistical data on housing and population (Table 4).

TABLE 4
HOUSING & POPULATION IN SWEDEN, 1940-1975

Year	No. of Housing Units	Total Population	No. of married couples	No. of dwellings per 100 inhabitants	No. of dwellings per 100 married couples
1940	1,960,000	6,371,000	1,330,000	31	147
1945	2,102,000	6,674,000	1,463,000	32	144
1960	2,675,000	7,498,000	1,783,000	36	150
1965	2,875,000	7,773,000	1,869,000	37	154
1970	3,180,000	8,080,000	1,927,000	39	165
1975	3,530,000	8,200,000	1,853,000	43	190

Sources: Number of housing units in 1940 according to official estimates in SOU 1945: Table 63, p. 228; data for other years from official censuses.

During the war years the rate of housing construction was relatively low, but still high enough to increase, marginally, the number of housing units per 100 inhabitants. The number of housing units per 100 married couples, however, declined slightly (from 147 to 144) due to the exceptionally high marriage rate during the war years. During the years after 1945, when the big shortage developed, the number of dwellings in Sweden increased at a considerably faster rate than both the total population and the number of married couples.

Conclusion

In the light of the above data it seemed sensible to reject the explanation that the housing shortage was a crisis product of the war years. We have now found that the population explanation does not stand the test either.

THEORY AND FORECASTING

Human life is a walk into a future filled with uncertainty. The purpose of science is to illuminate, like a searchlight, the road in front of us. Therefore, the touchstone of all knowledge is its ability to anticipate the future—the forecast. When our astronomers can forecast hundreds of years ahead the moment for an eclipse of the sun, they prove that their conception of reality, their "model" of the universe, is a realistic one.

The famous sociologist, Florian Znaniecki, has expressed this thesis in the following way: "Foresight of the future is the most conclusive test of the validity of scientific theories, a test perfected in experimental science. Prediction is thus the essential link between theory and practice."[5] The need for knowledge and forecasts about society is far stronger in a centrally directed "planned" economy than in a liberal market economy. The British economist, Sir Roy Harrod, has formulated this conclusion in the following terms:

"Lack of economic comprehension may not matter so much if the system is largely self-working. But when the working of the machine necessitates the constant vigilance of the supervisor, and the supervisor does not understand the mechanism, there is bound to be serious trouble."[6]

Judging from different forecasts, the decision makers behind the Swedish rent controls had highly imperfect knowledge about the structure and function of the housing market. For several years they thought that the housing shortage was a product of the war and for many years afterward they thought it to be a product of population changes. From such models of the housing market they made very optimistic forecasts, according to which the shortage after the war would quickly disappear.

The following "forecast" shows how Sweden's leading official expert on housing policy "anticipated" future developments as of 1944: "The liquidation of the housing market shortage is a once-for-all business, which ought to be accomplished in a relatively short time, though not over so short a period as one year."[7] As we have seen, subsequent developments were very much different.

A forecast of an entirely different nature was published by Professor Eli F. Heckscher, at that time the doyen of Swedish economic history and economics:

"It is probably a general opinion that the housing shortage is due to insufficient construction activity. But this is, by and large, an enormous mistake. In a free housing market no shortage would exist at the present rate of construction. On the other hand, no rate of construction activity can eliminate the shortage under the present order. It is like the tub of the Danaids, from which water was constantly flowing out at a faster rate than it could be poured in."[8]

I myself published a similar forecast a few months earlier:

"The cause of the housing shortage is to be found entirely on the demand side. As a consequence of rent control and the relative reduction of the rent—the manipulated low price—demand has increased to such an extent that an ever-widening gap between supply and demand has developed in spite of the high level of construction activity. Our great mistake is that we always seek the cause of a shortage on the supply side, while it is as frequently to be found on the demand side. The housing shortage will be our companion forever, unless we prevent demand from running ahead of production."[9]

It will be convenient to conclude this section with a now-classical statement by the late Professor Frank H. Knight, the "grand old man" of the Chicago School of Economics:

"If educated people can't or won't see that fixing a price below the market level inevitably creates a shortage (and one above a surplus), it is hard to believe in the usefulness of telling them anything whatever in this field of discourse."[10]

SINGLE PEOPLE INVADE THE HOUSING MARKET

"You need not eat the whole egg to feel it is rotten."
(Russian proverb.)

As indicated in Table 4 the number of housing units in Sweden during the period 1940 to 1975 rose by 1,520,000 (net), while the number of married couples increased by only 645,000. Even if every married couple had obtained their own home, there would still have been 875,000 dwellings available for other groups.

Which are the groups in Swedish society that have increased their occupation of dwelling space to such an extent that a serious shortage has developed? There are three groups of consumers in the housing market: married couples, previously married people (widows, widowers and the divorced), and unmarried adults (twenty years or older). Table 5 shows the size of each group at various years and

TABLE 5
NUMBER OF PERSONS BY GROUPS AND PERCENTAGE OCCUPYING OWN DWELLINGS, 1940-1975

Year	Married couples	%	Previously married persons	%	Unmarried adults	%
1940	1,330,000	98	435,000	65	1,453,000	23
1945	1,463,000	98	457,000	65	1,337,000	25
1960	1,783,000	98	575,000	75	1,047,000	36
1965	1,869,000	98	628,000	77	1,051,000	43
1970	1,927,000	98	717,000	80	1,073,000	50
1975	1,853,000	98	874,000	82	1,500,000	53

Sources: Official housing and population censuses.

Note: The sum total of *occupied* dwellings, calculated from Table 5 is not equal to the sum total of housing units in Table 4. At every time, even during shortage periods, there is a reserve of unoccupied empty dwellings. According to the housing census this reserve was 93,000 in 1965 and 129,000 in 1970.

the percentage living in dwellings (houses or flats) of their own.

Growth of demand among unmarried adults

All housing censuses indicate that, with few exceptions, married couples have always occupied housing units of their own. However, it is also true—even in a free housing market—that there is some "doubling-up"; for example, young married couples living with their parents for a while. The majority (65 percent) of the previously married also lived in dwellings of their own in 1940. Their share had increased by 17 percent by 1975.

The only dramatic change has been for unmarried adults of whom only one in four occupied a dwelling of his own in 1940, while 35 years later more than one in two did. Thus the supply of dwellings available for unmarried adults must have rapidly improved during the 35-year period (Table 6 is another way of viewing the information contained in Table 5).

TABLE 6
PERSONS WITHOUT DWELLINGS OF THEIR OWN
(In Absolute and Relative Numbers, 1940-1975)

	Married Couples	%	Previously Married	%	Unmarried Adults	%
1940	27,000	2	152,000	35	1,119,000	77
1945	29,000	2	160,000	35	1,003,000	75
1960	36,000	2	144,000	25	708,000	64
1965	37,000	2	144,000	23	611,000	57
1970	39,000	2	143,000	20	592,000	50
1975	39,000	2	157,000	18	705,000	47

Sources: Official housing and population censuses.

Table 6 shows that in both 1940 and 1945 over one million unmarried adults lacked housing units of their own.

The reason why the housing shortage—the demand surplus—was relatively small as late as 1945 in spite of this enormous reserve of demand was that only a small proportion of these persons were actively seeking dwellings of their own. The majority either lived—and were satisfied to live—with their parents, or they rented furnished rooms.

The majority of unmarried adults from the beginning accepted a passive role. The explanation of the housing shortage must be sought in the fact that this majority was later progressively transformed into active dwelling seekers who invaded the housing market and with energy and success hunted and occupied homes. As indicated in Table 5, the share of residents with own dwellings in this group has increased from 23 percent in 1940 to 55 percent in 1975. The implication of this strongly increased demand for dwellings among unmarried adults is that they occupied 416,000 more homes than they would have done had only the same proportion (23 percent) as in 1940 occupied their own dwellings. As the number of dwellings in Sweden increased by a net 1,520,000 from 1940 to 1975 more than 25 percent of the increase has thus been disposed of exclusively to satisfy the extra demand of unmarried adults.

What has brought about this upsurge in the demand of single persons for private dwellings? The reason of course is that the normal relation between income and rents has been entirely distorted by rent control. In the period 1942 to 1975 industrial wages grew to sixteen times what they were in 1942 while rents less than quadrupled. The distortion was particularly marked between income and rents of apartment houses built before 1942 (see Table 1).

That the share of persons with housing units of their own in the unmarried adult group increased from 23 percent in 1940 to 55 percent in 1975 by no means implies that the demand for dwellings by this group was satisfied. The longest queue at the housing exchange offices was, during all the shortage years, made up of unmarried adults.

Responsiveness of housing demand to changes in price

Would not a strong reduction in the rent-income ratio have

occurred even in the absence of rent control and the demand for dwellings have increased as consequence? Certainly, but the demand increase would have been less accentuated and, in particular, it would have been less among unmarried adults. It all depends on the "price elasticity" of demand. According to common experience, the price and income elasticity of demand for dwellings is low, as it is for other necessities like food and clothing.* It is on this basis that the supporters of rent control have attempted to build up a defence. If the demand for dwellings has a low elasticity, they argue, a relative reduction in rent levels could not have increased demand very much.

This general reasoning, however, is valid only for the married and previously married groups. For members of these groups private dwellings are a necessity and, as a result, price and income elasticities are relatively low. The situation is different for unmarried adults. For the majority in this group a self-contained housing unit is somewhat of a luxury, a non-necessity. Young people will often hesitate if they have the choice between going on living cheaply and comfortably with their parents or moving out and acquiring a dwelling of their own.

That unmarried adults occupy self-contained housing units of their own to a lesser extent than the married is not due to lower income. In fact, a comparison of income levels, taking account of the obligations of family men— that is, the number of persons living on one income — shows that the incomes of umarried adults are as high as those of the married. The unmarried have demanded dwellings to a lesser extent because they assign a higher priority to other things, such as clothing, amusements, travel, education, etc.

For the majority of unmarried adults a dwelling is a relatively dispensable commodity, and the demand for a

---

*Price (or income) elasticity of demand for a commodity is high if a given percentage change in price (or income) leads to a greater percentage change in the quantity demanded. Elasticity is low if the quantity demanded changes less (in percentage terms) than the change in price or income.—Ed.

commodity of this kind is normally highly sensitive to changes in price or income. The strong reduction in rents relative to other prices and to incomes (resulting from rent control) has, for this reason, considerably stimulated the demand for homes on the part of unmarried adults.

The data in Table 6 indicate that in 1945 more than a million unmarried adults in Sweden lacked housing units of their own. This represented a very large potential demand reserve that rent control unleashed on the housing market. The influx of this group into the housing market naturally created a demand which far exceeded supply.

HOUSING PRODUCTION GROSS AND NET

"In many cases rent control appears to be the most efficient technique presently known to destroy a city—except for bombing."
Assar Lindbeck[11]

Deterioration of the housing stock

It is well-known and documented that rent controls result in poorer maintenance, fewer renovations and modernizations, and, therefore, in the long run in a serious deterioration in the quality of dwellings. Because some requests for rent increases have been granted, the defenders of control have persistently contended that deterioration and slum development have not occurred. This argument is fallacious.

Rent control breeds slums

As a result of control and lower rental income, owners' ability to maintain their apartment houses has declined. In particular, their incentive for such upkeep which is motivated by an aesthetic or comfort point of view has dwindled.

In a free market there is always a surplus of dwellings and flats to let. If the owner in such a market does not keep his property in good condition he runs the risk of losing his tenants and being left with empty flats and losses in rental income. In a controlled market with severe shortages, the owner is under no such compulsion. However badly maintained his property, there are always long queues of homeless people willing to rent his shabby, poorly maintained flats.

Since there is no economic incentive to encourage the owners to repair, even basic upkeep, which in the long run is necessary to prevent serious quality deterioration (i.e. slums), is neglected. A development of this kind is difficult to describe in quantitative terms. But thanks to the detailed Swedish statistics on the number of new dwellings and the periodic housing censuses, an important aspect of the process can be documented (Table 7).

TABLE 7
GROSS AND NET HOUSING PRODUCTION, 1941-45 TO 1971-75

	Total new dwellings constructed (a)	Net increase in stock of dwellings (gain) (b)	Dwellings removed from housing stock (loss) (c)	"Loss Ratio" of (c) to (a) %
1941-45	180,000	142,000	38,000	20
1946-60	825,000	573,000	252,000	30
1961-65	415,000	200,000	215,000	52
1966-70	515,000	306,000	209,000	41
1971-75	469,000	350,000	119,000	25

Sources: *Housing Construction* (Swedish Official Statistics), and the housing censuses.

Rapid "loss" of houses

What is striking about Table 7 is the rapid increase in the

"loss" (column C) up to the year 1965. During the period 1941 to 1945 the net increase in the stock of dwellings was about 80 percent of new production and the "loss" only 20 percent. During the years 1961 to 1965, the net addition was barely 50 percent and the "loss" more than 50 percent. The "loss" in those years assumed such proportions that the authorities appointed a special committee with instructions to try to explain "the mystery of the disappearing dwellings." After 1965 the process of decontrol got into full swing, and from 1965 to 1970 the number of controlled private houses decreased from 900,000 to 600,000 and from 1970 to 1975 from 600,000 to 350,000. As a consequence, the number of "losses" decreased.

The anticipation of profits is the incentive to private enterprise to produce housing units. If this incentive is destroyed by regulations, and if it is made more profitable for the owner of apartment houses to rent his dwellings for commercial purposes, then it is not possible to prevent—in spite of prohibitions—a conversion of dwellings to offices, shops or storerooms.

It was of no avail to pour increasing amounts of public funds into the housing bag, as long as we did not patch up its holes. It was of no avail that since 1945 we had built more dwellings per head in Sweden than in any other country (according to the *UN Statistical Yearbook*). It was of no avail that we built more than 100,000 dwellings per year, when the 1967-1972 annual "loss" at the same time was about 40,000. A construction of 70,000 dwellings and a loss of 10,000 would have given us the same net addition. The system of control obviously caused an enormous and shameful waste of resources.

THE FALL AND REVIVAL OF SWEDISH RENT CONTROL

The rise and fall of house building

The Swedish government in 1965 made a bold promise

according to which one million new dwellings would be built during the decade 1965-1974. Until then the hunger for new dwellings had seemed insatiable, and the government did not provide for the possibility of a surplus of housing. Thanks to an overdimensioned building industry and extensive subsidies, the overambitious program could be fulfilled.

The gradual abolition of rent control plus extensive new construction laid the base for a surplus that from 1970 became really distressing. But a political "promise" is a "promise" and in spite of growing surpluses the building program had to be fulfilled. A Swedish construction record—110,000 new dwelling units—was reached in 1970, after which construction went on at a decreasing rate.

According to the socialist Swedish government, housing construction must be controlled in order to prevent the ups and downs of private unregulated production. But in spite of strict control, construction in Sweden went down from 110,000 in 1970 to 56,000 in 1976; a decrease of 50 percent in six years!

The growing vacancies in the first years of the 1970s were one reason for the setback, but as rent losses were mostly paid by government, they were of minor importance. The main reason was a control system which prevented landlords from collecting cost covering rents, leading to growing financial and maintenance troubles for the landlords as a consequence. Difficulties were so severe that private building of rented houses practically stopped, while council, or public, building drastically shrank.

Not only the volume but also the product mix radically changed. The share of small family houses in new production exploded from 30 percent in 1970 to 75 percent in 1978. An explosion with its roots in an unsatisfied demand had piled up during the long social-democratic era (1932-1976). The building of family houses was, however, less imposing in numbers than in percentages: 33,000 in 1970 compared to 40,000 in 1978. The reduction of apartment house building was still more conspicuous: 77,000 dwellings in 1970 compared to 14,000 in 1978.

The fall and rise of quality construction

During the years of shortage—created by rent control—apartments of low quality in dismal environments were mass produced. And having no choice, the homeless families in the queues had to accept them. The growing surpluses, however, created quite a new situation; the seller's market was transformed into a buyer's market. Housing enterprises had to compete for tenants, and this competition forced builders to use all their creativity to produce attractive flats. During the shortage years they could ignore the wants and wishes of the consumers, but now they had to respond to them.

Fewer "skyscrapers" are built, and more construction in Sweden now consists of low houses with one or two storeys and with an easy and intimate contact with the ground. Most families have out-of-door-rooms or green plots of their own. As a matter of fact, the changed market situation changed the quality of new construction—houses and environment—in a miraculous way. Because of inflation and rising costs, new flats must be more expensive than old ones, and so in a balanced market they can find tenants only if they are more attractive. The builders in Sweden, accustomed to the protection that shortages provide, are today adjusting to consumer sovereignty. A development made possible by the return to a situation with surpluses, a situation in this respect similar to a free market.

Cooperative housing

In Sweden, building societies own about 500,000 housing units in apartment houses. Nominally, these houses are owned by cooperative societies founded by cooperating families, but in reality these flats—with certain restrictions—are owner occupied.

In 1939 only 4 percent of new construction was built by the societies, but during the war years and the following decades cooperative housing was so encouraged by the government—and by the housing shortage—that the share of cooperative housing in 1959 reached a peak of 32 percent. In subsequent years the share of cooperative housing has been declining and from 1975 the share has been about 10 percent. Why?

Because special concessions by government are not enough, there must also be a shortage for a scheme of this sort to be successful. The gradual abolition of rent control from 1958 meant that the shortage reached its maximum proportions about that time. With gradually shrinking queues, the market for cooperative housing deteriorated year after year.

In order to become a member of a cooperative housing society a person must pay a rather large sum in cash, and in a shortage situation people have no choice. But as the market was permitted, by the return to more economic pricing, to provide a supply of alternatives, a preference for rented apartments in the private sector and for single family houses became evident. The demand for cooperative houses shrank to such an extent that it often happened that a family wanting to move could not find another family willing to take over and pay that sum in cash which they themselves had paid. As the risks of such losses became generally known, the demand for cooperative flats shrank still more. Because of low building levels during recent years, a growing scarcity has again increased demand for cooperative housing.

There is a class of organisms called "pathophiles" that detest healthy environments but thrive on sick plants and animals. So it is with council and cooperative housing enterprises. They had their golden age during the years when our housing market was fatally ill and disorganized by government regulations and shortage. But the more the shortage decreased, and the more the market recovered its balance, the more the status of these enterprises deteriorated.

Private housing enterprises, on the contrary, thrive only in healthy, balanced markets and react with pronounced "pathophobia" against pathological environments. During the worst control—and shortage—years, private housing suffered seriously.

The end of cooperative rent control

Every time a member of a cooperative society wanted to move, he had to "sell" his flat to a new member wanting to take over. But up to 1969 the society board had to calculate and approve the sum paid. No "speculation" was allowed.

In the Swedish housing market there is an intense competition between cooperative flats and family homes, and here the cooperative societies felt handicapped. Their members were not allowed to sell at free prices, which the homeowners could.

So in 1968 the big society organizations requested the social-democratic government to abolish cooperative rent control, and as a favor control for the cooperative sector was ended from 1 January 1969. From this time "speculation" with cooperative flats has been as flourishing as "speculation" with family homes.

Council housing

From 1932 to 1976 Sweden had social-democratic governments with an antipathy towards private housing, whether privately owned apartment houses or owner-occupied single family houses. The construction of council houses, owned by local authorities, and cooperative houses, owned by building societies, was encouraged by special concessions and subsidies, and as a consequence, out of 2,000,000 rented dwellings in 1975, 600,000 were council houses and 500,000 cooperative houses.

The government apparently believed that apartments in local authorities' projects would be cheaper, due to the absence of profits, and better than privately owned apartments. The managers of the local authorities' projects—often with a political career as their only merit—energetically tried to live up to that hope. But costs could not be conjured away. In the event, rents on the council apartments stayed, for a time, at about the same level as the rents on private apartments.

Political pressures ultimately had their effect, however, and for a number of years council project managers set rents lower than were to be found in private housing. This was done in spite of the fact that at the lower level rents did not cover costs. Gradually this policy led to a depletion of council project funds, and councils had to fight desperately against growing liquidity problems. In the face of such difficulties there was only one expedient—rent increases. And, as council houses had been freed from rent controls in 1958, rents were increased. Having allowed considerable increases in the rents on council houses, the government had to allow private rent increases, too.

From shortage to surplus

In the 1970s a considerable surplus—mostly municipal—developed. For the local authorities this surplus was a shocking experience. They had for several decades lived in a world without vacancies, a world they found natural. In their economic calculations there was no allowance—and no funds—for the losses associated with vacancies.

For municipal authorities this was an abnormal and undesirable phenomenon meaning economic catastrophe, and in 1972 the situation for municipal housing enterprises was so disastrous that the government had to hasten to their rescue. Bankruptcies would have meant political scandal, and 1973 was an election year.

So, loans on extremely advantageous conditions were given, and the local governments—the legal owners of the council houses—had to provide extensive subsidies as well. Up to 1975, vacancies—and vacancy losses—grew year by year, and with them the need for loans. Most of the borrowing enterprises are in such a precarious financial condition that there is little likelihood that they will be able to repay the interest on the loans, let alone the capital values. The losses, therefore, will be paid by the taxpayers.

The tenants take over power

Swedish rent control (launched in 1942) was gradually abolished after 1958, when council houses were exempted.

In 1975, when only 350,000 out of 2,000,000 rented dwellings were under control, the government decided to liquidate the remaining control between 1975 and 1978.

A puzzling element in the political fight for and against rent control was the maneuvering of the powerful National Association of Tenants (670,000 members in 1979—1,500,000 including families). From the beginning one of rent control's most fanatical defenders, it eventually changed its opinion and during the last decade acted as a hard critic.

During the last liquidation years, however, an explanation of this policy change emerged. The abolition of rent control was not—as could have been expected—followed by a free housing market. Instead a new regulation system was established, a negotiation system in which the Association of Tenants played a dominant role. From now on all rents in Sweden—like wages—were to be decided by negotiations between bargaining blocks of tenants and landlords.

Council rents function as guidelines

The biggest single landlord block was the Association of Local Authorities (representing 650,000 out of 700,000 council dwellings in 1979), and a main principle of the new system was that self-supporting nonprofit council rents were to function as guideposts for the rents in the 800,000 private dwellings, too. Since, according to popular opinion, big slices of private rents in free markets are profits, a result of this system ought to be lower—but nevertheless self-supporting—rents for tenants in private houses.

In theory this strategy seemed rational and streamlined. But, alas, it did not function this way in practice. Why?

For different reasons. First, local authority managers of council houses had a strong desire to be able to boast of lower rents than those charged in private houses.

Second, for still another important reason, council rents during the new negotiation system never were self-supporting. If you transform a market price into a political price, sooner or later the buyers will refuse to pay cost covering prices, with disastrous effects for production, provision, and distribution.

In a free market there is equality and power balance between individual sellers and buyers. As a rule this balance is upset as soon as government interferes in the market, supporting one party or the other by means of its power apparatus.

In the Swedish housing market, government is supporting the buyers—the tenants—not only by giving their association an official status as legal negotiator but also by making negotiation mandatory for the landlords, too. As an extra privilege government is granting the tenants legal security of tenure.

The housing crisis of 1978

Faced with an opponent armed with such powers, not only the landlords but government, too, had to surrender. The economic crisis, coupled with rapid inflation, created a need for substantial rent increases, but at the same time—because of economic stagnation—resistance from tenants was hardening. In the Fall of 1978 the local authorities demanded—and needed—18 crowns per square metre, while the Association of Tenants refused to offer more than 7 crowns. A deadlock situation beyond mediation soon developed, and a large-scale confrontation threatened. A conflict with extended rent strikes would very soon have created a financial catastrophe for the landlords, not least for the local authorities. And for the Liberal minority government that took over power in October, such a conflict would have meant political disaster.

The Association of Tenants was indeed a powerful political pressure group, disposing of more than one million votes among its members alone. A blackmail situation developed, and the new government had to pay the ransom—one billion crowns to the local authorities— bridging the gap between the rents they urgently needed and the rents the tenants were willing to pay.

The surrender of the government meant a triumph for the Association of Tenants, not only for the time being but for the future, too, since it set a precedent. At the same time, the new negotiation system, founded on self-supporting rents, was in ruins after a few years.

The revival of rent control

"If you expel the devil through the front door, he will return by the back entrance."
(Jewish proverb.)

The formal abolition of rent control never meant a return to free markets and free prices. In the new system substituted for rent control, rents are still manipulated by government, directly or indirectly.

In 1975 only 350,000 out of 2,000,000 rented dwellings were under control. The new system, launched in 1975, meant, however, a return from partial to almost total control (cooperative housing exempted). Under the new system, government has to pay that part of rents which tenants refuse to pay. This system means that a majority of 4,700,000 Swedes, living in farm houses, single family houses, and cooperative houses, have to pay part of the housing costs out of their taxes for a minority of 3,600,000 Swedes who live in rented houses.

As members of this minority are as well-to-do as those of the majority, no social reasoning can motivate the system. From this you may conclude that in future the majority will resist large government subsidies to the minority. Such resistance will mean inadequate funds for maintenance, gradually deteriorating accommodation, growing slum areas, and declining quality of life for renters—a development quite in accord with all historical experience of rent control.

In this system, one of the parties in the housing market, the tenants, is exploiting not only the taxpayers in common, but also—and especially—the other party, the landlords. To be sure exploitation like all immoral acts has general harmful effects. Not only the exploited, but also the exploiters, have to suffer. The two parties in a market are like Siamese twins with a common circulation. Every party trying to exploit—blood-tap—the other one is bound to suffer himself.

RENT CONTROL—DREAM AND REALITY

"Rent control has in certain western countries constituted, maybe, the worst example of poor planning by governments lacking courage and vision."
Gunnar Myrdal*

Good intentions confounded

"It is not for single persons that we have created our housing policy but in order to give families better dwellings."[12]

The ignorance of the authorities about the mechanism of the housing market explains their inability to lead development in the directions they themselves desire. They never wanted their policy to favor unmarried adults. Judging from the practical results, however, one is led to believe that favoritism of this kind has been the primary objective. Earlier we showed how the share of unmarried adults with their own dwellings has increased from 23 to 55 percent.

Unmarried adults have increasingly been given the opportunity to invade the housing market and occupy a gradually increasing share of homes. At the same time, tens of thousands of families with children have been unable to find homes of their own.

A free housing market always has a surplus—an available reserve of empty apartments. We call such a market a

*Gunnar Myrdal, co-winner with F.A. Hayek of the 1974 Nobel Prize in Economics, was described by Prof. Paul Samuelson, himself a Nobel Winner in 1970, as follows: "Dr. Myrdal has been anything but a believer in laissez-faire, having been an important architect of the Swedish Labor Party's welfare state." *The New York Times* (10 October 1974).—Ed.

buyer's market because the buyer has the upper hand. The normal situation in such a market can be said to be that a hundred landlords compete for each tenant. In such a market even a poor family has opportunities of finding and renting a flat. According to a housing census from the free market of 1940 (Table 5), 98 percent of all married couples then had dwellings of their own. In such a market, landlords often have the choice between only two alternatives—to leave flats empty or to accept poor families with children as tenants. Under such conditions the latter alternative is often chosen.

A deficit market, on the other hand, is always a seller's market. The normal situation in the tight Swedish housing market was that a hundred homeless potential tenants competed for every vacant dwelling. These hundred included both families with children and single persons. Heavily squeezed between the demands of tenants for repairs on the one hand and reduced rental income due to rent control on the other, it is understandable that landlords in many cases showed a preference for single persons. Wear and tear, and thus repair costs, will usually be lower with single tenants than with families.

Paradoxical benefits for richer people

"The aim of our housing policy is to favor the many poor and weak people, not the few rich."

As wealth and income grew, people demanded more living space. Therefore, government housing experts believed that the demand for small apartments with one to two rooms would gradually decline. According to one of several false forecasts, a growing surplus of such dwellings would develop. In fact, the shortage had all the time been most pronounced in small apartments. The authorities, however, looked upon small apartments with aversion and contempt as something unworthy of the wealthy Swedish welfare state. They had, therefore, consistently directed construction towards large apartments. While the share of new dwellings with four rooms or more was 14 percent in 1941 to 1945, this share had been raised to 37 percent by 1966.

During recent times, a growing surplus of large expensive flats compels the authorities to retreat. Only high-income families can afford to rent them. At the same time there is a crying need for smaller apartments for families with low incomes. Judging from the practical results, one gets the impression that the policies pursued have had as a primary aim to favor the rich and few, not the poor and numerous.

Long waiting lists for the poor

"In a free housing market the distribution of dwellings is determined by income. Through our 'social housing policy' we have attempted to invalidate this rule. Not the size of the purse but the strength of the need shall decide the allocation of dwellings."

Never before have people with low incomes found themselves in such weak and inferior positions as in the Swedish housing market. He who could only afford to rent a small dwelling could wait for years and years. The shortage was acute and the queues were long. Even families with children had to wait for years for dwellings of their own.

Large purses, of course, always meant advantages on the Swedish housing market, but never such enormous advantages as during the shortage years—the era of rent control. The rich man could solve his housing problem practically instantaneously. He could buy a house of his own. Or he could become part owner of a cooperatively built and owned property requiring a high investment in cash. Or he could rent a large, expensive, newly built flat (of which there was a surplus). And, finally, he had the opportunity of acquiring an apartment in the black market (always possible, but very expensive). Not so the man with the low income.

QUESTIONS AND ANSWERS ABOUT
RENT CONTROL

"People complain that housing policy has become so complicated that they no longer understand it. But just imagine their complaints if they had understood it."
The Economist

- *Is it really true that the abolition of rent control would introduce equilibrium in the housing market? Is the problem so simple?*

Yes, certainly. According to general experience the price in a free market automatically creates equilibrium between supply and demand. Expenditures in Sweden on automobiles, TV sets, summer houses, and foreign trips have increased at a much faster rate than expenditures on housing. Yet no signs of shortage have been noticed in these free markets.

That this situation can perplex even a Swedish minister of finance is evidenced by the following question: "How is it possible that we can solve the economic problems when we wish to acquire a car or a TV set, but have so great difficulties with a need which is so morally well-founded as that of a dwelling?"[13]

- *According to the critics, rent control creates both a shortage and a socially unacceptable distribution of dwellings. Unmarried persons with little need for dwellings of their own frequently displace married couples and families with more urgent requirements. Is not such a distribution even more characteristic of a free market, where wealthy persons with less pressing needs displace poor people with urgent requirements?*

This objection can be met from the housing censuses undertaken in 1940 in the five cities of Nörrkoping, Västeräs, Gävle, Kalmar and Kristianstad.[14] They show how the self-contained housing units available at that time (when the market was free) were distributed among the several groups of residents. Only 25 percent of unmarried adults lived in their own dwellings, while the share of married people—with the most pressing need—was 97 percent, and the previously married—with the next strongest need—78 percent. If a housing distribution authority had been responsible for the distribution, with "social justice" as the criterion, one would have expected the figure to have been about the same. Therefore, the distribution mechanism of the free market is perhaps not so arbitrary.

- *Would not the people in the old centrally located residential areas be unjustly hit if rent control were abolished?*

No. They have been privileged for decades. Abolition of the privilege would mean a change but no injustice. The wasteful disposition of homes in these areas is the principal cause of the housing shortage. Better economy in their use would have given room to the homeless, too.

- *Would not rent increases mean a lowering of standards by compelling more people to crowd into smaller and cheaper apartments?*

The housing shortage has developed because the groups privileged by rent control have been able to increase their consumption of dwellings above that which would be allocated by the supply. A return to a free market would compel those privileged by rent control to give up some of their surplus or "luxury" space, and, as a result, dwellings would be made available for the homeless. A free housing market, therefore, would mean a lower standard for those now privileged but a very large improvement for those who now lack dwellings of their own. The housing shortage is essentially a problem of distribution.

- *In a free housing market a natural reserve of empty flats always develops. Is not such an unused reserve an enormous waste?*

On the contrary, it is the absence of a reserve of this kind that is wasteful because it prevents free mobility and free choice by the citizens. If we had had the same situation in our shops, their shelves would have been empty long since. The customers would have had to form a queue, fill in forms listing their requirements, and then wait years for delivery.

* *Would not abolition of rent control result in unjustifiable profits for the property owners?*

The possibility of making profits is a driving force behind all private enterprise. Rising profits act as a signal to producers to increase the supply in the same way that falling profits (or losses) are a signal for a cessation of production. Normal development and expansion of private ownership and free enterprise is braked and prevented to the same degree as opportunities of making profits are curtailed.

Profits are in practice largely reinvested and function as a dynamic force for development and expansion. As a result of official attempts in Sweden to prevent private profits in housing, self-financing in this sector has gradually dwindled. The share of self-financing had in 1960 declined to 25 percent and in 1970 to 10 percent. It has been possible to provide the housing sector with necessary capital only by compulsory government measures. The sector has become parasitic; it can manage financially only by drawing capital from other sectors.

NOTES

1 *Human Action: A Treatise on Economics* (New Haven: Yale University Press, 1949), p. 758.
2 Svensk sparbankstidskrift, No. 2, 1948.
3 From the minutes of the Congress of the Swedish Real Estate Owners' Association in Malmö.
4 Svensk sparbankstidskrift, No 2, 1948.
5 "Proximate Future of Sociology: Controversies in Doctrine and Method," *American Journal of Sociology* (May 1945): 516.
6 "Britain Must Put Her House in Order," *World Review* (December 1951): 13.
7 Alf Johansson in *Ett genombrott*, 1944 (a dedication volume in honour of Gustav Möller, Minister of Social Affairs).

8 Dagens Nyheter, 15 May 1948.
9 Handelstidningen, 16 December 1947.
10 "Truth and Relevance at Bay," *American Economic Review* (December 1949): 1274.
11 *The Political Economy of the New Left* (New York: Harper & Row, 1972). Lindbeck, a professor of economics in Stockholm is, like Professors Oskar Lange and Abba P. Lerner, both a socialist and (partly) a supporter of a market economy.
12 Statement by Gustav Möller in the 1st Chamber of the Parliament, 20 January 1951. At that time Möller was Minister of Social Affairs and had the principal responsibility for housing policy.
13 Gunnar Strang at the Conference of Riksbyggen (a construction co.) in June 1958.
14 *Sociala medd*, No. 3 (1951).

Chapter Twelve
Apartment Shortages and Rent Control

BASIL A. KALYMON

12. Bomb Damage or Rent Control? See page 321 for the answer.

THE AUTHOR

BASIL A. KALYMON, born in 1944, is Professor, Faculty of Management Studies, University of Toronto, where he took his first degree (Honours Mathematics and Statistics) in 1966. Twice winner of Yale Fellowships and recipient of a Ford Foundation Fellowship, Professor Kalymon graduated from Yale, M. Phil. (Operations Research), 1968 and Ph.D. (Operations Research), 1970.

Before taking up his present post in 1975, Professor Kalymon taught at the University of California, the University of Toronto, and Harvard University.

He is the author, with G.D. Quirin, of "Changing Incentive Structures in Petroleum Exploration," a working paper prepared for the Canadian Tax Foundation. Professor Kalymon's other scholarly publications include "Economic Incentives in OPEC Oil Pricing Policy," *Journal of Development Economics* 2 (1975).

In 1977 Professor Kalymon contributed to the Fraser Institute book, *Oil in the Seventies: Essays on Energy Policy.* In the chapter co-authored with G.D. Quirin, Kalymon used the analytical techniques herein applied to the real estate industry to analyze prospects in the oil industry. He is the author of the 1978 Fraser Institute book, *Profits in the Real Estate Industry.*

Chapter Twelve
Apartment Shortages and Rent Control

BASIL A. KALYMON

Faculty of Management Studies,
University of Toronto

The introduction of rent control in Ontario in 1975 was an example of legislation aimed at short-run objectives which contained the seeds for long-term disruption. To the tenant, the appeal was direct, and the payoff immediate in reduced monthly payments. To the politician, controls can be translated into guaranteed votes whose lure is irresistible. Forgotten, in the scramble, are the lessons of past experience, the long-term welfare of city residents, the rights of the landlord minority, and, last but not least, the elementary principles of the behavior of our economic system.

SEQUENCE OF EVENTS

Let us review the chain of events which has brought legislated control of rents in 1975. Since Toronto is at the centre, the story focuses there. In 1960 Toronto was a city with a population of 1.7 million whose residents predominantly lived in single family housing. In the next decade, the city underwent tremendous growth. It had great attraction for large numbers of new immigrants arriving yearly in Canada as well as for those seeking a higher level of opportunity within the country. As a result Toronto was transformed into one of the major cities of North America, increasing its population by 35 percent in a decade. The proportion of residents living in apartment and row housing rose significantly, approaching half of the population by the early 1970s. In the mid 1970s, the growth of the city's population slowed, falling from its 3.4 percent rate of increase in the 1960s to approximately 1.3 percent annually.

FIGURE 1
RATIO OF RENT TO HOME OWNERSHIP INDICES

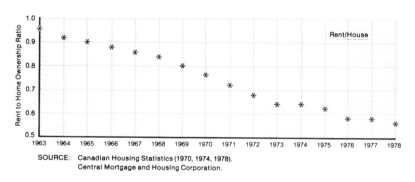

SOURCE: Canadian Housing Statistics (1970, 1974, 1978).
         Central Mortgage and Housing Corporation.

But why were no calls for rent controls heard until 1974? The first reason is clear from Figure 1 which shows the ratio of the Toronto rental index to the cost of home ownership. In every year from 1960 to 1973, the relative cost of renting accommodations *decreased*. Only in 1974 did this pattern briefly reverse itself, with rents rising faster than the cost of home ownership. By 1974, relative to their relationship to home ownership in 1963, Toronto rents had fallen by 30 percent.

To understand the historic rent pattern and also the outcry of 1975, consider Figure 2, which compares the annual rate of rent increase in Toronto and the general inflation as measured by the Consumer Price Index. We notice that rent rises over the 1963 to 1974 period almost invariably were lower than the overall inflation level. In fact statistical analysis shows that the average growth in rents was only some 80 percent of that in the real price level. Thus, from 1963 to 1974, not just the relative but also the real cost of rental accommodation in Toronto was falling.

FIGURE 2
RENT INCREASES AND INFLATION RATES

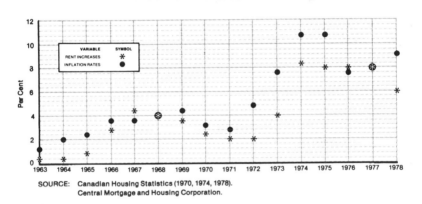

SOURCE: Canadian Housing Statistics (1970, 1974, 1978).
Central Mortgage and Housing Corporation.

In 1974, however, an unprecedented inflation took place, with prices spurting by 10.9 percent. Despite the fact that rents in 1974 rose by only 8.3 percent, the shift from historic nominal levels was pronounced. With these rent upsurges, calls for legislation to parallel the federal government's wage and price controls became vocal and, seemingly, irresistable. Assurances were of course provided that these would be "only temporary" and would expire with the general controls.

HISTORICAL EVIDENCE ON RENT INCREASES

To understand subsequent developments, it is important to consider the nature of the Toronto rental housing sector and the parameters which rule these markets in the absence of direct intervention. Economic theory suggests that the forces of supply and demand would raise rents as shortages develop and lower them in oversupplied conditions. Using the vacancy rate in Toronto as our empirical measure of market supply/demand conditions, Figure 3 clearly illustrates the countervailing nature of the relationship in Toronto. Thus, relatively significant rent increases occurred in years with low vacancy rates while smaller ones accompanied surplus conditions. In fact, vacancy rates were at a low point of their cycle in 1974 when open market corrective forces were pushing up rent levels at the fastest rate in the last fifteen years. Previous experience would have led to the expectation of an increased vacancy rate in the subsequent year, and, in fact, 1975 saw a small rise.

Analysis of the historical series shows that 83 percent of the variability in rent increases could be explained by the

FIGURE 3
VACANCY RATES AND RENT INCREASES

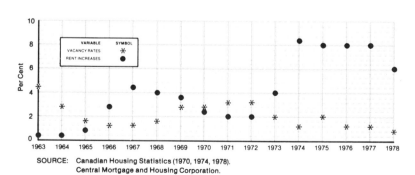

SOURCE: Canadian Housing Statistics (1970, 1974, 1978).
Central Mortgage and Housing Corporation.

two critical factors indicated above: inflation and the vacancy rate. Through econometric regression techniques it is found that, historically, an increase in the inflation rate of one percentage point appears to have induced a 0.7 percent rise in rents, while a reduction in vacancy rates of one percentage point raised rents by 0.6 percent.* This result must not be interpreted too literally by assuming that causality can be simply reversed. The factor simply suggests the historic rate of response of rents to market disequilibrium.** Substantial levels of statistical significance can be ascribed to these results which also indicate that the general inflation rate is an important determinant of rents. Figure 4 shows the forecasted value of rent increases based on the above response coefficients as compared to actual levels.

FIGURE 4
FORECASTED AND ACTUAL RENT INCREASES

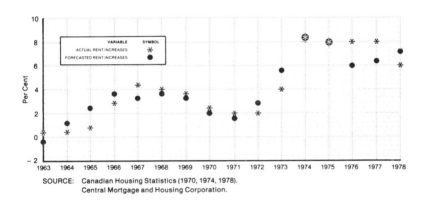

SOURCE: Canadian Housing Statistics (1970, 1974, 1978).
Central Mortgage and Housing Corporation.

*A reduction in the vacancy rate of 1 percent raises the rate of increase in rents by 0.6 percent so that if the vacancy rate were to be 1 percent lower for 3 years, the cumulative increase in rents would be almost 2 percent.—Ed.

**This does not imply any specific housing demand elasticity. For movements in the vacancy rate reflect not only demand side changes, but alterations on the *supply* side as well, brought about by new construction.—Ed.

The analysis demonstrates the effectiveness with which vacancy rates have, prior to 1975, controlled rent increases. Allowed to operate freely, the market was self-regulated with a resulting smooth cycle of low to high vacancy rates inducing high to low rental increases. This cyclical behavior was clearly broken in 1975-76 when vacancy rates failed to rise and rent increases did not abate. The severity of the disruptions which impacted on the rental market in 1975 would have resulted in some degree of deviation from historical patterns in rent increases, which possibly understate the immediate adjustment. Corrective market responses were, however, interrupted by the advent of rent control.

HISTORICAL EVIDENCE ON APARTMENT STARTS

An explanation of the events of 1975-1976 lies in the supply creation mechanism by which new apartment rental units are brought to the market. Figure 5 illustrates the almost continued decline in annual apartment starts in Toronto as measured by the percentage which new starts represent of total housing stock. (This measure will be used throughout this paper, and percentage changes refer to percentage point changes in this measure.)

FIGURE 5
APARTMENT STARTS AND VACANCY RATES

SOURCE: Canadian Housing Statistics (1970, 1974, 1978).
          Central Mortgage and Housing Corporation.

To explain this decline, many alternative factors must be considered. These include population growth rate, vacancy rates, interest rates, rent levels, and the construction cost index. Each can potentially influence the rate of new starts. Higher population growth increases the demand for housing. The vacancy rate signals the balance between current housing stock and demand. The interest rate significantly affects construction and operating costs and thus the potential profitability of any project. Finally,[1] rents directly influence the potential gross revenues from investment, while construction cost levels determine the size of the overall investment.

Through statistical regression analyses it is discovered that the most critical factor explaining housing starts was the ratio of the rent level and construction costs indices. This factor alone is able to explain 78 percent of the variability in apartment start rates.

Such a result is quite consistent with standard economic theory,* which states that the level of investment will be determined by the rate of profit. That such a result should be consistent with observed historical experience requires some further explanation. At first look, one may argue that the expected profitability on real estate rises with inflation and that the ratio of *current* rent levels to construction costs is not relevant. However, this argument ignores the fact that required returns also rise with inflation. In theory, these two effects leave expected *real* levels of profitability unchanged from new investments under equivalent cost and initial rent conditions. Thus, real profitability was falling sharply over the entire period of 1963-1978, and a lower rate of investment would be quite reasonable.**

---

*Standard economic theory assumes well adjusting markets that are at equilibrium and that price expectations are reflected in interest rates. —Ed.

**Although profitability may have been declining in the late 1960s it was still sufficiently high to bring forth a considerable level of construction activity. Expectations of *shifts* in rents or interest rates can create the perception of higher potential profits, even if subsequently unrealized.—Ed.

It is important to report that vacancy rates, in most of the explanatory models which fit, predictably show a dampening impact on housing starts. For each increase in the vacancy rate of one percentage point an approximate drop of 0.5 percentage points in construction start ratio occurs. However, the margin of error on this coefficient tends to be high, indicating that the level of response is quite questionable.

Most other factors are found to exercise basically imperceptible influences on the rate of construction starts, with the exception of one critical dimension: the presence or absence of rent controls during the period. In addition to the effects captured by the ratio of rents to costs and the vacancy rates, rent controls appear to have depressed housing start rates by an average of 1.5 percentage points below the levels which might otherwise have occurred. Thus, for example, for the given rent-to-cost ratio and vacancy rates, housing starts in 1976 might have been in the 4.5 percent rather than 3 percent range.

Of course, this figure relates only to the additional direct effect of controls and does not consider their influence on the rent-to-construction cost ratio which for each 1 percentage point rise would provide approximately 0.2 percent increase in the apartment start rate. Thus, if for example rent controls reduced the rental increase rate by 5 percent, then a total of 2.5 (1.5 + 1.0) percentage points drop in the apartment start rate would have been caused by rent controls. With declining population growth, such a change in start levels would have been sufficient to *reduce* vacancy rates by approximately 1.2 percent. Such a result did, in fact, occur in the rent control period from 1975 to 1978.

While the above response levels were in fact experienced historically, the reader must, of course, be cautioned against assuming that these relationships will be stable under sharply altered future conditions. Nevertheless, without other influences considered, these historic responses provide intuitively supportable indications of likely responses by the apartment construction start market.

The degree of predictability of the rate of apartment construction starts based on the rent-to-construction cost ratio, vacancy rate, and population growth can be seen in Figure 6. The 1975 and 1976 results show the large drop to actual from predicted levels which resulted from the initial introduction of rent controls. The 1977 and 1978 performances which exceed the low forecast levels are most likely explained by the fact that the amount of government subsidies to apartment construction increased substantially. The proportion of starts which depended on government support increased from 13 percent in 1974 to 91 percent in 1977. Further study of the future implications of this intervention will become critical as controls remain in place.

FIGURE 6
FORECASTED AND ACTUAL
APARTMENT STARTS

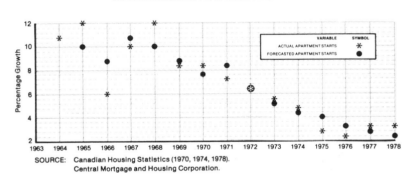

SOURCE: Canadian Housing Statistics (1970, 1974, 1978).
Central Mortgage and Housing Corporation.

EFFECTS OF CONTROLS

The evidence on the impact of rent controls appears to be clear and quite in keeping with simple economic reasoning. First of all, as shown in Figure 5 above, both vacancy rates and the rate of apartment starts declined with the introduction of the rent control program. It is interesting to note that this was "achieved" while rent increases were, according to Figure 4, probably rising not much slower than would have been the case if historic market forces had been operative. For example, only 1978 shows rent controlled increases below levels forecast by historical relationships. Here the role of expectations is clearly operative. Investors in rental accommodations reduced their level of activity as a response to concerns over future permitted rent increases. The historic relationship between the cost of housing starts and rental increases was broken. The decline of rents relative to home ownership continued under rent controls as is evident from Figure 1, even taking a further sharp drop in 1976 and 1978. The end result? Government subsidies finally appear through large interventions to prop up a drastically reduced start rate in 1977 and 1978.

OTHER INFLUENCES

Of course, in addition to the most critical factors which we could analyse explicitly, several other developments were interacting on the Toronto rental market.

In the 1970s a sequence of severe shocks hit the system. First came income tax reform legislation in 1971, under which real estate investment became less attractive to those in upper-income brackets and, in general, was required to bear an increased tax burden. The justice of the distributive effects of the tax legislation is a question of social values and, hence, apart from our concerns. Indisputable, however, is the effect on the cost of rental housing: new supplies became more expensive.

But this was only a start. By 1971, the homeowners of the city were ready to rebel against the further destruction of single family housing areas for redevelopment into large multiple dwelling apartment complexes. Being well-organized in traditional homeowners' associations, and politically visible and highly vocal as well, their dissatisfaction with the encroachment on their neighborhoods by apartment dwellers was soon converted into a reform council at city hall with a mandate to stop further highrise development in the city. Not fully realizing the longer-term implications for their own interests, the city's tenants did not effectively oppose the antidevelopment forces. But a price had to be paid, even for a goal as noble sounding as the preservation of residential neighborhoods of the middle and upper classes. The price, of course, fell not on the homeowners whose properties in fact soared in value, but on the tenants of the city who found inexpensive accommodation harder and harder to find as vacancy rates fell.

CURRENT AND FUTURE DEVELOPMENTS

This brings us to our current predicament. The painful adjustments to the significantly higher costs of providing rental housing appeared as sizeable increases in rental renewals in late 1974 and 1975. The visible causes were the landlords, who became the targets of tenant wrath. The rent control program was imposed without adequate considerations of true current costs and the recurring needs for new development; this caused major disruptions in our apartment vacancy cycle and severe inequities in the housing industry. Investment in anticipation of future needs virtually ceased. For example, the landlord who built or purchased rental units in 1973 did so at a cost unjustified by then prevailing rents. Such actions were undertaken strictly on the expectation of rent adjustment to replacement cost levels. (Pre-emptive activity of this sort plays a valuable role in the market by providing tenants with needed housing without serious time delays.) But this investor, after the imposition of rent controls, finds himself either losing money or earning a return completely inadequate to compensate him for the services he has provided. The need to recognize the return on funds invested as a cost which is every bit as legitimate as heating bills, wages, or any other costs of operations is essential, and in fact has traditionally been accepted as such in the regulation of utility companies.

The major problem which has arisen relates to the supply of new rental units. Since the cost of development has risen, new investment will be made only if substantially higher rents can be charged. With wide gaps between rents charged in old and new housing, no new housing can successfully be introduced until the general vacancy level is critically low. Furthermore, by implication, all tenants not fortunate enough to reside in an old unit will be required to pay substantially higher rents for similar new accommodations.

But potential investors recognize the swiftness with which new housing can be declared "old" under rent control legislation. Little such investment will be forthcoming if the current owners of "old" units are perceived to receive unfair treatment. If the annual rent increase fails to provide for recovery of lost purchasing power for past years' investment as well as adequate returns, the confidence of new investors can be undermined and the rate of rental housing construction will deteriorate.

POSSIBLE ALTERNATIVES

Given that rent controls in Ontario have now been in effect for four years (a remarkable longevity for a six-month "temporary measure"),* there appears to be only one way out of the predicament. Just as in the case of energy pricing, we require a declaration of intention by the provincial government that rent controls will be used only to moderate the rise of rents to market clearing levels dictated by the replacement costs and demand levels. Two factors ought to make the transition period easier: (1) if measures to lower the cost of home ownership in the form of interest relief are introduced by the federal government, the rental market demand would be weakened, possibly raising vacancy rates; (2) given the substantial tax income and avoidance of capital gains taxes, it is likely that rental arrangements will be progressively less attractive in the future as controls are lifted.

Gradual decontrol could be implemented both through less restrictive allowable rental increases and the decontrol of units upon vacancy. This would allow the measured re-establishment of realistic market rents without the need for massive government subsidies or direct investment.

---

*But nothing compared to New York City's 39-year stint of rent controls which were intended only for the duration of the "war time emergency": World War II!—Ed.

Legislative votes for controls can no more create cheaper housing than can government money printing make us collectively richer. Expansion of available rental units and an increased vacancy rate have served as effective controls on rent increases in the past, but cannot isolate the market from severe inflationary pressures on the costs of new developments. At best, rent control legislation, if viewed as temporary, could ease the tenants' burden in the transition to higher market rent levels. But if extensively continued, with the inevitable attendant disruption, government takeover of the development industry might well be the necessary result. It is important to support measures which recognize the costs of housing construction and the role that rents must perform in assuring present and future supplies. Only in this way can the current shortages be rectified to the common long-term interests of both tenants and landlords.

NOTES

1 While tax changes occurred during this period, altering profitability, their influence is inconsistent with initial increases due to Capital Cost Allowance tax rate changes followed by the decreases in taxes with the introduction of Multiple Unit Residential Buildings.

Chapter Thirteen
Decontrol

M.A. WALKER

13. Bomb Damage or Rent Control? See page 321 for the answer.

Chapter Thirteen
Decontrol

M.A. WALKER

Director,
The Fraser Institute

In places that have rent control, many people—home-owners, occupants of uncontrolled apartments, and landlords—stand to gain from its termination, though only landlords correctly perceive their interests. Occupants of controlled apartments will be the losers. A factor that looms large in the thinking of government officials is the uncertainty about exactly what will happen (or, about what will be said is happening). While it is impossible to remove this uncertainty completely, it is possible nevertheless to provide some analysis of the situation and, perhaps, thereby eliminate from the range of the possible some of the more extreme views of what will happen.

CONSEQUENCES FOR RENTS

What will happen to rents if rent control is removed? This is, of course, the essential question to be answered. The extent of the rent rise occasioned by decontrol will determine the amount of hardship imposed on occupants of controlled housing by the return to a free market and the amount of ill-feeling directed toward the government.

The answers to what will happen to rents are as numerous as there are separate housing market areas in the country. In each of these areas, the basic housing supply and demand conditions are different, and, accordingly, the reaction to a lifting of controls will be different in each case. The answers will also depend upon the duration and details of the rent control ordinance. Fortunately, for our analysis, the circumstance can only be of three basic kinds: (1) excess supply of housing, (2) excess demand for housing, (3) supply-demand balance.

Supply-demand balance involves rents that are mutually satisfactory to both tenant and landlord. In this case, decontrol of rents would have no impact since the market is already in a state of balance. Accordingly, in what follows we will not address ourselves to this case.

EXCESS SUPPLY OF HOUSING

Excess supply of housing exists if the actual number of vacant apartments exceeds the number that landlords would like to have vacant, or expected to have vacant on average when they built or bought the apartments. If there is an excess supply of apartments, landlords would find it difficult to raise rents since tenants have the option to move to other comparable apartments—the owners of which are glad to accept lower rents rather than have too many of their suites vacant. If there is an excess supply of apartments, it is unlikely that a rent control program would be effectively constraining rents. The market determined rents would be lower than the permissible ones, because of the competition among landlords to rent their vacant suites. Accordingly, rent control in these areas is redundant and its abolition would have no effect.

EXCESS DEMAND FOR HOUSING

There is excess demand for housing if, at the existing level of rents, people want to occupy more housing space (either space per unit or number of units) than is currently available. A condition of excess demand would normally cause rents to rise until people had adjusted their expenditures on housing (their demand for space) to coincide with the available supply. Of course, the rise in rents would also cause landlords to make more space available both in the short term (remodelling and speedy completion of projects underway) and in the long term (new construction). To the extent that supply expanded, the amount of adjustment required on the part of demanders of space would be correspondingly reduced. Rent control that effectively constrains rents produces an excess demand for, or shortage of, housing. Accordingly, the remainder of the discussion will assume that most areas concerned about decontrol are characterized by a condition of excess demand.

Supply response and decontrol

It is often said that the housing market is unlike other markets in that the supply of housing is "inelastic" or slow to respond to changing circumstances. In large measure this opinion arises from the fact that it takes time for new housing to be built. However, a significant degree of "elasticity" or responsiveness to changes in rents is provided by "doubling and undoubling." Doubling can take the form either of two households occupying the same housing unit or of an existing housing unit being remodelled to provide for separate double or multiple occupancy. The phenomenon of "doubling" represents a simultaneous decrease in the quantity of housing services demanded and an increase in the quantity of housing services supplied (more intensive utilization of the existing stock).

Analysis of the housing market that relies on published information about changes in the supply of housing is likely to fall very short of determining the actual condition of the market because of the existence of this "unofficial" segment of the market. Statistics collected by the Canadian Central Mortgage and Housing Corporation do not even attempt to cover housing units containing less than six suites. However, most of the short-term "action" in the market is likely to occur in precisely these units. The extent to which analyses of published figures is likely to be erroneous can be inferred from survey evidence in Vancouver which indicates that between 10 and 15 percent of the residential housing stock probably contains "illegal" suites.[1]

It seems reasonable to suppose that these conversions to multiple occupancy did not occur during periods of excess supply of housing. Rather it is highly likely that they occurred during times of excess demand when rents were rising and the official market appeared quite tight. To the extent that this is a correct assessment, analysis of official statistics would be quite misleading. In particular such analysis would underestimate the responsiveness of the supply of and demand for housing services to increases in rents.

Demand response and decontrol

The foregoing discussion notwithstanding, the principal adjustment to the rising rents necessary to eliminate excess demand would have to occur, at least in the short run, on the side of the demand for housing. A "shortage" of rental housing is symptomatic of—indeed is synonymous with— rents that are, relatively speaking, too low. At some level of rents there would be a glut of housing on the market as consumers, in an attempt to reduce their total outlays on housing, moved to increasingly smaller and less well-appointed quarters, doubled up, postponed leaving home, and so on.

Since North Americans are the best housed people in the world, there is obviously a considerable margin within which housing demand could contract without appreciably altering housing standards. Furthermore, most of the necessary adjustment could come about as a result of doubling of nonfamily households. Nearly a third of total household formations are currently undertaken by single, unattached individuals, and, reflecting their less pressing need for separate households, it is this group that probably would be most responsive to a rise in rents. Similarly, single individuals who have not yet left the homes of their parents may be encouraged by a rise in rents to delay their leaving.

This, too, would reduce the quantity of housing demanded.

The question that we must address in this section is *By how much would rents rise if, upon decontrol, all of the burden of adjustment had to be borne by the demand side of the market?*

In this regard, the first questions that arise are *What would determine the extent to which rents would rise? When would they stop rising?*

Rents would stop increasing relative to other prices when supply and demand were in balance. In terms of conventional measures of housing market conditions, supply and demand can be said to be in balance once the vacancy rate reaches its "natural equilibrium" level. The trick, of course, is to know what this "natural" vacancy rate is.

Estimates, based on published housing market information, made by Professor L.B. Smith, suggest that the natural vacancy rate for Canada as a whole was in the 5 percent range during the 1950s and 1960s.[2] Bearing in mind the deficiencies in the published information (as outlined above), I am inclined to suggest a figure of about 4 percent as a working estimate in the current circumstances.

Having fixed on 4 percent as the natural vacancy rate, we must now determine what increase in rents would be necessary to reduce the quantity of housing demanded so that this vacancy rate will be achieved. To do this we have to know to what extent consumer demand for housing is responsive to changes in the relative price of housing (that is, rents relative to the price of other things).

Various estimates of consumer responsiveness have been made and they range from insignificant to substantial. For example, some estimates indicate that a 10 percent relative change in rents (rents rising 10 percent faster than the overall consumer price index) would cause a 10 percent reduction in the quantity of housing services demanded by consumers. Other estimates place the reduction in demand caused by a 10 percent rise in rents at about only 1 percent.

The demand for housing that is relevant for any calculation related to the vacancy rate situation is the demand for physical housing units. The estimates of consumer responsiveness that we have cited relate to the demand for the services of these housing units. Fortunately, estimates have also been made for the responsiveness of the demand for housing units. On the basis of estimates calculated by L.B. Smith, an estimate of 0.4 seems appropriate as a working assumption of the responsiveness of housing unit demand to relative changes in rents.[3] The implication of this estimate is that, if average rents rise 10 percent and nothing else changes, the demand for housing units will fall by about 4 percent.

The required rise in rents

In order to illustrate the application of this formula, we will apply it to the current situation in the Vancouver area. The vacancy rate in the Vancouver area is currently hovering in the 1 percent range. If the natural vacancy rate is assumed to be about 4 percent, vacancies would have to rise by about 3 percent before rents would stabilize. The relative rise in rents required to achieve this, assuming that nothing else changes, would be about 7.5 percent. Since general inflation (the increase in the consumer price index) is proceeding at about 6 percent at annual rates, a rise in rents of 7.5 percent relative to other prices would require an increase in rents of about 13.5 percent.

Of course, this calculation ignores the fact that population growth and growth in family disposable income will both increase the demand for housing. The exact extent of these effects is not known but, on the basis of estimates that have been made for Canada and elsewhere,[4] it seems reasonable to assume that growth in real income (growth in incomes minus growth in prices) is reflected to the extent of about 30 percent in increased housing demand. New family formation, on the other hand, can reasonably be assumed to have a "one for one" effect on the demand for new housing units.[5] In other words, a 2 percent increase in the number of families would increase the demand for housing units by about 2 percent. Similarly, an increase in real family income of 2 percent would increase the demand for housing units by about 0.6 percent.

The above calculation of the required rent increase also

ignores the fact that at any given point in time there are rental units in the process of construction that will eventually come on the market regardless of changes in rents. For example, in the Vancouver area some 3,400 rental units are currently (March 1977) in process. This represents about a 3.8 percent eventual increase in the total "official" stock of rental accommodation in the city.[6]

If we revise the simple calculation made above to include the effects of population growth (2 percent increase in demand), income growth (1.5 percent increase in demand) and construction in progress (3.8 percent increase in supply), we arrive at an estimate of 6.8 percent as the relative rent increase. This yields 12.8 percent as the actual rent increase required to arrive at a vacancy rate of 4 percent. (Table 1 summarizes these calculations.)

This calculation and those preceding it have assumed that all of the adjustment would have to be borne by the demand for housing. However, as shown above, at least some of the adjustment to higher rents would come from the supply side of the market—even in the short run. If we assume that, say, one-tenth of the total adjustment would be made up by supply response in the short run, our final estimate for Vancouver is that an 11.7 percent rise in rents would increase the vacancy rate to about 4 percent by early in 1978. At that vacancy rate there would be no tendency for rents to rise further—other things equal. Since this estimate is based on a variety of assumptions, Table 2 presents a range of estimates based on different assumptions.

A note of caution is appropriate in the use of this formula. The starting point for the estimation is the actual vacancy rate at the point in time when the estimate is made. If rent controls have been in force for an extended period of time, the measured vacancy rate may underestimate the true extent of consumer demand that has been stimulated by the "bargain" rents under the rent control regime. The vacancy rate cannot be zero—however, the extent of demand may be such that it would more than fill all of the existing housing units, implying a "negative" vacancy rate. In some areas, the vacancy rate may well be "negative," and, if that is the case, the relative rent increase would have to be larger to offset this "queueing" or pent-up demand.

TABLE 1
CALCULATION OF RENT INCREASES
THAT WOULD OCCUR AFTER DECONTROL
(Using Vancouver Illustration)

Total rise in rents assuming no supply response .... A
   Equals

Growth in population .... B
   Plus

One-third the growth in real disposable family income C
   Minus

Growth in rental housing stock already in progress .... D
   Plus

The difference between the natural vacancy rate
and the actual vacancy rate .... E

All ((B + C) - D + E) divided by the rate of demand response   4
   Plus

The actual rate of general inflation (percentage
increase in the CPI) .... F
A = ((B + C) - D + E)/.4 + F
$12.8\% = ((2\% + 1.5\%) - 3.8\% + 3\%)/.4 + 6\%$

Total rise in rents assuming that supply response accounts
for 10 percent of the adjustment .... R
   Equals

Ninety percent of the total rise in rents assuming no supply response
R = A x .9
$11.5\% = 12.8\% \times .9$

1. Rents will rise until the "natural" vacancy rate is attained. The
   "natural" rate is assumed to be 4 percent.
2. A 10 percent rise in rents is assumed to reduce the demand for housing
   units by about 4 percent.
3. Population and real disposable income growth are assumed to affect
   the demand for housing units. A one percent increase in real income is
   assumed to generate a .3 percent increase in the demand for housing
   units. Growth in population is assumed to affect housing demand on a
   "one for one" basis.
4. Housing units in process are deducted from the net increase in
   demand.
5. Increases in supply are assumed to account for 10 percent of the total
   adjustment.

The consequence of decontrol

As the foregoing discussion makes clear, the effects of decontrol in each area will differ according to the situation. The principal variables that will determine the rate of rent increase in each area are: the vacancy rate gap, the rate of population growth, the rate of growth in real family income, and the rate of growth in the housing stock implied by projects currently underway. All of these variables can be roughly estimated for each area and the degree of uncertainty attaching to the consequences of decontrol thereby substantially reduced.

In the case of Vancouver the most pessimistic estimate suggests that decontrol would be accompanied by a rise in rents of about 18 percent. A more likely outcome is that rents would have to rise by about 13 percent to increase the vacancy rate to the 4 percent range. These estimates relate to the situation that would obtain during the first year.

Unfortunately, there is very little historical evidence against which we can compare our judgement about the current situation in Canada. This is because rent control, once installed, tends to become a permanent feature of the economic landscape and, hence, experience with decontrol is limited. Also, even in those cases where rents have been decontrolled, the documentation of the process has seldom been thorough. In the following paragraphs we will discuss the limited information available from decontrol experiences in the US.

The only experience with decontrol that has been accurately recorded in detail, of which we are aware, was that undertaken in the United States in the last months of 1949. The US Department of Labor conducted surveys in selected cities that were decontrolled to determine rents before and after decontrol. The results of this survey are contained in Table 3.

At the time decontrol came, in the last months of 1949, rent control had been in effect for eight years. During that period a general wage and price freeze was in effect. The general wage and price controls—except for rent—were dropped in 1946 under the pressure of events. (There were strikes in key industries because companies subject to price

TABLE 2
RENT INCREASES UNDER
DIFFERENT ASSUMPTIONS

	Text Assumptions %	Alternate 1 %	Alternate 2 %	Alternate 3 %	Alternate 4 %
Population growth	2.0	2.0	2.0	2.0	4.0
Real income growth	4.5	7.0	4.5	3.0	4.5
Housing growth	3.8	2.8	3.8	3.8	3.8
Vacancy gap	3.0	3.0	3.0	3.0	3.0
Demand response	0.4	0.4	0.2	0.4	0.4
Relative rent increase	6.8	10.8	13.5	5.5	11.8
Total actual rent increase (assuming 6% general inflation)	12.8	16.8	19.5	11.5	17.8
Total actual rent increase allowing for short-run supply response	11.5	15.1	17.6	10.4	16.0

Source: Author's computations.

control could not yield to even the reasonable demands of unions; shortages of various foods such as beef, butter, and oranges developed, and there was a general proliferation of supply crises and their bedfellows—black markets.) From 1946 to the end of 1949, the general price level in the US rose by 32.4 percent—a very large increase by the then existing historical standards and by current standards.[7]

Against this backdrop of general inflation, rents in aggregate rose by only 14.9 percent over the 1946-1949 period, and in the year of widespread decontrol, rents rose by only 3.5 percent.[8] In fact, it was not until 1954 that rents rose sufficiently to regain their prewar relationship with other prices.

The data in Table 3 indicate that only in three cases did the rent increase after decontrol exceed 15 percent (Dallas, Beverly Hills, and Knoxville). The average percentage increase in rents amounted to only 11.6 percent.

In the preceding analysis, it is assumed that all of the rental housing in the metropolitan area is controlled and

TABLE 3

INCREASES IN RENTS FREE TO RISE AFTER TERMINATION OF FEDERAL RENT CONTROL IN CITIES

ALL RENT RANGES

(Excludes units having continuous leases and units individually decontrolled before area-wide decontrol)

City	Percent of All Units Having Increases	Their Average Percentage Increase	Average Percentage Increase In General Rent Level*	Survey	Date of Decontrol 1949
Houston, Texas	31	41.3	10.7	8/15/49-11/15/49	10/19
Beverly Hills, Calif.	74	41.0	26.7	10/15/49- 3/ 1/50	12/ 7
Dallas, Texas	67	35.4	20.5	4/15/49-11/15/49	6/23
Topeka, Kansas	40	30.3	10.5	7/15/49-11/15/49	9/14
Eugene, Oregon	38	30.3	9.4	6/15/49- 2/15/50	8/18
Knoxville, Tennessee	61	26.8	15.8	5/15/49-11/15/49	6/14
Jacksonville, Fla.	56	26.2	12.3	6/15/49-11/15/49	8/ 5
Oklahoma City, Okla. 1	17	26.2	2.9	9/15/49- 1/15/50	11/23
Omaha, Nebraska	62	21.9	14.2	9/15/49- 1/15/50	11/ 2
Milwaukee, Wisc. 2	60	20.2	12.2	5/15/49- 2/15/50	8/ 5
Spokane, Washington	46	18.6	8.2	5/15/49-11/15/49	7/25
Wichita, Kansas	35	18.2	6.4	10/15/49- 3/ 1/50	12/29
Salt Lake City, Utah	46	16.2	7.1	6/15/49-11/15/49	8/ 5
Madison, Wisc.	51	12.3	5.9	6/15/49- 2/15/50	8/ 5

1 General Rent Increase of 20 percent granted prior to decontrol.
2 Includes all units—data on rents free to rise not available.
* (Includes rents which did not increase).

Source: "Hearings before the Committee on Banking and Currency, United States Senate," 1950, *Extension of Rent Control*, p. 462. Reprinted in "The Post War Rent Control Controversy," by Willys R. Knight, Director, Bureau of Business and Economic Research, Georgia State College, Research Paper Number 23, September 1962.

that each household occupies an apartment of the desired quality at the controlled price. Both assumptions are violated in many cases. Rent control is frequently enacted in one or two of the many political jurisdictions in an area. Within these jurisdictions, newly constructed units are frequently exempted from controls. In these cases, decontrol will affect the rents of uncontrolled as well as controlled units. Furthermore, since landlords have an incentive to respond to rent control by reducing their expenditures on maintenance, and the rent control law never requires a higher level of maintenance than that provided prior to the law, it is likely that controlled housing will decline in quality while the quality desired by its occupants will increase due to the lower price. In 1968 New York City's housing market had a large uncontrolled sector, and controlled units provided lower quality than desired by their occupants. It has been estimated that decontrol would increase the rents of controlled units by 41 percent and have no perceptible effect on the rents of uncontrolled units in the short term.[9] Over a longer period the rents of uncontrolled units would be lower as a result of decontrol.

CONCLUSIONS

The effect of decontrol on rents is important to government officials who must make a decision on this issue. The magnitude of this effect depends upon the severity and duration of the rent control ordinance and changes in other factors, such as population and real income, which underlie the demand and supply for housing. This paper has presented evidence on the effects of decontrol in the United States after World War II and estimates for two cities greatly differing in the severity and duration of their rent control. These estimates show that statements about the effects of decontrol can be removed from the realm of pure conjecture.

NOTES

1 A sample survey of residential housing in Vancouver indicated that 8.3 percent of the residences contained suites about which there existed no official record. In view of the fact that these suites are illegal, and since the enumerators had no power to coerce respondents to provide information, it is likely that the 8.3 percent estimate is conservative. (Divulging the information could have led to prosecution under the planning by-law.) In addition, there were 1,660 "illegal" suites officially known to exist. That is, 1,660 or 2.6 percent of those houses classed as single family dwellings were known to have more than one suite. In total, therefore, a minimum of 11 percent of the total single family residential housing stock was, at the time of the survey, housing two or more households. P. Johnston and D. Hayes, *Housing Conversion*, (City of Vancouver Planning Department, 1975), p. 8.

2 L.B. Smith, "A Note on the Price Adjustment Mechanism for Rental Housing," *American Economic Review* 64 (June 1974):478-81.

3 L.B. Smith, *Postwar Canadian Housing and Residential Mortgage Markets* (Toronto: University of Toronto Press, 1974), p. 30.

4 *Ibid.*, p. 30.

5 To some extent this assumption represents a summary of a variety of influences. The total demand from demographic sources arises from net household formation where household formation includes family and nonfamily households. Accordingly, it is often the case that zero population growth yields significant housing demand because of undoubling and young people leaving home to establish a separate household. Rather than launch into a discussion of household formation, I have simply assumed that the population growth number includes an allowance for this. In the range of estimates calculated below and reported in Table 2, I have used a high and low estimate of population growth.

6 The estimate of supply expansion ignores the potential effects that movements from the rental market encouraged by the Assisted Home Ownership Program will have on the supply situation. Research currently being conducted by Central Mortgage and Housing Corporation in Vancouver indicates that many of the people moving into AHOP housing are, in fact, leaving the Vancouver rental housing market. This means that, other things being equal, the net supply of available rental units will be larger than is implied in our calculations, and the rent increases necessary to eliminate the vacancy gap will be smaller.

7 US Department of Labor, Bureau of Labor Statistics, *Monthly Labor Review*, various years.

8 Some increases had been allowed by the "Housing Expediter" who was responsible for the administration of rent control.

9 These results are based on data in Edgar O. Olsen's "An Econometric Analysis of Rent Control," *Journal of Political Economy* (November/December 1972): 1091, and his unpublished calculations.

Part Four
Conclusions

Chapter Fourteen
Alternatives

EDGAR O. OLSEN

M.A. WALKER

14. Bomb Damage or Rent Control? See page 321 for the answer.

Chapter Fourteen
Alternatives

EDGAR O. OLSEN

Associate Professor of Economics,
University of Virginia

M.A. WALKER

Director,
The Fraser Institute

What matters in economic policy making is what is believed to exist and not what actually exists. Further, our understanding about the economy is highly imperfect and our measurement of its functioning, imprecise. Accordingly, there is considerable room for the exercise of judgement in the assessment of current economic events. So, to some extent, economic events are partially in the mind of the beholder, and the unfolding of economic events is, as much as anything, the development of a consensus amongst observers about what is happening. (After the fact, sometimes long after, our measurements are usually more precise, and there is often a final judgement about matters on the basis of more reliable evidence.)

In the case of economic policy, the economic consensus is only one of the many opinions that bear on the decisions that are made. Political considerations weigh heavily on policy makers as do the "high profile" and behind-the-scenes pleadings of special interest groups. The consequence is that economic policy is seldom, if ever, designed with the single-minded objective of dealing with an economic problem. More important, perception of the economic problem is often badly distorted because of the effect that other considerations have on the exercise of judgement in the interpretation of economic evidence.

Housing policy seems to have been particularly prone to this weakness, and rent control has been one of the consequences.[1]

THE ORIGINS OF RENT CONTROL

Rent control, in practice, is always adopted as a temporary measure to alleviate the hardship (real or imagined) that tenants are presumed to endure as a consequence of a rental housing shortage. For example, the British rent control scheme (now sixty-one years old), the Swedish rent control provisions of 1945 (finally abolished under pressure from tenants in 1975), the existing 1974 rent control provisions in British Columbia, and 1976 legislation in Alberta and Ontario all have this in common. The critical and determining factor in most of these cases was the widely held belief that the jurisdiction in question was experiencing a housing "shortage" of crisis proportions. A housing crisis demands an immediate dose of strong policy medicine—particularly if an election is in the offing or if the steps of parliament are daily occupied by vociferous, media attracting tenants. If, as will usually be the case, the short-term benefactors of rent control (*sitting tenants*) are more numerous than those who lose (*landlords*) the strong medicine for a housing crisis almost invariably takes the form of rent control.

From the point of view of the politically orientated policy maker, rent control has everything to offer. It silences (at least for a time) the noisy activists, it shows that the government is doing something about the housing crisis, and often as not it wins the political support of a large fraction of the voting public (over half of the households in most urban areas are tenants). Moreover, rent control does not involve the use of government resources and hence doesn't "cost" the government anything.

In addition, the bad side effects of control take a long time to emerge and are slow to affect tenants on average and hence slow to affect adversely the political fortunes of those who enact controls. In this respect, housing is unlike most other commodities. The supply of housing services is provided, for the most part, from fixed stock. Hence, controls on the price of these services cannot result in a rapid withdrawal of the service. It is this built-in inertia effect in the supply of housing that makes it particularly vulnerable to controls. The prices of other necessities of life such as food and clothing are seldom controlled, because the shortages produced by control are immediately evident. (The attempt to freeze food prices—Freeze II, 13 June 1973 to 11 August 1973—during the US anti-inflation program promptly produced food shortages and necessitated the introduction of food regulations. Similarly, price controls in the US following World War II were abandoned in the face of widespread shortages.) In short, given the nature of housing, rent control is excellent policy snake oil for squeaky wheels.

The process that leads to rent control usually begins during a time when the housing market is in the process of adjusting to the pressure of excess demand. The natural consequence of excess demand for housing services is an increase in rents. The rise in rents will, after a time, encourage landlords to increase the supply of housing that they bring to the market. In the very short term, however, the excess demand can only be accommodated by a more intensive use of the existing stock of housing.

However, the dearth of information concerning local housing markets (for example, the vacancy rate) makes it difficult to distinguish this situation from one in which rents are rising rapidly because the national government has printed too much money, with the result that all prices and wages are rising. If data on the vacancy rate are available and indicate a tight market, they usually find their way into the popular press. What rarely is available and almost never finds its way into popular discussions is evidence on the response of suppliers to the low vacancy rate. Has the number of new starts increased? Has the completion of housing in process been speeded? Has the rate at which units are removed from the stock been slowed? If the answer to these questions is "yes," then present increases in rents relative to other prices will be followed by future decreases in the relative price of housing services. In the midst of this ignorance about market conditions, enter the tenant activists whose objective it is to have rent control enacted.

Tenant activists generally do not start out from the premise that "we must first ascertain the facts." Quite the contrary. The objective of the tenant activist is to create a sense of crisis—to make policy makers and other tenants believe that the situation is truly desperate. A book entitled *Less Rent More Control*, which is "about rent control... and how tenants can organize to win and enforce it," advises:

> "Even if you can't get good statistics, it's often helpful to publicize specific cases of families paying a large portion of their incomes for rent."

> "Stories about specific families who are suffering from the housing crisis can be very useful in bringing statistics to life and in getting publicity for the rent control campaign."[2]

Since the process of market adjustments produces rising rents, and there are people in most communities whose incomes are low or slow to rise, the rent control campaign will not have to look very hard to find the evidence of a crisis. The media for its part, always happy to advance the cause of the underdog—an admirable objective taken by itself—willingly cooperates in making notorious the plight of the underprivileged. Coincidently, the rent control campaign attracts to it the support of a larger number of tenants who, owing to their own situations, would not have pressed for controls but who identify with the disadvantaged. (And besides, they do have something to gain because rent control does reduce the rate of increase in rents.)

At this juncture, whether or not there is a housing shortage, and whether or not increased supply is on the way, is irrelevant to the government involved because the general public believes that a crisis exists. Hard facts to dispel this belief are not available and, when available, are discounted by the emotional content of the evidence of hardship cases. As so often happens, the government "can't do nothing." In this situation, careful demonstrations by economists of the disastrous long-term effects of rent control are unlikely to get a careful hearing. Besides, rent controls are only a temporary measure!

It would be foolish to pretend that rent controls are always adopted in circumstances like the foregoing. In the case of British Columbia, pressure for rent control actually came from within the government itself. During a program of general wage and price controls, rent controls are simply imposed as an adjunct to the general program—whether or not there is tenant pressure for controls. Nevertheless, our characterization of the process is important because it highlights the essential elements—namely, the lack of information and the plight of the disadvantaged.

THE EFFECTS OF RENT CONTROL

Although more complete information on the current state of local housing markets is highly desirable, an informed decision on the merits of a proposed rent control ordinance requires predictions of its effects. To make accurate predictions for particular localities within the relevant time frame is virtually impossible. An alternative approach is to consider the effects of rent control ordinances in different times and places. This book brings together much of the available evidence. We summarize the main points here.

Rent control worsens housing "shortage"

Rent control makes rental housing relatively cheaper than it would otherwise have been. Accordingly, it increases the demand for housing. At the same time it reduces the profitability of investment in rental housing and hence reduces the supply. If we use the vacancy rate (the percentage of suites unoccupied) as a measurement of the shortage, observable evidence of the effect of controls is available in the New York City housing market. This area has both a controlled and an uncontrolled market. The vacancy rate in the rent controlled market is consistently half that in the uncontrolled market.

Currently the Canadian experience with rent control is producing evidence that seems to conflict with this view that rent control increases housing shortages. The evidence is that, in spite of rent control, vacancy rates are starting to rise—especially in Toronto and Vancouver. This evidence must be carefully interpreted.

The principal reasons for the incipient increase in vacancy rates relate to government policy to make production of rental accommodation more attractive and to make home ownership an attractive option for many current renters. Construction of rental accommodation has been made more attractive by the reinstatement of the provision, abandoned in 1971, that allowed landlords to "write off" the capital cost of buildings against their other income. The abandonment of that provision in 1971, with its associated effects on supply, was a principal factor in the rise in rents that occurred during 1973-1975.

Rental accommodation is also being directly subsidized by the government. There has been widespread adoption of assisted rental programs which subsidize the capital cost of projects in return for controls on the rents that will be charged. In effect, these programs are an acknowledgement of the fact that rents are too low and should be viewed as the first step in what could be a disastrous journey. The provision of these subsidized units will "take the pressure off" the rental market in the short term but will succeed in maintaining rents that are increasingly unrelated to the market in the long term. Thus, while seeming to improve the situation, these programs will ultimately create a situation where no construction is undertaken unless it is subsidized.

Various programs have been adopted to increase the attractiveness of home ownership. These subsidized home ownership programs have the effect of artificially shifting demand from the rental sector to the home ownership sector at a faster rate than is justified by the underlying economics of these two submarkets. As a consequence, the short-term condition of the rental housing market will improve—but the improvement is illusory and must not be permitted to deflect attention from the fact that rents are below the long-term or equilibrium level.

Rent control causes deterioration of the housing stock

Faced with a rate of return on investment that is too small, many landlords recoup their losses on a current basis by allowing the physical stock of houses to depreciate at a faster rate. That is, regular maintenance and repair is neglected. While this improves the landlord's financial situation, it has an obviously disastrous effect on the housing stock over the long term.

From the landlord's point of view, rent control reduces the capital value of the buildings supplying the housing service.[3] The extraction of capital in the form of repair and maintenance forgone is a rational way of equalizing the rent controlled rate of return with the expected rate of return before rent controls.

Rent control redistributes income in haphazard fashion

Rent control is a form of tax that is levied on landlords, the proceeds of which are given to tenants. The amount of tax and subsidy varies according to the difference between the market rent and the controlled rent. It is often supposed that the redistribution effected by rent control is from high-income earners to low-income earners. While there is not much firm evidence on the matter, what evidence there is does not support this view. For example, taxation statistics for Canada (1973) show that about half of all rents reported were earned by landlords with incomes of less than $13,000. A detailed study of US data by D. Gale Johnson did not support the hypothesis "that landlords have significantly higher incomes than tenants." Further, he concludes, "if one of the objectives of rent control is to aid low-income people. . .it does not achieve that objective."[4]

Rent control leads to discrimination

To the extent that they are unable to discriminate amongst tenants on the basis of price, landlords find it expedient to do so on the basis of race or other characteristics.[5] Groups particularly vulnerable are those tenants that may cause higher costs for the landlord, such as large families or families with children (more "wear and tear" on housing unit) and people whose jobs require higher than average mobility (less stable tenancy).[6]

Rent control shifts the incidence of property taxation

Rent control reduces the value of rental property. With a given revenue requirement, governments that rely on the assessed value of property as a tax base must increase the tax rate on all property. Since the assessed value of owner-occupied housing will, in all probability, rise under a rent control regime, the burden of property tax is gradually shifted to homeowners.

Recent evidence of this effect of rent control has been compiled for the City of Cambridge, Massachusetts, where, against an inflationary backdrop similar to Canada's, the total assessed value of real property actually fell during the 1972-1974 period. The city assessor, in commenting on the situation, noted that as a consequence of the shrinking tax base, the tax *rate* had been increased by 70 percent over the 1970-1974 period.[7]

Rent control reduces labor mobility

Occupation of a rent controlled apartment is an asset. The yield on this asset is the difference between the market rent and the controlled rent. Moving from one unit with controls to another without controls therefore entails a "capital loss." The extent of this effect normally increases with the length of time that controls are in force.

Rent control does not improve housing conditions of the poor

It is often supposed that since rent control makes housing cheaper it, therefore, improves the housing condition of the poor. The evidence suggests that the effect of rent control is to cause tenants to increase their expenditures on goods and services other than housing. In other words, under rent control people tend to occupy about the same standard of housing that they would occupy in a free market. The extra disposable income that they have because of rent control is used to buy things other than housing.

Rent control does not eliminate price rationing

One of the functions of price in a market is to ration the supply of a good or a service amongst the people that want it. Proponents of rent control argue that this *ability-to-pay criterion* ought not to be applied in the housing market because of the essential nature of housing and because the existing income distribution is such that there is wide variability in ability to pay. This argument for rent control is advanced in the belief that eliminating the formal price rationing mechanism will eliminate rationing on the basis of ability to pay.

In practice, imposing rent control on the market price rationing scheme doesn't have this effect, because rent control doesn't much affect the existing distribution of income. Key money, large security deposits, phoney offers to buy, bribes to officials and the like take the place of formal rent increases, and ability to pay, as ever, determines who gets what. Indeed, since rent control reduces the total supply available, and accordingly the need for rationing is more acute, the ability to pay could potentially be a more significant determinant of housing conditions in a rent controlled market than in a free market.

The tendency for black and gray markets in housing (that is, informal price rationing) to arise in the presence of rent control also has side effects on the structure of rental housing supply. Since black and gray market activities are generally illegal, many landlords are reluctant to become involved. However, since the return from such activities is fairly high and becomes higher the farther controlled rents move from free market rents, people who do not have a distaste for marginal illegalities are attracted to the market. And, since property values based on market rents are artificially depressed, such potential landlords find the cost of *buying into the market* quite attractive. The potential effects of this sort of evolution and the situation that could arise do not tax the imagination. Certainly, the *property management* techniques of the sort of landlord that thrives on the intralegal margin are well known.

ALTERNATIVE MEANS TO WORTHY ENDS

The only noble motivation for rent control that we have been able to unearth is a concern for the well-being of low-income households. However, rent control is far from the best way to express this concern. If aid to such families is in the public interest, then equity requires that the cost of providing it be spread among concerned families. There is no justification for requiring almost the entire cost to be borne by the small proportion of the population who own rental property. Furthermore, there is no justification for providing aid to middle- and upper-income families as is typical of rent control.

If aid to low-income families is to be financed by taxes on other families, then taxpayers' preferences should be taken into account in determining the form of the aid. Clearly, if we want to help low-income families, think that these families know better than others what is good for themselves, and have no other reason for being concerned about how they spend their money, aid should be in the form of unrestricted cash grants. On the other hand, if we have some special interest in inducing these families to occupy better housing than they would choose were they given unrestricted cash grants (perhaps because we do not consider them to be the best judges of what is good for themselves), some other form of aid is desirable.

Evidence strongly suggests that some form of housing allowance is the most efficient and equitable means of subsidizing housing.[8] For example, low-income families could be given a cash grant on the condition that they occupy housing meeting certain standards. The amount of the grant could be greater for families with lower incomes and more members. The US Department of Housing and Urban Development (HUD) has been conducting full-scale housing allowance programs of this sort in two urban areas since the mid-1970s.[9] Studies of these programs and HUD's traditional new construction programs (for example, conventional public housing and Section 236) show that housing services are produced less efficiently under the traditional programs. The smallest estimate of the extent of the inefficiency is 10 percent.

Furthermore, in their early years, the new construction programs provide their participants with much better housing than that typical of families just above the upper-income limits of eligibility. Section 8 New which accounts for the bulk of the additions to the stock of newly constructed, subsidized units in the United States is a perfect example. The mean rent of the Section 8 New units added in fiscal year 1978 was about $400 per month; the mean rent of families at the upper-income limits of eligibility was only $190.

To look at the same phenomenon in a different way, about 60 percent of all households are ineligible for this program but very few of these families occupy units renting for more than the typical Section 8 New unit. As a consequence of providing luxurious housing to low-income families, the per-unit subsidy is enormous (about $3,800 per household for Section 8 New in fiscal 1978) and Congress has never been willing to appropriate enough money to serve all eligible households. Indeed, together, all of HUD's housing subsidy programs serve fewer than 25 percent of the households in every income class.

The result is that some low-income families receive

enormous subsidies while the majority of equally needy families receive nothing. As a new construction program matures, the preceding inequities are gradually replaced by inequities among recipients. Some units under the program are old and poorly maintained; others are new. Since the rent paid by participants in HUD's programs does not depend on the desirability of the unit, occupants of old, poorly maintained units receive much smaller benefits than occupants of newer, better maintained units. This is the situation today in conventional public housing.

Housing allowances avoid the inefficiencies of traditional new construction programs by subsidizing households directly and reduce the inequities substantially by offering equally situated households the same cash grant under the same conditions and providing a subsidy to all eligible families who wish to participate. The major objections to housing allowances have been that they would result in higher rents without leading to better housing and that they would be too costly.

Research has shown that these objections are incorrect. The full-scale housing allowance programs conducted by HUD in two urban areas did not result in higher rents for units that were not improved. For units that were upgraded, increases in rent were consistent with the extent of the improvements. Furthermore, the average subsidy under the housing allowance programs is far less than that under the traditional new construction programs. In 1978, it was about $900 per year for the housing allowance programs and $3,900 for Section 8 New. Since recipients are required to occupy housing which meets current standards for decent, safe, and sanitary housing, and since a substantial fraction of all substandard units were either upgraded or vacated in response to the housing allowance program, it is clear that housing allowances are a much cheaper means of attaining our goals than the new-construction programs.

Since unconditional cash grants and housing allowances do not lead to any of the problems associated with rent control, one or the other should be supported by anyone who has supported rent control out of a concern for the well-being of low-income families. Rent control is an inferior means to its ends.

STRATEGY FOR DECONTROL

Clearly, the best way to achieve an uncontrolled housing market is to resist rent control in the first place. It is easier for politicians to refuse to grant favors in the first place than it is for them to alienate potential supporters by withdrawing a subsidy to which they have grown accustomed. Furthermore, the longer tenants have enjoyed the unrealistically low controlled rents, the more difficult it is for them to adjust to a free market situation. Nonetheless, given that the case against rent control is overwhelming, and that there are many places which currently have rent control programs, some ways of making the transition from a controlled to an uncontrolled market are better than others, and it is appropriate to discuss decontrol strategies.

Most arguments against immediate decontrol are similar to those used to justify controls in the first place, and they have the low-income tenant as their centrepiece. It is argued, for example, that overnight decontrol would impose tremendous hardships on those with low incomes. The rise in rents would force these people either to move to truly desperate living quarters or to drastically reduce their spending on other necessities.

We believe that these arguments overlook several important points. In the first place, the number of people for whom this could potentially be true is usually exaggerated.[10] Secondly, the fact that market adjustment causes hardship for some is not an argument for intervention in a particular market. It may be an argument for an income supplement of some form or for an expansion of existing supplements. It is clear that if hardship for low-income groups does occur, it is a result of an inadequate income supplementation scheme and should be treated as such.

If, as is sometimes the case, the "hardship" referred to is the fact that all tenants will, upon decontrol, have to pay a market rent for accommodation, it is very difficult to be sympathetic to this view. The burden of adjustment back to a market rent will fall on roughly the same group of people who enjoyed the "benefits" that accrued from control. The only way tenants as a group can lessen the burden is by reducing the amount of housing that they demand. This is precisely what is required in a situation of excess demand. Unless the market is allowed to adjust, new entrants to the housing market (of all incomes) are forced to have less housing than they would like (or where new construction is not controlled, pay more for it) because of the preferred position of sitting tenants.

Although we think that speedy decontrol is desirable, we feel that it would be a mistake to end all controls instantly. If this were done, it is possible that market rents on some types of housing would rise substantially until private builders were able to react with the production of new rental housing units. Although rents would fall when these new units become available for rent, the political pressure to re-establish controls prior to that development might be too strong for politicians to resist. In such a situation it would be easy for rent control advocates to convince the public that the rapid rent increases are a permanent feature of decontrolled housing markets.

We also feel that it would be a mistake to try to achieve decontrol through a very gradual liberalizing of rent control procedures. This is particularly true if the authority to reimpose controls is retained. Potential investors are likely to remain skeptical about the sincerity of the decontrol effort, and the outcome is likely to be one where all of the drawbacks of decontrol are experienced, but few of the advantages.

What we advocate is a gradual but specific decontrol program. Initially, new units, high-rent units, and vacated units should be exempted from controls where such provisions do not already exist. In this way the proportion of people living in rent controlled units will be diminished. Also, annual rent increases in excess of increases in costs should be allowed. In this way, controls will gradually become ineffective as controlled rents rise to free market levels and as more units come into the high-rent category. Finally, a firm commitment should be made to completely terminate controls as of a specific date a couple of years in the future. The adoption of this provision would encourage the construction of new units which will come onto the market as controls are terminated, and it should help to bring an end to the excessive conversion of rental units to condominiums.[11] If these proposals are adopted, it is quite likely that the transition to decontrol will be very smooth, with the termination date being scarcely detectable.

NOTES

1 For an analysis of Canadian Housing Policy in the 1970s, see L.B. Smith, *Anatomy of a Crisis—Canadian Housing Policy in the Seventies* (Vancouver, The Fraser Institute, 1977).

2 Emily Achtenberg, *Less Rent More Control* (Cambridge, Mass.: Urban Planning Aid Inc., 1973), pp. 2, 29, 27. Ms. Achtenberg is better known in Canada in her role as project leader on rent control in the 1975 study undertaken by the Government of British Columbia. One of the objectives of that study was to assess the impact of rent control and advise as to its place in government housing policy. This study is discussed by Raymond Heung in *The Do's and Don'ts of Housing Policy*, (Vancouver, The Fraser Institute, 1976).

3 The capital value is determined by the expected revenue from rents in the future.

4 See Heung, *The Do's and Don'ts of Housing Policy*, p. 75.

5 See Elizabeth Anne Roistacher, "The Distribution of Tenant Benefits Under Rent Control," (Ph.D. diss., University of Pennsylvania, 1972). Possibly in recognition of this effect of rent control, the National Association for the Advancement of Colored People (NAACP), as early as 1974, was opposing the institution of rent control in California.

6 Under the New York City ordinance, more mobile tenants are preferred by landlords because the controlled rent is increased each time a unit is vacated.

7 Charles R. Laverty, Jr., Assessor, City of Cambridge, Massachusetts, to the Honorable Donald R. Gaudetter, House Chairman, Joint Legislative Committee on Local Affairs.

8 See, for example, US Department of Housing and Urban Development, *Housing in the Seventies*, A Report of the National Housing Policy Review (Washington, D.C.: Government Printing Office, 1974), Chapter 4; *Fourth Annual Report of the Housing Allowance Supply Experiment*, R-2302-HUD (Santa Monica: Rand

Corporation, May 1978); and Helen E. Bakeman, Stephen D. Kennedy, and James Wallace, *Fourth Annual Report of the Housing Allowance Demand Experiment* (Cambridge, Mass.: Abt Associates, 1977).

9 More limited experiments with other types of housing allowances were conducted by HUD in ten additional cities during this period.

10 See M. Walker, "What Are the Facts?" in *Rent Control—A Popular Paradox* (Vancouver: The Fraser Institute, 1975).

11 In saying this, we are assuming that investors believe the government officials who announce the termination of controls. Unfortunately, there is no way of binding a government to its word, since future legislative bodies have the power to reverse any decision made by the present one.

Chapter Fifteen
Postscript:
A Reply to the Critics

WALTER BLOCK

15. Bomb Damage or Rent Control? See page 321 for the answer.

THE AUTHOR

WALTER BLOCK is Senior Economist at the Fraser Institute and a member of the Economics Department at Rutgers University. Born in Brooklyn, New York, in 1941, Dr. Block received his B.A. from Brooklyn College in 1964 and his Ph.D. from Columbia University in 1972. He has taught Micro-economics, Industrial Organization, Urban Economics, and Political Economy at Stony Brook, State University of New York; the City College of New York, New York University; and Baruch College, City University of New York; and has worked in various research capacities for the National Bureau of Economic Research, the Tax Foundation, and *Business Week* Magazine.

Professor Block is Editor of The Fraser Institute's sixth book in its Housing and Land Economics series, *Zoning: Its Costs and Relevance for the 1980s.* In addition, he has published numerous articles on economic theory in *Growth & Change, Theory & Decision, The American Economist, The Journal of Libertarian Studies, Real Estate Weekly, The International Journal for Housing Science,* and *Inquiry.* A former Cato Institute Fellow, Earhart Fellow, and New York State Regents Fellowship winner, he is the author of *Defending the Undefendable,* published by Fleet Press, New York, in 1976.

Chapter Fifteen
Postscript:
A Reply to the Critics

WALTER BLOCK

*Senior Economist,
The Fraser Institute*

Although there are no competent economists on any side of the political spectrum who have advocated rent controls, there are several pundits, journalists, and social critics enamored with this idea. Their arguments are hardly of the greatest intellectual moment; even though seemingly launched at the professional economists who make the anticontrol case, many of their diatribes are not even relevant to the topic. It is no wonder, then, that professional economists have disregarded their journalistic critics who favor rent control.

But this has been a mistake. First of all, although economists do in fact have a greater input into public policy decision making than mere numbers would suggest, other groups have even more political clout. How else is one to account for their virtually unanimous opposition to rent control—and for the increasing popularity of this legislation on the part of the general public? If the "dismal scientists" wish the public to take cognizance of the evidence they have uncovered on the effects of rent control, they must make this information known to the average intelligent citizen. And they can only do this by addressing, not ignoring, the few popular journalists who oppose them. Secondly, a continued refusal to "enter the fray" will be interpreted by the rent control advocates and their supporters as an admission that the challenges were unanswerable. Given the overwhelming evidence of the harm created by rent control, this would be particularly unfortunate. It is for these reasons that the present essay addresses the views of journalist advocates of rent control.[1]

THE CASE AGAINST RENT CONTROL DOES *NOT* REST ON THE ASSUMPTION OF PERFECT COMPETITION

One of the most widely heard refrains is that the brief against rent controls incorrectly assumes the existence of, variously, "a perfectly functioning market," "pure competition," "perfect competition,"[2] or some similar idealistic system which, according to the critics, exists only in the minds of conservative economists.

Let it be said, once and for all, loud and clear: there never was, is not now, and never will be perfection with regard to fallible mankind, or any of his institutions, economics specifically included. It would be nice if markets were perfect (although the actual meaning of a "perfect market" is far from clear). Unfortunately perfection is denied mankind while on this side of heaven. So the objection is undoubtedly correct; there is no perfect market in rental housing.

But what precisely follows from this insight? Is it that rent control, despite all the arguments presented in this book, somehow becomes an efficacious program? Hardly. Is it that government action is justified because of market "imperfections?" Not at all.

The undeniable existence of market imperfections has absolutely no implications for the efficacy of rent control! Just because the free market is "imperfect," it does not logically follow that government action will improve matters.[3] If the market were "perfect," even the critics would presumably have to concede the harmfulness of rent control. An imperfect or real world market will, to be sure, be worse than a perfect one in all aspects. But an imperfect world without rent control is still preferable to an imperfect world *with* this law. And this is what is shown throughout this entire book. Friedman and Stigler, Hayek, and de Jouvenel do not conjecture about a mythical world of "perfect competition." On the contrary, they analyse the actual effects of rent control on real world economies as disparate as the US, Austria, and France.

THE RENTAL HOUSING MARKET IS *NOT* MONOPOLISTIC

Then there is the charge that capital, particularly in housing, has a tendency to concentrate, resulting in a decidedly uncompetitive urban land market.[4] This can easily be refuted, however, and in two basic ways.

First of all, the *facts* do not bear out this contention. Taking Canada as an example, Basil Kalymon[5] notes that the largest 29 real estate firms own less than 20 percent of total industry assets, and that neither the top 11 nor the big 4 even reach the 15 percent level, as is shown in Table 1. The leading firm, moreover, weighs in with slightly less than 3.5 percent, the second in line tips the scale on the small side of 3 percent, and no other member of the industry exceeds 2 percent.

Low concentration ratios

When the concentration ratios are defined in terms of revenues, an even lower measure is derived. Here, the comparable figures for the top 29, 11 and 4 firms are 15 percent, 12 percent and 8 percent.*

Four-firm concentration ratios, the most widely used

*Similar evidence for Toronto and for Mississauga, a municipality in the Greater Toronto Metropolitan Area, is provided by Professors Markusen and Scheffman in The Fraser Institute book *Public Property? The Habitat Debate Continued* (1977), pp. 149-167. Their work is concerned with land ownership concentration, a substitute for housing unit concentration.—Ed.

TABLE 1
SHARE OF TOTAL REAL ESTATE INDUSTRY
(1976)

	% of Assets	% of Revenue
Cadillac-Fairview	3.41	2.63
Trizec Corporation	2.94	2.05
Campeau Corporation	1.57	1.88
Oxford Development	1.55	0.75
Abbey Glen	1.27	1.30
Bramalea	0.97	0.70
McLaughlin	0.84	0.79
Daon Development	0.68	1.37
MEPC	0.59	0.32
Markborough Properties	0.46	0.36
Orlando Realty	0.39	0.17
Top 4 Firms	9.47%	7.93%
Top 11 Firms	14.67%	12.32%
Total CIPREC[1] (29 companies)	19.2%	15.1%

Source: Report of the Canadian Institute of Public Real Estate Companies; Statistics Canada, Corporation Financial Statistics.

[1] CIPREC: Canadian Institute of Public Real Estate Companies

measure, are especially important. By using them, we may compare the supposedly monopolistic real estate industry with other possible "malefactors." Table 2 shows the critics' claim for the fabrication it is. Even the twentieth most concentrated industry, typewriter supplies manufacturing, has a ratio (78.3 percent) *far* in excess of urban land developers (9.5 percent).*

---

*It is also worth noting in this context that the Canada Mortgage and Housing Corporation owns approximately 30,000 housing units, and, together with homes owned by provincial and municipal housing authorities, these exert considerable competitive pressures in the housing market.—Ed.

TABLE 2
TWENTY CANADIAN MANUFACTURING
INDUSTRIES WITH THE HIGHEST
FOUR-FIRM (VALUE-OF-SHIPMENT)
CONCENTRATION RATIOS, 1972

Rank 1972	Industry	CR4
1.	Cotton yarn and cloth mills	97.5
2.	Tobacco products manufacturing	97.1
3.	Glass manufacturing	97.0
4.	Breweries	96.5
5.	Fibre and filament yarn manufacturing	93.8
6.	Cane and beet sugar processing	93.7
7.	Aluminum rolling, casting and extruding	89.0
8.	Wood preservation industries	87.1
9.	Miscellaneous vehicle manufacturing	86.6
10.	Abrasives manufacturing	86.2
11.	Manufacturing of lubricating oil and greases	85.9
12.	Cement manufacturing	83.7
13.	Office and store machinery manufacturing	82.7
14.	Copper and copper alloy rolling, casting and extruding	81.9
15.	Distilleries	79.7
16.	Battery manufacturing	79.3
17.	Manufacturing of electrical wire and cable	79.2
18.	Clock and watch manufacturing	79.0
19.	Smelting and refining	78.6
20.	Typewriter supplies manufacturing	78.3

Source: *Report of The Royal Commission on Corporate Concentration,* 1978, p. 40, Table 2.8.

The market is dynamic, not static

A second line of refutation is to call into question the presumed relationship between high concentration ratios and "nefarious" monopolistic activities.[6] The difficulty with this critique is that it views the economy in a static manner, at a single point of time. It treats as identical companies which have *earned* a large market share through the competitive process itself (by means of innovations and improvements, new raw material discoveries, continual cost and price cutting, for example) with those that arrived at this lofty position through a premeditated short circuiting of competition (by exploiting government subsidies, grants, tariff protections, and discriminatory regulations which apply only to competitors).

If the competitive game was fair, then the winner is an example of *competition*, not its absence. (Unless this distinction is firmly kept in mind, we risk labelling as monopolists—and antitrusting to death—some of our most able, competitive, and productive corporations.)

EXCESSIVE PROFITS ARE *NOT* COMMONLY EARNED IN REAL ESTATE

This claim,[7] too, must be rejected on both a factual and a theoretical basis. The Canadian experience, for example, does not bear out this contention. Based on data collected for 1969-1970, two years of low inflation, and for 1973-1974, a period of high price rises, Basil Kalymon concludes that "the returns on equity invested in the real estate industry were very similar to those achieved by industry in general."

But the major problem is the lack of economic understanding behind the objection. Let us suppose, only for the sake of argument, that the critics are correct, and that an enormously higher profit rate exists in real estate compared to all other industries. Specifically, assume a rate of return of the order of 50 percent in real estate, and only 10 percent elsewhere.

This would imply that the gap between prices and costs is much greater in housing than in other industries. This, of course, would be symptomatic of a severe housing shortage, and relative satiation of other consumer desires. (Such an example might arise if an enemy destroyed half our housing but miraculously left untouched everything else: automobiles and capital equipment such as household furnishings and utensils, for example. Perhaps one could imagine a bug that attacked housing and nothing else).

TABLE 3

FINANCIAL RESULTS: REAL ESTATE COMPARED WITH ALL INDUSTRIES (Other than Financial)

	All Industries (Non-financial)				Real Estate Operators and Developers*			
	1969	1970	1973	1974	1969	1970	1973	1974
	(Millions $)							
1. Income Reported	4,706	4,119	9,766	12,333	254	228	424	686
Percent of Equity	9.37	7.75	13.43	15.04	10.51	8.58	11.29	14.79
Percent of Equity less Inflation	4.77	4.45	5.83	4.24	5.91	5.28	3.69	3.99
2. Income Adjusted by Inventory Profits	3,885	3,500	7,667	8,125	229	206	288	391
Percent of Equity	7.73	6.58	10.55	9.92	9.46	7.75	7.67	8.43
3. Income Adjusted by Inventory Profits and Understated Depreciation	2,855	2,202	4,559	3,296	69	33	(59)	(152)
Percent of Equity	5.68	4.14	6.27	4.02	2.85	1.24	(1.57)	(3.28)
4. Income + Depreciation + Deferred Taxes	9,075	8,847	16,768	20,939	522	515	930	1,207
Percent of Equity	18.07	16.64	23.09	25.54	21.50	19.33	24.78	26.02
5. Dividends Paid	2,004	2,248	3,475	4,526	83	85	225	298
Percent of Equity	3.99	4.23	4.78	5.52	3.41	3.21	6.00	6.43
6. Income as Percent of Capital Employed	5.8	4.7	7.3	8.1	2.4	2.0	2.9	3.3

Consumer Price Increases (percent): 1969 — 4.6; 1970 — 3.3; 1973 — 7.6; 1974 — 10.8

Source: Corporation Financial Statistics, Statistics Canada, cited in Basil Kalymon, *Profits in the Real Estate Industry*, Vancouver, The Fraser Institute, 1978, p. 18.

*Statistics Canada's definition of "real estate operators and developers"—establishments primarily engaged in owning and operating real estate or in developing or improving unimproved real property. This includes operators of nonresidential buildings, apartment buildings, trailer sites of a "permanent" nature, other dwellings, owners of agricultural, forest, mining, railroad, public utility and other kinds of real property which are rented out to the operators. This industry includes establishments primarily engaged in subdividing and developing real estate.

But even under these exceedingly unlikely conditions, the high profits in real estate would soon be dissipated. For profits in the market economy play the part of a beacon at sea.[8] Let them rise in any one sector, and entrepreneurial investment from all over is attracted to them. Money would flood into housing construction and away from other alternatives. This movement will tend to reduce the great profits earned in real estate and raise the rates everywhere else until similar returns prevail in all sectors of the economy (taking into account risk, uncertainty, subjective entrepreneurial preferences, and so on). Extremely different rates of return, then, can only be short-run phenomena. They tend to be quickly erased by profit seeking behavior on the part of all entrepreneurs.

If profits in real estate are high, they will be dissipated. But, as we have seen, they are *not* greater than those earned elsewhere. One might even make a case that, when risk is taken into account, profits in real estate are *lower* than elsewhere, for although reported earnings are similar to other industries, risks are greater.[9]

TENANTS ARE *NOT* "EXPLOITED" IN THE ABSENCE OF RENT CONTROL

In the unregulated market, it is charged, tenant exploitation will take place in the form of rents higher than the true value of apartments.[10]

The difficulty is that there are no "true values" of dwelling units or of anything else, for that matter. This idea relies on the false assumption of objective value: that the worth of an item is an inherent characteristic, in much the same way as is weight, volume, shape, or colour.[11] Objective values require that every good (and service) in nature would have to come labelled with a price tag; but no one, of course, has ever seen anything of the sort. Nor do human beings have any special powers of discernment which can determine implicit "natural" prices. Moreover, there is a wealth of contrary data ready to hand. The value of horses plummeted with the introduction of the "horseless carriage" at the turn of the century, because people had a preferable transportation alternative—not because of any basic change in this barnyard animal. The "pet rock," hitherto worthless, was suddenly infused with value solely upon the "discovery" of pet like characteristics. The price of hula hoops rose from virtually nothing in the 1950s to something just under \$5 in the 1960s, and fell back again to virtually zero in the 1970s—in accord with changing consumer evaluations—notwithstanding the fact that the hula hoop was physically identical throughout this period.

There is no "true" or objective value in economics. Price is rather established on the basis of how choosing individuals evaluate the available stock of the commodity or service. This is entirely a subjective phenomenon.

Thus rents (or any other price) *cannot* be greater than the "true value" of an apartment. For there is no true value, apart from the level agreed upon by the acting individuals concerned in the specific bargaining situation.

A tendency toward comparable rents

There is on the market, to be sure, a tendency for rents of similar housing units to approach the same level. Landlords charging lower rents and tenants paying higher ones both have a financial incentive to alter their behavior.

But what of tenants who pay higher (lower) rents than people who occupy other, physically similar, units? Are they exploited? Do they exploit their landlords? (Even if we accept the idea of objective value, there should be no presumption that rents are *higher* than "true values." It is just as likely for rents to be below this level).

The charge of exploitation is unwarranted, for what counts in value determination is not physical similarity but subjective or psychic factors. The view, noise levels, proximity to friends, for example, may all play a part in the rent levels a tenant is willing to pay. Similarly, psychic income elements may affect the property owner's deliberations.

The same rent for equally attractive dwelling space, moreover, is only a *tendency* of the free market, not a precondition, not a definition, and not even, except in equilibrium, a conclusion. But it is a patent absurdity to expect equilibrium, an exact balancing of all supplies and demands, in the real world. Such a situation can only be reached in an artificial theoretical construct, where all economic actors (1) know everything there is to be known, and (2) never alter their plans nor change their minds about anything. Equilibrium is possible only when all human action, as we know it, vanishes completely. It is only in such a world that all prices for the same good would have to be equal.

Small divergences

The critics, of course, are barking up the wrong tree. While rents may not be identical in the real world, the market forces of competition keep the divergence down to small proportions.* But these elements are either completely lacking or heavily retarded under a regime of rent controls. It is here, and here alone, that truly notorious rent spreads have been registered. With the complexity of decontrolled, uncontrolled, rent controlled, and rent stabilized sectors in New York City, for example, and given a bewildering array of reductions, exemptions, and exceptions, it is not uncommon to find a rent divergence for similar units in the same building of 500 percent or more!

RENT CONTROL SHOULD *NOT* BE PART OF A COMPREHENSIVE GOVERNMENT HOUSING PROGRAM

Many critics[12] advocate rent control as part of a general housing policy, along with zoning, urban renewal, and public housing.[13] The difficulty with this plan is that the "cures" it offers are all highly questionable. Moreover, they are widely known as creators of the very problem supposedly solved by rent controls: high rents.

---

*High rent *variance*, the subject under consideration here, should not be confused with high *rents* (rent "gouging") a subject which is also discussed in the Ault contribution to this volume.—Ed.

Zoning laws* for example, have catapulted the prices tenants must pay by stifling the construction of highrise residential dwellings. By enshrining the single family unit, which allows for minimal occupancy per acre of developed land, these restrictions have reduced the supply of housing available in desirable areas. Tenants, especially poor ones, have had to bear the brunt of this burden in the form of higher rents.

Urban renewal

Urban renewal, the governmental program which allows sound structures to be condemned and then demolished in order to make reality conform to the city planners' utopian vision, is another case in point. At least insofar as practiced in the United States, this policy has been one of ripping down housing mainly occupied by the poor (thus *raising* the rents paid by the lower-income classes) and building luxury accommodations either occupied by the rich (thus *lowering* their rents) or used primarily by them (like symphony halls, opera houses, and museums). The authority in the field has gone so far as to label urban renewal ''Negro (or poor people's) Removal.''[14] See Table 4 for housing stock changes caused by urban renewal.

Public Housing

The case against public housing is as thorough as it is devastating. The gigantic 2,900 unit Pruitt-Igoe development in St. Louis, which cost $36 million to build in 1956, became a ''vertical slum'' of such staggering proportions that it had to be completely demolished—by the same authorities that had built it—when it was less than twenty years old.[15] Nor is this case unrepresentative. Public housing projects, in their short half century of existence, have become synonymous with crime, abject poverty, hopelessness, and a prisonlike atmosphere. Thousands of US units have decayed, been boarded up, and eventually abandoned,

---

*See The Fraser Institute book *Zoning—Its Costs and Relevance for the 1980s,* by Michael Goldberg and Peter Horwood (1980).—Ed.

TABLE 4
HOUSING STOCK CHANGES CAUSED
BY URBAN RENEWAL

Fiscal Year	Housing Units Razed*	New Housing Units Completed	
		Total*	Public, low & moderate income*
1967	383,449	106,961	42,601
1968	422,817	124,781	52,399
1969	460,482	144,317	63,021
1970	499,407	169,224	80,696
1971	538,044	200,687	101,461

*All data are cumulative.

Source: Department of Housing and Urban Development, unpublished data. Cited by John C. Weicher in *Perspectives on Housing and Urban Renewal* (New York: Praeger, 1974), p. 190.

despite the existence of a seeming bottomless municipal purse.

Part of the reason is that the architects of public housing, drawing their aesthetic judgements from the nineteenth-century British "Garden Cities" movement, have shown an almost pathological hatred of all things commercial. Accordingly, their central city buildings have been surrounded by large vistas of grass and trees.

In order to understand why this has been a disaster, a few brief remarks on urban crime are in order. One of the things that makes the large city tenement neighborhood far safer than it would otherwise be, given its congestion, density, and social and economic problems, is the phenomenon called "eyes on the street":[16] If large numbers of people, both travelling on the sidewalks and looking down on them from windows above, have their "eyes on the street," then crime is severely reduced. This is because criminals naturally prefer to commit their acts of aggression far from the glare of public recognition. But a housing project surrounded by grass and trees, with the nearest playground, candy store, or bar and grill perhaps a quarter of a mile away, attracts neither passers-by nor onlookers from above. It is a dull empty space where muggers may prey at will and in relative isolation.

Income limits

A second policy pursued by public housing project officials has been the establishment of a strict upper-income requirement for occupancy. People who earn above "poverty" incomes are not accepted, and tenants whose earnings rise above these levels are summarily evicted.

The problem with such limits is that they exclude the very people who might function as neighborhood leaders, that is, members of minority or impoverished groups whose ambition has enabled them to rise above their unfortunate initial circumstances. Moreover, of the people admitted as tenants, those who fill the leadership gap are precisely the ones likely to see their incomes rise beyond "acceptable" levels. Then they too must leave.

This is a process which continually weeds out those who are widely looked up to, the ones who are a stabilizing influence on the entire community—and the people who can be most counted upon to quell the mischievous tendencies of the youngsters and teenagers who are, statistically, the most given to crime. Instead this process leaves in its wake the helpless, the old, the infirm, female and single heads of households—with hordes of children and teens they are unable to control. The end result is crime, neglect, and decay.

No profit-and-loss system

Let it not be thought that these horrendous policies were only "accidents," that public housing, run by more enlightened managers, would be an improvement. The problem is much deeper. What is lacking in public housing is not good ideas and skilful executives, *but a process whereby innovation and competence are rewarded and their opposites punished.* This is precisely what obtains in the ordinary workings of the free market—in the absence of rent control—through the profit-and-loss system.

Proven real estate managers can, of course, be hired by the public housing authorities. Even this is insufficient, however. For past success is no guarantee of present abilities. Unless the invigorating winds of market competition are brought to bear on a day-to-day basis (demunicipalization of public housing), there will be no rescue for these projects.

RENT CONTROL DOES *NOT* HALT THE "ABSENTEE LANDLORD MENACE"

Perhaps the favorite whipping boy of the rent control advocate is the "absentee landlord."[17] He is bitterly reviled on all sides, charged with everything from falling plaster and rodent infestation to tenant harassment, "unconscionably" high rents, and neighborhood deterioration. Fear of the absentee landlord is widely incorporated into rent control legislation. For example, New York City exempts buildings with six or fewer units, ostensibly on the ground that these are likely to be owner occupied.

It is difficult to say exactly what accounts for this phenomenon. Absentee owners of restaurants are not similarly lambasted. We do not ban stock exchanges, the greatest creators of absentee ownership the world has ever known. Indeed the very idea is ludicrous. But if there were any harm in absentees *per se*, such prohibitions would make sense.

A grain of truth

However, although rent control advocates have *misdirected their efforts in aiming at the wrong target,*[18] absentees, their concern is not completely without foundation. There is a legitimate case against landlords, but, as we shall see, this too stems directly from rent controls.

In a free market, residential property owners (and all other businessmen) earn profits by providing the highest quality housing service the rent dollar can buy. Their every decision, their every instinct, is bent toward this purpose. But when rent control enters the picture, incentives become all turned around. Landlords are no longer rewarded for providing better service: the process by which they can collect for it is either completely blocked or fraught with obstacles. Instead, the system now rewards them for an entirely different set of activities: for *decreasing* services, not increasing them; for *allowing* rodent infestations, not curing them; for *destroying* property (and/or standing idly by while tenants also do so), not protecting it; for *evicting* tenants (in order to raise rents) not attracting them; for *burning* residential complexes (to collect insurance money) not building them.

If *this* is what earns profit under rent control, it should occasion no surprise that an entirely different sort of landlord will be drawn into the real estate industry, owners with temperaments and abilities suitable to these new ends. When quick repairs and good service are rewarded, only landlords able to comply are successful. Under rent control, however, profits can be made not through these good deeds but by harassing and evicting tenants from perfectly sound houses and by renovating, demolishing, rebuilding, or replacing them with occupants at much higher market rents. Is it any surprise that under such a system the entrepreneurial role should be undertaken by those with such skills, and that landlords of this type should prove successful?

The good old days of prohibition

It must be reiterated, however, that there is nothing improper about landlords *per se*, absentee or not. Their antisocial and uneconomic acts are the result of rent control. They were unknown before the advent of this legislation and will disappear after decontrol.

An analogy may serve to highlight this. Nowadays, it

would be farfetched indeed to cast aspersions on the morality or character of the brewers of beer or the distillers of liquor. Indeed, the owners, executives, and managers of the alcoholic beverage industry are pillars of the community. It was not so always. Under prohibition in the 1930s, an entirely different element entered the field—one that has not been seen there before or since. For, just as in the case of rent control, the profit incentives were reversed. A premium was placed on entirely different qualities: not the production of a quality product, but speed, ability to dodge bullets, pay bribes, suborn, threaten, and the like.

There is, of course, no necessary connection with these qualities and people for either industry. Entrepreneurial unscrupulousness is a function of the degree of government control. Since rent controls are a lesser involvement than prohibition, only *some* landlords exhibit these characteristics, and to a lesser degree.

HOUSING IS *NOT* A BASIC HUMAN RIGHT

All rights have corresponding obligations. If I have a right to property, you have an obligation to refrain from stealing it or trespassing upon it. If you have an inviolable right in your person, I, and everyone else, have an obligation to leave you unmolested. Note that these are *negative* rights. They make it incumbent upon people to refrain; to cease and desist; to avoid certain aggressive behavior. But they impose no positive obligations whatsoever.[19] Rights such as these, the rights to person and property, have been acknowledged since time immemorial. They are at the core of the Magna Cartas, the constitutions, and the principles of all western democracies; they are, indeed, the very backbone of western civilization.

Of late, however, a new type of "right" has arisen.[20] Widely trumpeted, these include a claim to everything from a "decent" level of clothing, food, housing, and medical care to rock music, sexual orgasms, and meaningful relationships. If this were only an emphasis of everyone's right to seek happiness in whatever manner chosen, provided no one else's rights were infringed in the process, it would be unobjectionable. Indeed this is the essence of the right to person and property. But something quite different is meant by those who hold—for example—that "housing is a basic human right." What is claimed here is not the right to be left alone, free to build, buy, or rent whatever shelter one can afford. *Now* demanded is a right to housing which implies an obligation on the part of other people to provide it. This claim, in other words, is for a so-called *positive* right, not the negative rights of classical origin. But what is actually at stake here has nothing to do with rights at all. On the contrary, it is a disguised, and therefore quite insidious, demand for *wealth*. In the case of rights, proper, all that is required of outsiders is noninterference; but in this fraudulent case, there is an unwarranted claim for a myriad of material goods and services.

The new positive rights

In order to see just how radical a departure are the new "positive" rights, consider the following: mankind could at one fell swoop, if it were so minded, completely banish all violations of negative rights. All that need be done is for each and everyone of us to resolve not to initiate physical violen. or fraud and then act on this basis. But all the agreement in the world would not be sufficient to provide the level of wealth necessary to fulfil our so called positive rights to health, happiness, and so on.

There are other grave problems with this contention. First of all, if housing is a basic right, imposing ethical imperatives upon strangers, then each of us is immoral—not only if any of our countrymen are without "decent housing," but as long as *anyone in the world* is so lacking. For rights know no national boundaries. If it is morally incumbent on anyone to supply a good or service without his contractual agreement, then this applies to everyone.

Another logical implication is even more insidious. For rights, by their very nature, are egalitarian. It is clear that all of us, rich or poor, old or young, have *equal* (negative) rights: we are all equal in that, for example, murder committed upon *any* innocent person is wrong, and to the identical degree. The mass murderer is guilty of the *same* immorality in *each* of the specific acts he perpetrates.

Coercive egalitarianism

If positive claims are also rights, then people must not only have a right to "decent" shelter, but to an absolutely equal share of the world's housing. Since there is no logical stopping place for positive rights (if housing, why not medical care? If medical care, why not clothing? If clothing, why not recreation?) the claim of basic human needs as rights really amounts to a demand for absolute income equality. And the situation is even worse. For there is nothing in the logic of the argument to prevent the demand for equal intelligence, equal beauty, equal athletic and sexual prowess, and even equal happiness, if these things could somehow be accomplished.

No. We must reject this claim, and with it the moral swamp it necessarily leads to. We must question, moreover, the relevance of this claim. For even were it *correct*, it could not justify rent control—the provision of a housing subsidy to rich and poor tenants alike, at the cost not to all society, but to one small group, the landlords.

THE MARKET DOES *NOT* PLACE PROFIT ABOVE HUMAN NEEDS

"Housing should be for people not profits, but private enterprise is interested only in profits, not in supplying housing for human needs."[21]

In the real world, profits exist as an incentive and a learning device. They attract investments to the areas most desired by consumers; they are the means through which entrepreneurs try to anticipate future demands—in the periods before presently ongoing productive processes will come to completion.

No real dichotomy

There is no dichotomy between profits and the needs, desires, and aspirations of the people. On the contrary, it is only by finding out what people's demands are, and catering to them in minute detail, that the businessman can earn a profit. He produces cherry pies, not mud pies, because the former, not the latter, are in accord with human needs. He spends millions of dollars for market research in an attempt to ascertain what people really want, or rather, what they *will* want by the time the goods can be produced. Executives with a knack for spotting future trends are rewarded by the profit system, which places consumer desires at centre stage.

The real estate developer in the private sector earns profits only insofar as he provides the kinds of housing people want, at the lowest possible cost. If the people want split-level ranch houses with formica kitchens and barbecue pits, then *this* is the avenue toward profits, despite the wishes of central planners, socialistic housing experts, and other do-gooders for communal kitchens, playrooms, and "efficient" housing projects.

Profits as consumer's leash on landlord

Profits are the leash by which the people direct the efforts of the construction industry. Public authorities are completely cut off from this tie and thus may build whatever they choose, secure in the knowledge that they can suffer no personal financial loss, no matter how ill-received are their products. But the private residential rental sector is always under the thumb of tenant likes and dislikes.

Consider a change in tastes: one that is desired to the extent that tenants are actually willing to pay more rent if their new desires are met. Although some humanitarian public official *might* alter existing plans, he need not. He certainly has no personal financial stake in so doing. Usually, he will only make changes after a long and tedious political process. The private landlord, on the other hand, not only has the incentive to passively "go along with" the new mode, but he will profit by *anticipating it*, and *leading* the way towards its fulfilment. All recent innovations in residential rentals—singles developments, ski chalets, the combination of residential, commercial and office space in one building with shopping malls and boat marinas in the basements, even nudist apartment dwellings—have followed this pattern.

A "WINDFALL PROFITS" TAX ON LANDLORDS IS *NOT* JUSTIFIED

"Controls ought not to be ended without an associated windfall profits tax on landlords—or they will benefit unfairly," it is sometimes claimed.[22]

An important purpose for decontrolling rents is to give landlords a much needed incentive to repair, maintain, upgrade, and build new housing. But rent decontrol coupled with a windfall profits tax takes away with one hand what it gives with the other. True, *if* the landlord stays in business, he will be tempted to supply more dwelling space, and certainly tenants will be led to economize on housing. But if the additional tax is calibrated precisely to remove all the gains of decontrol, the landlord will be in no better position than before, and will have no more funds with which to continue operations than he did under rent control.

The prognosis for housing is even more pessimistic because the decontrol-tax plan will only further aggravate matters. One factor which presently ensures that the rate of deterioration under rent control is no worse is the hope that the law will be rescinded and that the landlord will be able to reap enough profit to compensate for his present losses on that glorious day. This expectation[23] is an important explanation of why the owner does not abandon his rental property any sooner.

But tying decontrol to a windfall profits tax will shatter this hope. The landlord will know that what lies at the end of the rainbow is not a pot of gold but rather "more of the same." Repairs will come slower, abandonments more quickly, and new construction less frequent and in smaller proportions.

The windfall profits tax, moreover, is a levy on returns that are abnormally high *only from the postdecontrol perspective*. For example, a landlord who registers a profit rate of 10 percent for the nine years preceding rent decontrol and then 150 percent immediately afterward, he averages only 6 percent for the entire ten-year period (not counting time preference discounts). If he is taxed at the rates applicable to the supposed "excessive" amounts earned in the last year, he is clearly overburdened. He is forced into a "heads-you-win, tails-I-lose" situation. If rents go up after decontrol, he is socked with an excess profits or windfall tax. If there is no decontrol, he is left holding the bag. The result can only be a massive rechannelling of resources from industries with high variable returns towards those with unchanging yields. This is a misallocation, stemming from an ill-designed antiwindfall policy, and not from any shift in consumer desires. Carry-forward and carry-back provisions in the tax laws of most countries can, at best, only partially offset this particular problem.

They leave unchallenged, moreover, the basic flaw in the very concept of windfall profits: the phenomenon of low elasticities of supply and demand. This means that small changes in quantity demanded or supplied will lead to large movements in price. (Since the supply of authentic Rembrandts is strictly limited, slight demand vacillations will translate into large price alterations; if there are absolutely no substitutes for a needed drug, wide variations in price will be the result of small differences in supply).

Most commentators have concentrated on changes which produce price *rises*, and consequently windfall *profits*. "A housing shortage of quite small dimensions will be sufficient to raise house rents and prices substantially," is a typical refrain. It is true that low supply elasticities for rental housing imply great price rises (and an increase in profits, *ceteris paribus*) for a given increase in demand. But it is also true that the lower the elasticity the greater the price *fall* and "windfall" *losses* associated with a given decrease in demand. In other words, the lower the elasticity, the greater the *risk* of highly varying prices.

This phenomenon, however, will tend to be capitalized

into the relative sale prices of "low-elasticity industries" compared to "high-elasticity industries." Presumably, if the marginal investor is a risk avoider (one who prefers a low variance to a high variance in investment projects with the same expected or average return), then low-elasticity industries such as housing will have their assets capitalized at a lower value than would otherwise be the case, and they will show a higher expected return. If this is so, then gains to the landlord should be interpreted not as an unexpected windfall, but as a compensation for risk bearing!

APPENDIX A

A Gradual Rent Control Phase-Out is *Not* Needed to Prevent Housing Market Disarray

There is a somewhat more sophisticated argument made on behalf of a gradual rent control phase-out[24] based upon a unique characteristic of housing: its low supply elasticity. The following contentions are made: supply is fixed in the short run; it takes a long time to build new units; the stock of apartments is large relative to the flow; that is, only a very small proportion of the total can be built in any one year. Any exogenous increase in rents—from the demand side, for example—will therefore be relatively large and of long duration.

The argument is sometimes made by utilizing a diagram similar to Figure 1,

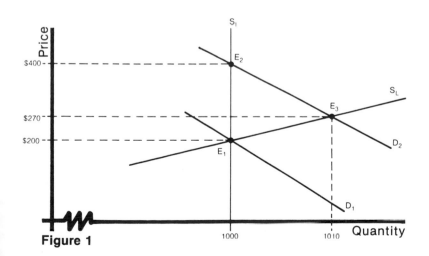

Figure 1

where P, Q, S_1, S_L, D_1, and D_2 are, respectively, price (rent), quantity of housing, immediate and long-run supply curves, and demand curves before and after an increased desire for rental housing space. E_1, E_2, and E_3 are the initial, immediate, and long-run equilibrium points associated with the change (presumably caused by rising incomes, population, tastes, and the like).

It is assumed in this case that 1,000 homogeneous units were originally in existence, renting for an average of $200 per month ($E_1$), and that in a free market prices would immediately rise by 100 percent to $400 ($E_2$), only to fall to $270 in the long run, after the new construction (10 units) was put into place (E_3).

It is then argued that allowing this temporary rise to $400 is inefficient (because it calls forth no additional supplies of housing in the short run), irrational (because it necessitates a price rise from $200 to $400 and then back down again to $270, a process which could easily be short-circuited, and forced to move directly to its final resting place of $270 in gradual, nondisruptive steps), and inequitable (since it imposes a quite unnecessary rent of $400 on the entire society). True, this high rent would be in effect only in the short run; but the "short run" in housing may be long indeed (three-to-five years?), and the poor may ill be able to afford an increase for this duration, even if it is considered only "temporary" by some "heartless" economists.

This line of reasoning has a certain veneer of sophistication. It does not accept a simplistic rent control, at $200 in this example, for its proponents realize full well that at this level demand would exceed supply, and all the evils pointed out by the critics would come to pass: reduced housing maintenance and labor mobility, the ruination of the tax base, the development of black markets, landlord-tenant strife. They know, moreover, that at the artificially low $200, a new supply of 10 units would not be forthcoming. So they advocate a "moderate" position of phasing out rent controls in a manner so as to ensure that the market gradually but directly adjusts to its long-run position (1,010 units renting for $270 at E_3). They contrast this to the "extremist" free market position which allows prices to go on a needless and harmful "roller coaster."

Although seemingly compelling, this line of argument has little merit.

First of all, it rests on the fallacious assumption of full knowledge on the part of the rent control authorities: it presumes they can have all the information imparted by Figure 1, whereas, in the real world, this is a chimera.

Economists have great difficulty determining whether or not a simple demand shift will take place. In fact, even armed with the latest, most up-to-date tools of econometrics, there is still wide disagreement regarding the analysis of demand *in the present*. Such constructs as leading, lagging, and coincident indicators have had to be employed in an attempt—far from always successful—to determine merely what is *presently* occurring in the economy. So the assumption that the rent control bureaucrat could fully anticipate a *future* $D_1 D_2$ shift is folly indeed.

This argument also assumes that the authorities can know the configuration and elasticity of the supply curve to the precise degree necessary to foretell a new equilibrium at 1,010 units and $270.

There is, of course, no guarantee that the increased demand for housing, coupled with the supply function, will come to any such resting place. Demand might reverse itself and fall back to its old levels; a sudden decrease in the desire for dwelling space might completely swamp the initial change, resulting in *lower* prices than before; just as likely, from the *a priori* perspective, is an even greater shift, implying long-run rents far in excess of $270. Supply, too, is liable to similar but unforeseen alterations. Moreover, even if the move from E_1 to E_3 could have been predicted based on present conditions, there is every reason to believe that changes will intervene long before such a shift could have taken place. For the market is a *process*, continually buffeted by the winds of competition: new tastes, technologies, substitutes, complements, desires, styles, and management techniques are the continual order of the day, and each has its repercussions on the real estate sector. No sooner had the bureaucrats fully understood any one state of the market (as if they ever could) when another, and yet another, would become relevant.

The account of the economy underlying this argument has

no room for entrepreneurship—the continual groping toward the "correct" or equilibrium concatenation of price quantity vectors. An accurate picture of business as actually conducted would have to acknowledge the woeful *ignorance* under which all market participants labor. Not for them the false niceties of the blackboard diagram; the clear road ahead where the goal, E_3, is depicted in flashing lights. No. Their path is strewn with false leads, abandoned assumptions, blunders of a heroic nature, partial successes, and only once in a very great while, the measure of exactitude blithely assumed on behalf of the rentalsman.

The man of business operates in (at best) partial darkness. He uses the price system as a blind man uses a cane. Take this crutch away and his actions can no longer be counted upon to be in the public interest. This applies to rent control, as we have seen again and again; but it also applies to the present scheme of short-circuiting the "roller coaster" path that would otherwise take place in the free market.

If rents are not allowed to wend their natural way from E_1 to E_3 *via* E_2 (stipulating, now, for the sake of argument, that this is precisely what would occur in the absence of government intervention) then several deleterious effects will ensue:

- There will be no conserving of space on the demand side in the immediate short run. Tenants will have no incentive to "double up" or to move to smaller quarters.

- On the supply side, no reaction will be possible, short of new construction. Highly temporary responses such as tents, quonset huts, and mobile homes will be effectively barred. The same holds true for such medium-run measures as conversions of commercial and industrial to residential space, which can take place more quickly than new construction.

Supply is actually a family of curves S_1, S_S, S_M and S_L (see Figure 2) depicting the immediate, short, medium and long run (and as many other in-between steps as one wishes to draw), not merely the two extreme members of Figure 1.

These are traced out by the coincidence of a series of vertical lines (showing the amount of housing space available at any one time) with the demand curve D_2. For example, in Figure 2,

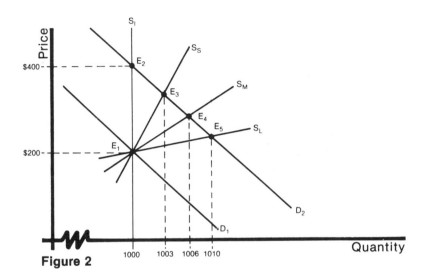

Figure 2

the housing market will call forth 1,003, 1,006 and then 1,010 units in the short, medium and long runs at equilibrium points E_3, E_4 and E_5. We should note, also, that housing is no different from any other commodity in this regard. Strictly speaking, *all* items, no matter how insubstantial, are available only in fixed supply at any one given time. Moreover, what is relevant in this case is the *service* supplied, not the stock of housing itself. Low, short-run supply elasticity is therefore not unique to housing, despite the long lead time necessary to bring an apartment dwelling to completion. The only difference is that all ameliorating responses will take *longer*. Moreover, market action depends upon incentives needed to overcome risk, inertia, and lack of knowledge. The higher the initial rent, the more profit to be earned, *ceteris paribus.* Thus, the greater will be the alacrity and enthusiasm with which entrepreneurs will seize the opportunity to make additional housing space available.

But the case is even worse when a beeline movement is imposed on dynamic equilibrium. Unless the system is allowed to move through each intermediate state, it will not arrive at E_5 (E_3 in Figure 1) at all! This is because the market's evolution to point E_5 is predicated upon no interference with its prior functioning (the extra provision of short- and medium-run supplies; the doubling-up effect on the demand side).

If there is government intervention, these space generating phenomena cannot occur; the final resting place* of the system will have to be at a greater price, and lower quantity, than it otherwise would have attained.

Nor let it be thought that the initial rent of $400 at E_2 represents a real tragedy for everyone. As we know, there are usually apartment leases in force which preclude rent rises for the duration.

In addition, rent bills are usually discharged by the month. Hence, on average, tenants are paid up for two weeks in advance. But if rents were really to double (from $200 to $400), some response would take place even within this short period, thus ameliorating the effects even for the very few people concerned. Afterward, as we have seen, supply and demand reactions would have more time to occur, and rents would be drawn further down from the $400 level.

This high rent plateau should be interpreted not as a long-term immiseration of tenants. Rather, its existence is transient, and it is punctured by the very attempts of all market participants to attain it. But it is of great and abiding importance for all that, for without it, businessmen will not act as effectively to alleviate the housing shortages

---

*The simplistic model assumes that all trades take place at the equilibrium price. But in the real world, lack of knowledge, impatience, etc. lead to transactions at other prices. This "false trading" diverts the market process from the path which would have taken place had all transactions taken place at equilibrium prices.—Ed.

as otherwise.

We may conclude by probing the consistency of the "cut-out-the-intermediate-price-adjustments" argument. We have seen how it works with regard to an upward shift in demand; let us now consider the opposite case.

In Figure 3, D_A, and D_B are the demand curves before and after the change;

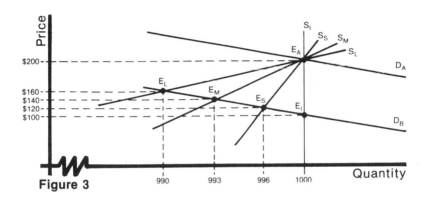

Figure 3

S_I, S_S, S_M, and S_L are the immediate-, short-, medium- and long-run supply curves which successively ensue over time; E_A, E_I, E_S, E_M, and E_L are the corresponding initial and successive equilibrium points, depicting, respectively, rents of $200, $100, $120, $140, $160 and 1,000, 996, 993, and finally 990 housing units.

Would the proponents of this view argue that prices should not be allowed to fall from $200 to $100 and then move up to $160, but should be made to creep down gradually, from $200 directly to $160? If they do, tenants will be cheated out of the low $100 rent. True, this would have been temporary in any case, and not widely distributed (given the institution of leases, monthly rents). But just as in the previous case, legal prohibition will have negative side effects.

Insisting upon an immediate price of $160 will create a

large stock of needless vacancies (the excess supply at this rent level will be equal to 10 units in our example). This, at a time when the problem facing society is not a housing shortage, but the very opposite: finding enough people to occupy the now superabundant housing stock.

If the drop in demand is of great enough magnitude, a rational plan might be to entirely vacate certain residential buildings, either so as to economize on such things as oil bills and repairs or to free them for conversion to commercial or industrial uses, and to relocate the tenants to other apartment houses where there are vacancies. This will take place to some degree at the artificially high rent level of $160. Tenants, however, will have greater incentives to act in this manner if they can take advantage of $100 rents. Their *attempts* to do this will, of course, soon raise rents from $100 to $120 to $140 and finally to $160 and thus dissipate the temporary bargains. But if the $100 option is frozen out by law, the dynamic process will be slower and less efficient. Tenants will also tend to spread out more effectively, or "undouble," under a regime of lower ($100) rents, and this too is rational, given the decreased costs involved.

We must conclude by rejecting the cut-out-the-intermediate-price-adjustments argument. Although preferable to a strict rent control, and perhaps more sophisticated, this attempt to impose "gradualism" on the market is nonetheless an unjustified government intervention. Its complete innocence of any understanding of the dynamic economic process is its fatal flaw.

NOTES

1 Since the present volume is the second Fraser Institute contribution on this issue, it is only fitting that we concentrate on the critics of the prior book, *Rent Control: A Popular Paradox* (Vancouver: The Fraser Institute, 1975).

2 See for example, Emil Bjarnason, "Rent Control—Fact and Fiction" in *Pacific Tribune* (19 December 1976), p. 3, who states: "The economic theory underlying the Fraser Institute Book [*Rent Control: A Popular Paradox*] and all the articles of its contributors, is good old fashioned eighteenth-century free enterprise economics. They are assuming a rational, perfectly functioning market which never did,

and certainly does not now exist." See also "Rent control debate" by Klaas Bylsma *City Magazine* (March 1977), p. 46, who opines: "The principal assumption underlying all the arguments raised by the authors [of *Rent Control: A Popular Paradox*] is that there is competition or a 'free market' in housing in Canada. Such an assumption is obviously absurd. Anyone with even a minimal understanding of the housing economy must reject such an assumption." And "The hearth of the matter" by Wally Seccombe *Books in Canada* (May 1976), p. 32, charges: "...the days have long since passed when Canada had anything faintly resembling a competitive open housing market."

3 Cf. "The Meaning of Competition" in *Individualism & Economic Order* by F.A. Hayek (Chicago: University of Chicago Press, 1948).

4 Says Wally Seccombe, "The hearth of the matter," pp. 32, 33: "The theoreticians of free-market magic present more than 200 pages of argument in this book without once mentioning the rapid monopolization of the urban land market and the development industry that has occurred in Canada in the past 20 years. Contrast this [Fraser Institute] 'study,' for instance, with the recently baked (sic) one by Peter Spurr (commissioned for the federal government's Central Mortgage and Housing Corporation), which thoroughly documents the monopolization of marketable residential property in Canada's major cities. Meticulously, Spurr demonstrates that more than one half the price of new housing lots in 1972-73 in Toronto and Vancouver was siphoned off by developers and speculators as pure profit. He calculates that the major development firms presently own sufficient acreage in and around cities to supply housing at the current rate of construction and density for the next decade." And Klaas Bylsma, "Rent Control Debate," pp. 46, 47, points to: "the growing power of a small number of developers who are acquiring a monopoly control on the market. Best illustrated by the authors of *Highrise and Superprofits* (Dumont Press Graphix, Kitchener), these corporations are able to control the market through their success at attaining vertical integration (control of the whole process, from land development and raw materials through construction itself, to the sale or rental of new housing or buildings). They can then set their own prices and reap unbelievable profits. The increasing control of the whole housing market by a limited number of monopolistic corporations is probably not very encouraging for the authors of *Rent Control: A Popular Paradox,* who seem to have taken their ideas from the golden era of their mentor, Adam Smith!"

5 See his Fraser Institute book *Profits in the Real Estate Industry* (1978), pp. 4-7.

6 See *Man, Economy & State* by Murray N. Rothbard (Princeton, New Jersey: D. Van Nostrand & Co., 1962) pp. 586-592; "Why Regulate Utilities?" and "Industry Structure, Market Rivalry & Public Policy" both by Harold Demsetz, in *The Journal of Law & Economics*, 4/68 & 4/73, respectively; "The Antitrust Task Force Deconcentration Recommendation" and "Bain's Concentration and Rates of Return

Revisited," both by Yale Brozen in *The Journal of Law & Economics*, 10/70 & 10/71, respectively; *The Myths of Antitrust* by Dominick Armentano (New York: Arlington House, 1972); *Planning for Freedom* by Ludwig von Mises (South Holland, Illinois: Libertarian Press, 1969) pp. 114-15; "Austrian Monopoly Theory—a Critique," by Walter Block, *Journal of Libertarian Studies* (Fall 1977).

7 Says Klaas Bylsma, "Rent Control Debate,": "...the price of existing housing is skyrocketing, reflecting the high levels of profits which are to be made in investing in rental housing." "Rent control is instituted to attempt to block landlord profiteering in a period of housing shortage."

8 See *Profits, Interest and Investment,* by Friedrich A. Hayek (Clifton, New Jersey: Augustus M. Kelley, 1975), pp. 24-29; *Human Action*, by Ludwig von Mises (Chicago: Henry Regnery, 1949), pp. 257-326; *Competition & Entrepreneurship*, by Israel Kirzner (Chicago: University of Chicago Press, 1973).

9 Cf. Kalymon's analysis, "Profits," pp. 4-11.

10 In the words of Klaas Bylsma, "Rent Control Debate," p. 46: "The timing of this book [*Rent Control: A Popular Paradox*] could hardly have been more appropriate from a landlord's point of view. At a time when governments in Canada are under pressure from tenants groups to institute effective rent control—to limit rent gouging—the free-market advocates launch a broadside claiming to show that rent control hurts everybody, both landlords and tenants." And the *Regina Leader Post*, 28 March 1977, sees rent control "as a hedge against rent gouging during a period of distress in the housing field, particularly for low-income families."

11 See, for example: *Principles of Economics*, by Carl Menger (Glencoe, Illinois: The Free Press, 1950), especially pp. 51-55, 77-84, 114-149, 226-236, 292-302; *Human Action*, by Ludwig von Mises (Chicago: Regnery, 1963), especially pp. 21, 119-126, 331-338; *The Common Sense of Political Economy*, by Philip Wicksteed (London: Routledge Kegan Paul Ltd., 1967), especially Book I, Chapters I and II, and Book II, Chapters II and III, pp. 759-765; *Lectures on Political Economy,* by Knut Wicksell (New York: Augustus M. Kelley, 1967), especially pp. 13-34 in Volume I and pp. 146-152 in Volume II; *Capital & Interest* by Eugen von Bohn-Bawerk (South Holland, Illinois: Libertarian Press, 1959), Volume I, pp. 271-274; Volume II, Book III, part A; Volume III, Chapters VII-X; *The Theory of Political Economy,* by W. Stanley Jevons (New York: Augustus M. Kelley, 1963); *Man, Economy & State,* by Murray N. Rothbard (New York: D. Van Nostrand, 1962), pp. 1-27, 290-93; "A Comment on 'The Extraordinary Chain of Praxeology' by Professor Gutierrez," by Walter Block, in *Theory & Decision* (June 1973); *Cost and Choice,* by James Buchanan (Chicago: Markham, 1969), especially pp. 20-37.

12 Wally Seccombe, "The hearth of the matter," concedes: "Yes, it is true that rent control is not 'the solution.' In the absence of measures by government to provide more housing, controls will tend to decrease

housing supply. . . . The current popular push for rent control has the same weakness as the drive to toughen up zoning by-laws that preceded it. Both are single-pronged state interventions in the economy that *constrict the market without undercutting it.* The result is that the most visible problem recedes at one point only to crop up as an 'unintended effect' (as planners call it) elsewhere." And the solution: ". . . governments must enter the development industry to build low-cost housing on a mass scale instead of continually sugaring the carrot for developers by subsidizing their profits, as is presently done in the limited-dividend schemes. . . . If rent control were accompanied by such a program, then the developers' threat to withdraw capital if rent controls are imposed could be given the Bronx cheer it so richly deserves." And in the view of Klaas Bylsma, op. cit., "As the [Fraser Institute] authors claim, rent control cannot solve a housing shortage. Governments may make the mistake of assuming that they are solving the problem by instituting rent control and then not develop programs to build the necessary new housing. However very few people would make the claim that rent control can solve a housing crisis. . . . Citizens' groups involved in housing in Canada must continue to fight for effective rent control to protect tenants' interests in the present context. But, at the same time, they must exert pressure on governments to begin to respond to the housing crisis by intervening directly in the housing sector and not through the aegis of private enterprise which has failed so miserably in supplying the needed housing."

13 In addition, some otherwise noninterventionist supporters of rent control recognize the inadvisability of government housing. They argue, however, that public housing projects may not be needed. But they are wrong. Since rent control seriously reduces the supply of private rental units, direct government construction or assistance for rental housing becomes politically irresistible as these results take effect.

14 Cf. Martin Anderson, *The Federal Bulldozer—A Critical Analysis of Urban Renewal 1949-1962* (Cambridge, Mass.: M.I.T. Press, 1964).

15 Cf. *Engineering News Record* (6 September 1973), p. 14.

16 See Jane Jacobs, *Death and Life of Great American Cities* (New York: Random House, 1961).

17 One example of a gratuitous attack on the absentee landlord is provided by Wally Seccombe, "The hearth of the matter": "The ghost of Adam Smith is apparently alive and well, in residence in the Fraser Institute in Vancouver. Smith's undiluted disciples are hard at work in *Rent Control: A Popular Paradox* (the Institute's first volume in a series on housing), arguing that there is absolutely nothing wrong with the housing situation in Canada that a return to the "free market" would not cure. Now if you happen to suspect that a housing market already exists where developers and landlords are only too "free" to make a killing, please be informed by Messrs. Walker, Hayek, Friedman, et al. that you have been brainwashed by scheming socialists after being softened up by misguided liberals. Please be

further informed that the poor developers and landlords are being driven right out of business by punitive government interference and are taking their capital elsewhere. *That* is the cause of the housing crisis, the Fraser Institute's assembled authorities cry in unison. Ergo, the solution,—*raise* rents, ban all controls, and if the poor cannot afford to line the pockets of *absentee landlords*, give them a subsidy to do so. Higher rents will reap fatter profits, attract more investment, lead to more construction and thus "solve" the housing supply problem. To believe, of course, that reality really does work this way requires a complete suspension of all one's critical faculties and several acts of voluntary amnesia." (*Emphasis added*) "Absentee" can apply to landlords who do not live on the premises, to foreign owners, and also to those who have relinquished control to professional real estate management companies.

18 See *A New Radical's Guide to Economic Reality*, by "Angus Black" (New York: Holt, Rinehart & Winston, 1971), Chapter 8: "Off the Absentee Landlord."

19 See Robert Nozick, *Anarchy, State and Utopia* (New York: Basic Books, 1974); Murray Rothbard, *Power and Market* (Kansas City: Sheed, Andrews, and McMeel, 1977), *Egalitarianism as a Revolt Against Nature* (Washington, D.C.: Libertarian Review Press, 1974), and *For a New Liberty* (New York: Macmillan, 1973); Friedrich A. Hayek, *The Road to Serfdom* (Chicago: University of Chicago Press, 1944), *The Constitution of Liberty* (Chicago: Henry Regnery, 1960), and *Studies in Philosophy, Politics & Economics* (New York: Simon & Shuster); and Walter Block, *Defending the Undefendable* (New York: Fleet Press, 1976).

20 Says Wally Seccombe, "The hearth of the matter," in this regard: "Let us begin by stating unequivocally that we consider decent housing to be a right, and its construction must not depend upon luring private capital with the promise of higher profit rates than can be made elsewhere." And in the view of Klaas Bylsma, op. cit.: "With regard to the...objection that rent control is responsible for excessive demands for housing, the answer is quite simple. No one has defined or has the right to define the normal pattern of occupancy of housing. If single people or older citizens prefer to live on their own, this is their right, and their needs must be responded to with proper policies."

21 Other statements of this ilk are supplied by Wally Seccombe, "The hearth of the matter," who calls for "a comprehensive program based on human need and not on profit;" by Klaas Bylsma, "Rent Control Debate," who complains that "Financial institutions prefer to invest in other sectors [than housing] because higher rates of profit on shorter terms are available," and claims that "our own experience in Canada shows that...private enterprise is primarily interested in profits and not in supplying housing at equitable and affordable rents and prices. Government must intervene directly in the housing economy by encouraging the construction of new housing on a *non-profit basis*," and by Geraldine Finn, *The Ottawa Citizen*, 29 November 1975, p. 17:

"...the assumption of the [Fraser] Institute's economics is the capitalist one: 'Canada has had a tradition of allowing economic decisions to be made on the basis of individual pursuit of individual goals'—perhaps it is time to question this political assumption."

22 Wally Seccombe, "The hearth of the matter," complains of landlords who "reap windfall profits."

23 The "expectations" literature includes the following: Ludwig M. Lachmann, *Capital & Its Structure; Capital, Expectations and the Market Process* (Wichita, Kansas: Institute for Humane Studies Press, 1961 & 1978), and *Macro Economic Thinking and the Market Economy* (Institute of Economic Affairs, 1977); Israel Kirzner, *Market Theory & The Price System* (New York: Van Nostrand, 1963) pp. 82-83, 113, 199-200, 224-25, *Competition & Entrepreneurship*, (Chicago: University of Chicago Press, 1973), especially p. 71, and "Methodological Individualism, Market Equilibrium, and Market Process," *Il Politico* 32, no. 4 (1967), especially pp. 794-796; "Economics & Knowledge" in *Individualism & Economic Order* by F.A. Hayek; *Expectations in Economics* by G.L.S. Shackle (Cambridge University Press, 1949).

24 In the opinion of the *Regina Leader Post*, 28 March 1977, "Saskatchewan's 18 months of experience in rent control has not been a failure. It has set the stage for *a more orderly rental market*, and there is no doubt that it has headed off some rent gouging. It's time now to put it behind us." (*Emphasis added.*)

BOMB DAMAGE OR RENT CONTROL?
THE ANSWERS

As Assar Lindbeck wrote in 1971, "...next to bombing, rent control seems in many cases to be the most efficient technique so far known for destroying cities..."

The photos illustrating this book show the effects of both bombing and rent control. On first glance, it is not easy to distinguish one from another.

Unlike bombs, of course, rent controls do not directly destroy property, and they offer no parallel to the human suffering caused by warfare or terrorism.

Nevertheless, the similarity between the photos is evidence of just how destructive rent control can become in the long run, through abandonment and consequent vandalism. No one contends, of course, that rent control is *necessary* to create slums. Other conditions such as poverty, ignorance, neglect, arson, etc. (which existed long before the advent of this legislation) are also responsible for housing decay. But rent control is a *sufficient* condition for the deterioration of the urban environment: when practiced strictly, widely, and for a long duration, as in the case of New York City, the havoc created by this policy can be truly astounding. Rent control, moreover, creates an economic environment which encourages the conditions which can independently lead to housing destruction.

Abandoned city blocks, shown in the illustration of New York City, begin with one or two individual apartments struck by fire and vandalism, then an entire floor, then the whole building, and then the next. The steady process gradually devastates entire neighborhoods.

Photo 1 (page 3). Bomb Damage. Aachen, Germany (photo by H. Armstrong Roberts).

Photo 2 (page 35). Rent Control. The Bronx, New York City (photo by J.P. Laffont, Sygma).

Photo 3 (page 53). Bomb Damage. Hiroshima, Japan (photo by Keystone Press Agency Inc.).

Photo 4 (page 85). Bomb Damage. Nagasaki, Japan (photo by CP Picture Service).

Photo 5 (page 105). Bomb Damage. Hiroshima, Japan (photo by World-Wide Photos/CP Picture Service).

Photo 6 (page 123). Rent Control. The Bronx, New York City (photo by CP Picture Service).

Photo 7 (page 149). Rent Control. The South Bronx, New York City (photo courtesy of William Moses, Community Housing Improvement Program, Inc., New York).

Photo 8 (page 161). Bomb Damage. Nagasaki, Japan (photo by CP Picture Service).

Photo 9 (page 169). Bomb Damage. Nagasaki, Japan (photo by CP Picture Service).

Photo 10 (page 187). Bomb Damage. Aachen, Germany (photo by H. Armstrong Roberts).

Photo 11 (page 199). Rent Control. The South Bronx, New York City (photo by Brian Alpert, Keystone Press Agency, Inc.).

Photo 12 (page 231). Rent Control. The South Bronx, New York City (photo courtesy of William Moses, Community Housing Improvement Program, Inc., New York).

Photo 13 (page 247). Bomb Damage. Hiroshima, Japan (photo by World-Wide Photos/CP Picture Service).

Photo 14 (page 265). Rent Control. The South Bronx, New York City (photo by CP Picture Service).

Photo 15 (page 283). Rent Control. The South Bronx, New York City (photo by Brian Alpert, Keystone Press Agency, Inc.).

BIBLIOGRAPHY*

Achtenberg, Emily. *Less Rent More Control.* Cambridge, Mass.: Urban Planning Aid Inc., 1973.

Achtenberg, Emily P. "The Social Utility of Rent Control." In *Housing Urban America,* edited by Jon Pynoos, Robert Schafer, and Chester Hartman. Aldine: Atherton, 1973.

Anderson, Martin. *The Federal Bulldozer—A Critical Analysis of Urban Renewal 1949-1962.* Cambridge, Mass.: MIT Press, 1964.

"Builder/Owners Called to National Rent Control Fight." *Apartment Construction News* 40 (July 1976).

Armentano, Dominick. *The Myths of Antitrust.* New York: Arlington House, 1972.

Arnault, E. Jane. "Optimal Maintenance under Rent Control with Quality Constraints." *American Real Estate and Urban Economics Association Journal* 3.2 (Summer 1975): 67-83.

Baar, Kenneth. "Rent Control in the 1970's: The Case of the New Jersey Tenants' Movement." *Hastings Law Journal* 28.3 (January 1977): 631-683.

Baar, Kenneth and Keating, W.D. "The Last Stand of Economic Substantive Due Process—The Housing Emergency Requirement for Rent Control." *Urban Lawyer* 7 (1975): 447.

Bakar, Gerson. "Rent Control—decreases housing supply, fails to benefit the poor." *The Mortgage Banker* 37 (May 1977): 68-71.

Bakeman, Helen E.; Kennedy, Stephen D.; and Wallace, James. *Fourth Annual Report of the Housing Allowance Demand Experiment.* Cambridge, Mass.: Abt Associates, 1977.

"Disaster Area, Rent Control Has Helped Turn Gotham Into One." *Barron's,* 21 April 1975.

"Gotham's Future—If It Is To Have One, Rent Control Must Go." *Barron's,* 13 December 1976.

Barton, David M. and Olsen, Edgar O. "The Benefits and Cost of Public Housing in New York City." *Institute for Research on Poverty,* Discussion Papers, No. 372. Madison: University of Wisconsin, 1976.

Bjarnason, Emil. "Rent Control—Fact and Fiction." *Pacific Tribune,* 19 December 1976.

Black, Angus. "Off the Absentee Landlord." In *A New Radical's Guide to Economic Reality.* New York: Holt, Rinehart & Winston, 1971.

Bleiberg, Robert M. "Ceiling Zero? Rent Control is Threatening to go Nationwide." *Barron's,* 12 December 1977.

*The National Rental Housing Council's aid in the compilation of this bibliography is hereby gratefully acknowledged.—Ed.

Block, Walter. "A Comment on 'The Extraordinary Claim of Praxeology' by Professor Gutiérrez." *Theory & Decision* 3.4 (June 1973): 377-387.

_____. *Defending the Undefendable.* New York: Fleet Press, 1976.

_____. "Austrian Monopoly Theory—A Critique." *Journal of Libertarian Studies* 1.4 (Fall 1977): 271-279.

Bloomberg, Lawrence M. *The Rental Housing Situation in New York City 1975.* City of New York Housing and Development Administration, Department of Rent and Housing Maintenance, 1976.

Blumberg, Richard. "Federal Rent Control Policy." A memo prepared for the National Housing and Economic Development Law Project, 3 May 1973.

Blumberg, Richard E.; Robbins, Brian Quinn; and Barr, Kenneth K. "The Emergence of Second Generation Rent Control." *Clearinghouse Review* 8 (August 1974): 240-249.

von Bohn-Bawerk, Eugen. *Capital & Interest.* South Holland, Illinois: Libertarian Press, 1959, Vol. I, 271-274; Vol. II, Book III, Part A; Vol. III, chapters VII-X.

Brenner, Joel F., and Franklin, Herbert M. *Rent Control in North America and Four European Countries.* Rockville, Maryland: Mercury Press, 1977.

Brown, Betsy. "Nobody Wants Rent Control." *Empire State Report* 3.5 (May 1977): 185-189.

Brownstein, Philip, and Schomer, Morton. "Implications for Rental Housing of Rising Rent Control Interest." *Legal Times of Washington* (18 December 1978).

Brozen, Yale. "The Antitrust Task Force Deconcentration Recommendation." *The Journal of Law & Economics* (October 1970).

_____. "Bain's Concentration and Rates of Return Revisited." *The Journal of Law & Economics* (October 1971).

Bruce-Briggs, B. "Rent Control Must Go." *The New York Times Magazine* (18 April 1976).

Bry, Barbara. "Rent Control? It's a Subject for Lively Debate." *The Sacramento Bee* (6 November 1977).

Buchanan, James M. *Cost and Choice.* Chicago: Markham, 1969.

Buchanan, J.M. and Thirlby, G.F. *Essays on Cost.* London: Weidenfeld & Nicolson, 1973.

"A New Ground Swell Behind Rent Control Loss." *Business Week* (24 October 1977) 106.

Bylsma, Klaas. "Rent control debate." *City Magazine* (March 1977).

California: Legislature: Assembly. *Rent Control: An Interim Report to the Assembly Committee on Housing and Community Development.* 15 September 1975.

"Rent Control Ordinances Declared Invalid—Two Cases, One in New York and One in California." *California Real Estate* 52 (August 1976).

Catalina, Frank E. "From the Legislatures." *Real Estate Journal* 6 (1977).

"Three Wise Men on Rent Control." *Chicagoland's Real Estate Advertiser* (24 November 1978).

Chicago Rent Control Committee. *Chicago Rent Control Committee Report to Mayor Michael A. Bilandic.* Chicago, Illinois (14 March 1977).

Coalition for Housing, Los Angeles, Ca. *Rent Control and the Housing Crisis in Southern California* (1977).

Cogen, Holt and Associates. *Housing and Local Government: An Evaluation of Policy-Related Research in the Field of Municipal Housing Services.* New Haven, Conn., January 1975.

"Residential Rent Control in New York City." *Columbia Journal of Law and Social Problems* 1-3 (1965-1967).

"Recent Statute: The New York Rent Stabilization Law of 1969." *Columbia Law Review* 70 (1970): 156-177.

Community Housing Improvement Program, Inc. "Rent Control Must Go." *Housing Crisis Report.* New York: 16 May 1977.

The Community Research and Publications Group, Urban Planning Aid. *Less Rent, More Control: A Tenant's Guide to Rent Control in Massachusetts.* Cambridge, Mass.: 1973.

Comptroller General of the US, General Accounting Office. *District of Columbia's Rent Establishment Policies and Procedures Need Improvement.* Report to Congress. 1978.

Cragg, J.G. "Rent Control Report." In a report commissioned by the British Columbia Rentalsman. Mimeo, 1974.

Cronin, Paul T. "Rent Control: Solution or Diversion?" *The Advocate* (Suffolk Law School) 6 (Spring 1975).

Davidson, Harold A. "The Impact of Rent Control on Apartment Investment." *Appraisal Journal* 46 (October 1978): 570-580.

Demsetz, Harold. "Why Regulate Utilities?" *The Journal of Law & Economics* (April 1968).

————. "Industry Structure, Market Rivalry & Public Policy." *The Journal of Law & Economics* (April 1973).

Dorfman, Dan. "The Bottom Line: The Landlords' Tax Revolt." *New York Magazine* (14 April 1975): 10.

Durst, Seymour B. "If the Cities Go Down, So Goes the Nation: An Urban Analysis and a Prescription for Housing Revival." *Journal*, The Institute for Socioeconomic Studies, 11.4 (Autumn 1977): 25-32.

Eagleton, Thomas F. "Why Rent Controls Don't Work." *Reader's Digest* III.664 (August 1977): 108-111.

Field, Mervin D. "Poll Finds Californians Support Rent Control." *The Sacramento Bee* (13 June 1979).

Finn, Geraldine. "The Case Against Rent Curbs." Review of *Rent Control: A Popular Paradox. The Ottawa Citizen* (29 November 1975).

First National City Bank of New York. "How New York Fell Behind On Its Rents." *Monthly Economic News Letter* (May 1974).

Fisher, Ernest M. "Twenty Years of Rent Control in New York City." In *Essays in Urban Land Economics.* Los Angeles: University of California, 1966.

"Constitutional Law—State Constitutions—City of Miami Beach Lacks Power Under Home Rule Provision of 1968 Florida Constitution to Enact Rent Control Ordinance." *Florida State University Law Review* 1 (Spring 1973): 360-369.

"Municipal Corporations—Rent Control—City of Miami Beach May Not Enact Rent Control Ordinance Under Municipal Home Rule Powers Act." *Florida State University Law Review* 3 (Winter 1975): 137-150.

"Sock the Landlord." *Forbes* 116.6 (15 September 1975): 103, 105.

Fougner, Robert S. "Rent Control in 1975." *Real Estate Forum* (December 1974).

_____. "33 Long Years of Rent Control." *Real Estate Forum* 10 (January 1977).

The Foundation for Economic Education, Inc. *Popular Essays on Current Problems.* I.2. New York: 1946.

Fowler, George. "The Bitter Fruit of Rent Control." *Nation's Business* 66 (August 1978): 63-6.

Frieden, Bernard J., and Solomon, Arthur, *et.al. The Nation's Housing: 1975 to 1985.* Cambridge, Mass.: Joint Center for Urban Studies of MIT and Harvard University, 1977.

Gately, Blair. "City Losing Thousands of Rental Units as Landlords Switch to Condos, Other Uses." *The Washington Post* (22 June 1978).

Gehrels, Franz. "Truth and Relevance at Bay." *American Economic Review* (December 1949): 1273-1278.

Gilderbloom, John. *Report to Donald E. Burns, Secretary, Business and Transportation Agency, on The Validity of the Legislative Findings of AB 3788 and the Economic Impact of Rent Control.* California Department of Housing and Community Development, Sacramento, California, 7 September 1976.

————. *Supplemental Report on Rent Control*. California Department of Housing and Community Development, Sacramento, California, 1 August 1977.

————. *The Impact of Moderate Rent Control in the United States: A Review and Critique of Existing Literature*. California Department of Housing and Community Development, Sacramento, California, March 1978.

Goldberg, Michael and Horwood, Peter. *Zoning—Its Costs and Relevance for the 1980s*. Vancouver: The Fraser Institute, 1980.

Government of the District of Columbia Commission on Residential Mortgage Investment. *Strategy for Change, Housing Finance in Washington, D.C.* Washington: January 1977.

Grampp, William D. "Some Effects of Rent Control." *Southern Economic Journal* 16 (April 1950): 425-447.

Grant, James. "Disaster Area: Rent Control Has Helped Turn Gotham Into One." *Barron's* 55 (2 May 1975).

Gruen, Gruen & Associates. *Rent Control in New Jersey: The Beginnings*. San Francisco: October 1977.

Van den Haag. "Economics is not enough—notes on the anticapitalist spirit." *The Public Interest* (Fall 1976).

Hamilton, S.W. and Baxter, David. *Landlords and Tenants in Danger: Rent Control in Canada*. The Research and Development Fund, Appraisal Institute of Canada. October 1975.

"Mini-Revolution in Berkeley—Rent Control is Guillotined." *H&H Housing* 14 (July 1977).

Harbridge House, Inc. *Why Rent Control is Needed*. Boston: Harbridge House, 1974.

Hartman, Chester. "The Big Squeeze." *Politics Today* 5 (May-June 1978): 40.

Hayek, F.A. "Das Mieterschutzproblem: Nationalokonomische Bertrachtungen." *Bibliothek fur Volkswirtschaft und Politik* 2, Vienna, 1929.

————. *The Road to Serfdom* (Chicago: University of Chicago Press, 1944).

————. "The Meaning of Competition." In *Individualism & Economic Order*. Chicago: University of Chicago Press, 1948.

————. *The Constitution of Liberty*. Chicago: Henry Regnery, 1960.

————, ed. "The Present State of the Debate." In *Collectivist Economic Planning*. Clifton: Augustus M. Kelley, 1975.

————. "Economics & Knowledge." In *Individualism & Economic Order*. Chicago: University of Chicago Press, 1948.

_____. *Studies in Philosophy, Politics & Economics.* New York: Simon & Schuster, 1967.

Heung, Raymond. *The Do's and Don'ts of Housing Policy.* Vancouver: The Fraser Institute, 1976.

Hirsch, Werner. "Let's Control Our Rent Control Fervor." *Los Angeles Times* (18 July 1978).

US House of Representatives Report No. 93-259, Authorizing the District of Columbia Council to Regulate and Stabilize Rents in the District of Columbia (5 June 1973).

Hsia, Richard Chi-Cheng. "The ABC's of MBR: How to Spell Trouble in Landlord/Tenant Relations (Up Against Crumbling Walls)." *Columbia Journal of Law and Social Problems* (October 1974): 113-176.

International Labour Office. *Housing and Employment.* Studies and Reports, New Series, no. 8. Geneva: 1948.

Jacobs, Jane. *Death and Life of Great American Cities.* New York: Random House, 1961.

James, Franklin J. and Lett, Monica R. *The Economics of Rental Housing in N.Y.C., the Effects of Rent Stabilization.* Prepared for the Rent Stabilization Association of New York City, 1976.

Jevons, W. Stanley. *The Theory of Political Economy.* New York: Augustus Kelley, 1963.

Johnson, D. Gale. "Rent Control and the Distribution of Income." *American Economic Review* 41 (May 1951): 569-582.

Johnston, P. and Hayes, D. *Housing Conversion.* City of Vancouver Planning Department, 1975.

Joiner, Robert C. "Trends in Homeownership and Rental Costs." *Monthly Labor Review* 93.7 (July 1970): 26-31.

Kalymon, Basil A. *Profits in the Real Estate Industry.* Vancouver: The Fraser Institute, 1978.

Kanner, Gideon. "Rent Control: Needed Restraint or Taking of Private Property?" *The Appraisal Journal* 46.3 (July 1978): 460-466.

Katz, Larry. "Rent Control Rears Head Again." *Rental Property Management* (February 1975): 7.

Katz, Sheldon. "Rent Control Continues Nationwide Spread." *American Banker* (31 October 1978): 12.

Kautsky, B. *Schriften des Vereins fur Sozialpolitik* 177 III (1930).

Keating, W. Dennis. "Rent and Eviction Control: A Selected Annotated Bibliography." Berkeley, California: National Housing and Economic Development Law Project, 1976.

Keen, Howard Jr. and Raiff, Donald L. "Rent Controls: Panacea, Placebo, or Problem Child?" *Business Review,* Federal Reserve Bank of Philadelphia (January 1974): 3-9.

Kirzner, Israel. *Market Theory & The Price System.* New York: Van Nostrand, 1963.

_____. "Methodological Individualism, Market Equilibrium, and Market Process." *Il Politico* 32.4 (1967).

_____. *Competition & Entrepreneurship.* Chicago: University of Chicago Press, 1973.

Kriegsfeld, Irving M. "Rental Property Controls—Where Will They End?" *Realtor Magazine* (Washington Board of Realtors). Washington, D.C. (October 1974): 14-19.

_____. "The Cost of Meeting Rent Control Requirements." *Journal of Property Management* (Institute of Real Estate Management). Chicago, Illinois (March/April 1975): 68-70.

_____. "Are Rent Controls Here to Stay?" *The National Apartment Association News Briefs* (July 1976).

_____. "Rent Control: A Plague on Property." *Journal of Property Management* 4 (September/October 1977): 229-233.

Kristof, Frank S. "Economic Facets of New York City's Housing Problems." Prepared for the Institute of Public Administration. Mimeographed. New York: 1970.

_____. "The Impact of Vacancy Decontrols on New York's Rental Market." Mimeographed. 1973.

_____. "Rent Control Within the Rental Housing Parameters of 1975." *American Real Estate and Urban Economics Association Journal* 3.3 (Winter 1975): 47-60.

_____. "Housing and People in New York City, A View of the Past, Present, and Future." *City Almanac.* Newsletter, New York City Affairs of the New School for Social Research (February 1976).

_____. "The Effects of Rent Control and Rent Stabilization in New York City." Fifteenth Interim Report to the Mayor by the Temporary Commission on City Finances. June 1977.

Krooth and Altman. *Rent Control in the District of Columbia.* Development Economics Group, Center for Urban Policy Research, Rutgers University, April 1977.

Kruschwitz, Carl. *Schriften des Vereins fur Sozialpolitik* 177, I (1930).

Lachmann, Ludwig M. *Capital & Its Structure; Capital, Expectations and the Market Process.* Wichita, Kansas: Institute for Humane Studies Press, 1961 & 1978.

_____. *Macro Economic Thinking and the Market Economy.* London: Institute of Economic Affairs, 1977.

Laverty, Charles R., Jr. "Rent Control Highlights, Effect on Property Valuations and Assessed Valuations for Ad Valorem Taxation, or a Probable Predicament." Mimeographed. Cambridge, Mass.: October 1976.

"Local Rent Control." *Law Project Bulletin* II.5 (June 1972): 12.

Lee, Tong Hun. "The Demand Elasticities for Non-Farm Housing." *Review of Economics and Statistics* 46 (February 1964): 82-89.

de Leeuw, Frank. "The Demand for Housing: A Review of Cross-Section Evidence." *Review of Economics and Statistics* 53 (February 1971): 1-10.

Lesher, Richard. "The Best Way to Destroy a City." *Vermont Business World* (November 1978).

Lett, Monica R. "Rent Control: The Potential for Equity." *American Real Estate and Urban Economics Association Journal* (Spring 1976): 57-81.

_____. *Rent Control: Concepts, Realities, and Mechanisms.* New Brunswick, New Jersey: The Center for Urban Policy Research, Rutgers University, 1976.

_____. "The Regulation of Rental Housing via Rent Control." In *Methods of Housing Analysis,* edited by James W. Hughes. New Brunswick, New Jersey: Center for Urban Policy Research, Rutgers University, 1977.

Levy, H. "Rent Control in New York City: Another Look." *New York State Bar Association Bulletin* 47 (April 1975): 193-195, 224-228.

Lindbeck, Assar. *The Political Economy of the New Left.* New York: Harper & Row, 1972.

Lindsey, Robert. "Rent Controls Gain in the Nation as a Cause Pressed by the Young." *The New York Times* (15 April 1979).

Lowry, Ira S., ed. *Confronting the Crisis: Rental Housing in New York City, Vol. I.* New York City: Rand Institute and McKinsey Company, prepared for New York City Housing and Development Administration, 1970.

Lowry, Ira S. "How to Rescue New York's Vanishing Housing Stock." *New York Affairs.* Summer 1973.

Marshall, Alfred. *Principles of Economics,* 8th ed. London: Macmillan, 1920.

City of Boston. *Report of the Mayor's Committee on Rent Control.* Submitted to Honorable Kevin H. White, Mayor. September 1977.

Menger, Carl. *Principles of Economics.* Glencoe, Illinois: The Free Press, 1950.

Meyer, Herbert E. "How Government Helped Ruin the South Bronx." *Fortune* XCII. 5 (November 1975): 140-146, 150, 154.

von Mises, Ludwig. *Human Action: A Treatise on Economics.* New Haven: Yale University Press, 1949.

_____. *Epistemological Problems of Economics.* Princeton: Von Nostrand, 1960.

_____. *Planning for Freedom.* South Holland, Illinois: Libertarian Press, 1969.

_____. *Profits, Interest and Investment.* Clifton, New Jersey: Augustus M. Kelley, 1975.

Mitchell, Laura. "When Housing is Tight, Are Rent Controls Necessary?" *California Journal* (February 1978): 53-56.

"European Experience With Rent Controls." *Monthly Labor Review* 100 (June 1977): 21-28.

Moorhouse, John C. "Optional Housing Maintenance Under Rent Control." *The Southern Economic Journal.* XXXIX. I (July 1972): 93-106.

"Rental Housing: An Endangered Species?" *Mortgage Banker* 39 (February 1979): 52.

"National Council Ready to Fight Rent Controls." *Multi-Housing News* 12.5 (May 1977): 73.

"New Anti-Control Drive Is On." *Multi-Housing News* 11.12 (December 1976): 1.

Muth, Richard F. "The Demand for Non-Farm Housing." In *The Demand for Durable Goods,* edited by Arnold C. Harberger. Chicago, Ill.: University of Chicago Press, 1960.

National Apartment Association (Washington, D.C.). "Rent Control and Resident Managers." *Units* 1.1 (September 1977): 21.

National Association of Realtors. *Rent Control: A Non-Solution.* Chicago, Ill.: 1977.

National Rental Housing Council. *Fighting Rent Control.* Fact book of rent control materials updated on a monthly basis.

"End Rent Control." *New York Amsterdam News.* (1 May 1976).

New York. City Rent & Rehabilitation Administration. *People, Housing & Rent Control in New York City.* New York: 1964.

New York State Study Commission for New York City (Scott Commission). *The Management of the Maximum Base Rent (MBR) Program by the Housing and Development Administration of New York City—from 1970 to October 1972.* New York: 1972.

New York Temporary State Commission on Living Costs and the Economy. *Report on Housing and Rents.* New York: 1974.

New York. Temporary State Housing Rent Commission. *People, Housing & Rent Control in Buffalo.* New York: 1956.

Niebanck, Paul L. *Rent Control and the Rental Housing Market in New York City.* New York: Housing and Development Administration, Department of Rent and Housing Maintenance, 1968.

Nozick, Robert. *Anarchy, State and Utopia.* New York: Basic Books, 1974.

Olsen, Edgar O. "An Econometric Analysis of Rent Control." *Journal of Political Economy* 80 (November/December 1972): 1081-1110.

Oser, Alan. "Rent Limit Squeezes Manhattan Landlord." *The New York Times* (11 May 1979).

"Realtors Say Rent Control Makes Rather Than Solves Housing Ills." Honolulu *Pacific Business News* (9 November 1978).

Page, Robert E. "Rent Control: An Evaluation." *Journal of Property Management* 39 (May/June 1974): 111-113.

Palmer, Jeffrey. *The Effect of Rent Control on New Construction.* Wharton School, University of Pennsylvania, December 1977.

Peck, James M. "The Case for Ending Rent Control." *New York Law Journal* (14 April 1976).

Penzer, Dr. Michael L. "The Rent Control Issue in California." *Special Publications Series Research Report.* San Francisco: Federal Home Loan Bank, 1977.

Phillips, David L. "Analysis and Impact of the Rent Control Program in Lynn, Massachusetts." Office of the Mayor, 1974.

Pierce, Neal R. "The Creeping Cancer of Rent Control." *The Washington Post* (15 August 1977).

"Case Against Rent Controls." *Professional Builder and Apartment Business* (December 1976): 33.

"Rent Controls: Pressure for Phase Out in New York." *Professional Builder and Apartment Business* (August 1976): 39.

"Rent Control Raises Its Head." *Properties* (July 1976): 8.

Quigley, Elizabeth. "RAM Corner" editorial on Rent Control. *The RAM Digest.* Washington, D.C.: The National Association of Home Builders. Spring 1976, inside front cover.

Radock, Monte. Preliminary Staff Report. *Real Property Abandonment in New York City.* New York: Savings Bank Association of New York State, 1974.

The Rand Corporation. *Fourth Annual Report of the Housing Allowance Supply Experiment.* R-2302-HUD. Santa Monica: Rand Corporation, May 1978.

Rapkin, Chester. *The Private Rental Housing Market in New York City.* Prepared for New York City Rent and Rehabilitation Administration (December 1966).

"Spreading Rent Control Seen as Threat to Housing Supply." Chicago *Real Estate News* (20 November 1978).

Real Estate Research Corporation, Coalition to Save New York. *A Policy Review of Rental Housing in New York City*. New York: April 1975.

"Study Calls for End to Controls." *Real Estate Weekly* (14 February 1977): 1, 13.

"Rent Control: Nobody Wins, Everybody Loses." *Realtors Review* 1 (February 1977): 1-5.

Reid, Margaret. *Housing and Income*. Chicago: University of Chicago Press, 1962.

"Rent Control and the Eastern Experience." *Rental Property Management* (January 1975).

Roistacher, Elizabeth Anne. "The Distribution of Tenant Benefits Under Rent Control." Ph.D. dissertation, University of Pennsylvania, 1972.

_____. *The Removal of Rent Regulation in New York City*. New York: Department of Housing and Urban Development, 1977.

Rothbard, Murray N. *Individualism and Economic Order*. Chicago: University of Chicago Press, 1948.

_____. *The Counter Revolution of Science*. Glencoe, Ill.: The Free Press, 1952.

_____. *Man, Economy, and State*. Princeton: Van Nostrand, 1962.

_____. *For a New Liberty*. New York: Macmillan, 1973.

_____. *Power and Market*. Kansas City: Sheed, Andrews, and McMeel, 1977.

Rothenberg, Jerome. *Urban Housing Markets: An Analytical Model and Its Application to the Impact of Rent Control*. Discussion Paper 32, Fels Center of Government, University of Pennsylvania, 1973.

Samuelson, Paul. *The New York Times* (10 October 1974).

San Francisco Planning and Urban Research Association. *Rent Control Versus Production of Housing*. Report 152. San Francisco: May 1979.

Seccombe, Wally. "The hearth of the matter." *Books in Canada* (May 1976).

Seldon, Arthur, ed. *Verdict on Rent Control*. London: Institute of Economic Affairs, 1972.

Selesnick, Herbert L. *Rent Control: A Case For*. Lexington, Mass.: Lexington Books, 1976.

Serruya, Leon M. and Chau, To Minh. "Effects of Rent Control on the Decision to Invest in Residential Construction: Some Empirical Evidence." *Appraisal Institute Magazine* (of Canada) (July 1977).

"Municipal Governments—Police Power—New Jersey Municipalities Have the Power to Enact Rent Control Ordinances—*Inganamort v. Fort Lee.*" *Seton Hall Law Review* 4 (Fall/Winter 1972): 360-378.

Shackle, G.L.S. *Expectations in Economics.* Cambridge: Cambridge University Press, 1949.

Sharav, Itzhak. *Vacancy Decontrol, An Examination of the Effect on Rents, Maintenance and Improvements.* New York: Community Housing Improvement Program, 1974.

Shenkel, William M. "Rent Control: A Critical Review." *Journal of Property Management* 39 (May/June 1974): 101-110.

Shock, Jim. *Where has all the Housing Gone?* San Francisco: New American Movement, 1979.

Smith, L.B. *Housing in Canada.* Ottawa: Central Mortgage and Housing Corporation, 1971.

_____. "A Note on the Price Adjustment Mechanism for Rental Housing." *American Economic Review* 64 (June 1974): 478-481.

_____. *Postwar Canadian Housing and Residential Mortgage Markets.* Toronto: University of Toronto Press, 1974.

_____. *Anatomy of a Crisis—Canadian Housing Policy in the Seventies.* Vancouver: The Fraser Institute, 1977.

Stanfield, Rochelle L. "Caught in the Squeeze of the Rental Housing Market." *National Journal* 11 (17 February 1979): 262-265.

Statistics Canada. *Perspective Canada.* Ottawa: Statistics Canada, Information Canada, 1974.

Sternlieb, George. *The Urban Housing Dilemma.* New York: City of New York Housing and Development Administration, 1972.

_____. *Housing and People in New York City.* The City of New York Housing and Development Administration Department of Rent and Housing Maintenance. January 1973.

_____, *et.al. The Realities of Rent Control in the Greater Boston Area.* New Brunswick, New Jersey: Center for Urban Policy Research, Rutgers University, 1974.

_____, *et.al. Rent Control in Fort Lee, New Jersey.* New Brunswick, New Jersey: Center for Urban Policy Research, Rutgers University 1975.

_____ and Elizabeth Brody. "The Pitfalls in Rent Control." *Real Estate Review* (Spring 1975).

_____, *et.al. Housing and Economic Reality: New York City 1976.* New Brunswick, New Jersey: Center for Urban Policy Research, Rutgers University, 1976.

_____, *et.al. A Study of Rent Control in the Greater Miami Beach Luxury Housing Market.* New Brunswick, New Jersey: Center for Urban Policy Research, Rutgers University, 1977.

Stumberg, Robert and Weiner, Elizabeth. *The Need for Rent Control.* Washington, D.C.: D.C. Public Interest Research Group, February 1974.

Teitz, Michael, ed. *The Impact of City Programs. Rental Housing in New York City, Vol. IV.* New York: New York City Rand Institute and McKinsey Company, prepared for New York City Housing Development Administration, May 1970.

Teplin, Albert M. *The Scope of Residential Rent Control Laws: A Preliminary Study.* Washington, D.C.: Federal Reserve Board, January 1977.

Thirlby, G.F. "The Subjective Theory of Value and Accounting 'Cost'." *Economica* (February 1946): 32-49.

US Department of Housing and Urban Development. *Housing in the Seventies.* A Report of the National Housing Policy Review. Washington, D.C.: Government Printing Office, 1974.

US Department of Labor, Bureau of Labor Statistics. *Price Index of Operating Costs for Rent Stabilized Apartment Houses in New York City.* Regional Reports: 45 (July 1975); 50 (July 1976); 54 (July 1977).

"Landlords v. Tenants: Why Clashes Spread." *U.S. News and World Report* (22 January 1979).

US Senate Committee on Banking, Housing and Urban Affairs, Committee print (17 May 1976).

"Rent Control by Municipal Ordinance—Not Within Home Rule Power." *University of Miami Law Review* 27 (Spring/Summer 1973): 518-524.

"Residential Rent Control: *Stoneridge v. Lindsay.*" *University of Pittsburgh Law Review* 31 (Spring 1970): 457-475.

USC Center for the Study of Financial Institutions. *Rent Control: A Survey of the Theoretical and Empirical Findings.* Staff report, October 1977.

"Rent Control in New York City: A Proposal to Improve Resource Allocation." *Urban Affairs Quarterly* 11 (June 1976): 511-522.

The Urban Land Institute. *New Housing Production in the District of Columbia: Toward Possible Solutions to a Public Policy Dilemma.* Prepared for the Federal City Council, Washington, D.C.: September 1975.

_____. *Prospects for Rental Housing Production Under Rent Control: A Case Study of Washington, D.C.* Washington, D.C.: 1976.

"Rent Control as a Municipal Function in Florida." *Urban Law Annual* 7 (1974):355-361.

"Residential Rehabilitation and Rent Control: The Massachusetts Priority." *Urban Law Annual.* St. Louis, Missouri: Washington University (1976): 319-332.

Urban Planning Aid. *People Before Property: A Real Estate Primer and Research Guide.* Cambridge, Mass.: 1972.

_____. "An Analysis of the Realities of Rent Control in the Greater Boston Area." Cambridge, Mass.: 1975.

Utt, Ronald D. "Rent Control—Sixty Years of Unlearned Lessons." *The Trustee.* National Association of Real Estate Investment Trusts, May/June 1977.

Vas, P. *Die Wiener Wohnungszwangswritschaft von 1917-1927.* Jena: 1928.

Walker and Dunlop. "Rent Control: Are the Benefits Worth the Costs?" *Portfolio* (Spring 1976).

Walker, Michael, ed. *The Illusion of Wage & Price Control.* Vancouver: The Fraser Institute, 1976.

_____. "What Are The Facts?" In *Rent Control—A Popular Paradox.* Vancouver: The Fraser Institute, 1975.

Weber, Adolf. *Die Wohnungsproduktion.* Tubingen: 1914.

Wetherington, Wade. "The District of Columbia Rental Housing Act of 1977: The Effect of Rent Control on the Rental Housing Market." *Catholic University Law Review* 27.3 (Spring 1978): 607-626.

Wicksell, Knut. *Lectures on Political Economy.* New York: Augustus M. Kelley, 1967: Vol. I, 13-34; Vol. II, 146-152.

Wicksteed, Philip. *The Common Sense of Political Economy.* London: Routledge Kegan Paul Ltd., 1967, Book I, chapters 1 and 2; Book II, chapters 2 and 3.

"The Politics of Rent Control." *Working Papers for a New Society* 6 (March/April 1979): 55-63.

"Britain Must Put Her House in Order." *World Review* (December 1951): 13.

Yousem, Joseph L. "Rent Control Destructive to Private Enterprise." *Journal of Property Management* 41 (September/October 1976): 204.

_____. "Rent Controls 'Destructive in Principle and Practice' According to President of Real Estate Management." News Release. 20 September 1976.

Znaniecki, Florian. "Proximate Future of Sociology: Controversies in Doctrine and Method." *American Journal of Sociology* (May 1945): 514-521.

THE FRASER INSTITUTE
Member of the Association of Canadian Publishers
and the Canadian Booksellers Association

Books on Current Economic Issues

PRIVATIZATION: THEORY AND PRACTICE
Distributing Shares in Private and Public Enterprises:
BCRIC, PETROCAN, ESOPs, GSOPs

In March 1979, the government of British Columbia launched a unique, new experiment in economic policy by divesting itself of the ownership of the British Columbia Resources Investment Corporation and giving the shares to the citizens of British Columbia.

T. M. Ohashi, Senior Vice President and Director of Research, Pemberton Securities Limited, Vancouver, provides for the first time the real story of how BCRIC was born as a private, widely-held corporation. He also provides an analysis of the largest common stock offering in Canadian history (which was made at the same time as the "giveaway"), who bought it, and what impact it has had on Canada's financial markets.

In the second part of the book, **T. P. Roth**, Chairman of the Department of Economics and Finance at the University of Texas at El Paso and a Senior Economist with the U.S. Congress Joint Economic Committee's Special Study on Economic Change in Washington, D.C., examines the effects of Generalized Stock Ownership Plans, particularly of the sort espoused by Louis O. Kelso. Given that some of the claims made by Kelso have been repeated by those who support BCRIC-type experiments, it is important at this time to re-examine his ideas. Also included is a theoretical overview of privatization and the public interest by **Zane Spindler**, an Associate Professor of Economics at Simon Fraser University in B.C., as well as an analysis of the prospects for privatizing the Alberta Heritage Savings Trust Fund by **Melville McMillan** and **Kenneth Norrie**, both Associate Professors of Economics at the University of Alberta in Edmonton.

256 pages   extensive bibliographical notes $12.95 paperback   ISBN 0-88975-036-X

TAX FACTS
The Canadian Consumer Tax Index and YOU

A major Fraser Institute book showing how the consumer tax burden in Canada has risen dramatically in recent years. Topics covered include *The Canadian Tax System; Personal Income Taxation in Canada; How Much Tax Do You Really Pay?; The Consumer Tax Index;* and *The Relative Burden of Taxation.*

By **Sally Pipes**, an Economist at the Fraser Institute, and **Michael Walker**, the Institute's Director, "Tax Facts" is a unique and highly readable analysis of the extent of direct and indirect taxation in Canada. In the case of some Canadians, hidden taxes make up more than 60 per cent of their tax bill. How much hidden tax do **you** pay? Do you want to know? Can you afford not to know!

The book contains a glossary of commonly-used terms, bibliographical notes and tables. It is an up-to-date sequel to the Institute's previous best-selling book "How Much Tax Do You Really Pay?"

140 pages   9 charts   29 tables $3.95 paperback   ISBN 0-88975-027-0

THE HEALTH CARE BUSINESS
International Evidence on Private Versus Public Health Care Systems

Professor Åke Blomqvist, Associate Professor of Economics, University of Western Ontario, having studied the health care systems in Canada, the U.S., Britain and Sweden, recommends sweeping changes to Canada's system of medical insurance in *The Health Care Business*. In the process of ensuring equity in access to medical services, Blomqvist contends, the current Canadian system has become unacceptably inefficient and costly. The response of government to rising costs has been to increasingly intervene in the market for health services — gradually moving the Canadian system closer to the British system of "choice by bureaucrats". In the opinion of Professor Blomqvist, the result of this trend could well be a substantial reduction in the effectiveness of Canada's health service system — currently among the best in the world.

The Health Care Business sets out a series of changes to current medical and hospital insurance schemes in Canada which would have the effect, over time, of reducing the built-in cost escalation without materially affecting access to medical care. Blomqvist's recommendations are aimed at increasing competition amongst suppliers of medical services, breaking the conflict of interest that medical practitioners currently find themselves in and establishing an economically realistic basis for the delivery of hospital services.

208 pages   7 tables $5.95 paperback   ISBN 0-88975-026-2

THE SCIENCE COUNCIL'S WEAKEST LINK
A Critique of the Science Council's Technocratic
Industrial Strategy for Canada

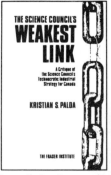

The Science Council of Canada recently published a study by two of its researchers — "The Weakest Link" — which purports to prove that the root of the country's economic malaise can be found in the "technological underdevelopment of Canadian industry." One solution, the Council's book proposes, is the adoption of an "Industrial Strategy" based on "technological sovereignty" involving wide-ranging and potentially massive intervention by government in the country's industrial structure.

Because the Science Council's views on Industrial Strategy are acquiring increasing attention in government policy circles and what many believe to be a credibility that is undeserved, this Fraser Institute book, by **Kristian Palda**, a Queen's University Professor of Business Economics, represents a searching critique of what is becoming the "Science Council view"; as such, it is a particularly useful contribution to the on-going debate about one of the most fundamental issues of our time.

73 pages   6 charts   7 tables $4.95 paperback   ISBN 0-88975-031-9

CANADIAN CONFEDERATION AT THE CROSSROADS
The Search for a Federal-Provincial Balance

The eleven Fraser Institute authors examine carefully the extent to which the current allocation of powers and functions in the Canadian system of government serves the economic and cultural interests of all Canadians. Since the issues raised involve many aspects of our society, the book spans the broad mosaic of Canadian life from economic policy to legal uniformity; from broadcasting to urban development policy.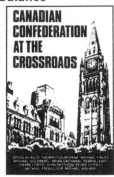

Canadian Confederation at the Crossroads: The Search for a Federal-Provincial Balance asks whether much of what is interpreted as **separatist** sentiment in Quebec in fact represents a deeply-rooted reaction to a rising feeling of alienation from government: a reaction as strongly rooted in the West and the Maritimes as in Quebec. As a solution, this book therefore looks at the ways personal and regional independence can be achieved within the framework of our existing constitutional structure. Can we produce a workable and acceptable federal-provincial balance that will reinvigorate our confederation?

Authors include. **Michael Walker**, Director, the Fraser Institute (Introduction); **Perrin Lewis**, Assistant Economic Adviser, Bank of Nova Scotia, Toronto (on the tangled tale of taxes and transfers); **John C. Pattison**, Assistant Professor, School of Business Administration, University of Western Ontario (on dividing the power to regulate); **Thomas J. Courchene**, Professor of Economics, University of Western Ontario (on the transfer system and regional disparities); **Peter Shiroky**, Fraser & Beatty, Toronto and **Michael Trebilcock**, Director, Law & Economics Programme, University of Toronto (on the uniformity of law); **Pierre Lortie**, Executive Vice-President, SECOR, Inc., Montreal (on education, broadcasting, and language policy); **Douglas A. Auld**, Professor of Economics, University of Guelph (on fiscal policy); **Brian A. Grosman**, Professor of Law, University of Saskatchewan and **Michael J. Finley**, Legal Research Officer, Law Reform Commission of Saskatchewan (on law enforcement); and **Michael A. Goldberg**, Professor & Chairman, Urban Land Economics Division, Faculty of Commerce & Business Administration, University of British Columbia (on housing and urban development policy).

381 pages	33 pages of extensive notes and bibliographical references	
10 tables	$9.95 paperback	ISBN 0-88975-025-4

FRIEDMAN ON GALBRAITH
...and on curing the British Disease

Why is it that **John Kenneth Galbraith's** theories have become widely accepted by the general public when there is almost a total lack of support for them in the economics profession? Is Galbraith a *scientist or a missionary*? **Milton Friedman**, Nobel Laureate in Economics 1976, addresses these and other questions about Galbraith as economist and prophet in this Fraser Institute book. Whatever the reader's view of Galbraith, this book by Friedman is must reading. It is said that Canada and other countries are on the same path as Britain — to some, the *British Disease* is the logical ending of Galbraith's story. In the second essay in this book, Professor Friedman outlines a cure for the British Disease: the principles that Friedman develops in this essay are of immediate Canadian interest as they point out the necessity to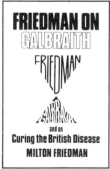

adopt gradualist corrective policies *now* before the more jarring policies currently required in the U.K. are necessary here.

66 pages	$3.95 paperback	ISBN 0-88975-015-7

OIL IN THE SEVENTIES
Essays on Energy Policy

Edited by **G. Campbell Watkins**, President, DataMetrics Limited, Calgary and Visiting Professor of Economics, University of Calgary and **Michael Walker**, Director of the Fraser Institute.

In Part One, *Energy in the Marketplace*, contributors include **Russell S. Uhler** of the University of British Columbia (on economic concepts of petroleum energy supply); **Ernst R. Berndt** of the University of British Columbia (on Canadian energy demand and economic growth); and **G. Campbell Watkins** (on Canadian oil and gas pricing).

In Part Two, *Government in the Marketplace*, contributors include **Walter J. Mead** of the University of California, Santa Barbara (on private enterprise, regulation and government enterprise in the energy sector); and **Edward W Erickson** of North Carolina State University and **Herbert S. Winokur, Jr.**, of Harvard University (on international oil and multi-national corporations).

In Part Three, *Oil in the Seventies: Policies and Prospects,* contributors include **G. David Quirin** and **Basil A. Kalymon**, both of the University of Toronto (on the financial position of the petroleum industry) and **James W. McKie** of the University of Texas at Austin (on United States and Canadian energy policy).

320 pages	17 charts	25 tables	index
$9.95 hardcover			ISBN 0-88975-018-1

THE ILLUSION OF WAGE AND PRICE CONTROL
Essays on Inflation, its Causes and its Cures

A look at the causes of inflation and an examination of responses to it in Canada, the United States, and the United Kingdom. Contributors include **Jack Carr, Michael Darby, Jackson Grayson, David Laidler, Michael Parkin, Robert Schuettinger** and **Michael Walker.**

258 pages	16 charts	7 tables	$2.95 pocketbook	ISBN 0-88975-005-X

WHICH WAY AHEAD?
Canada after Wage and Price Control

This book draws together the research and ideas of fifteen well-informed Canadian economists. It presents a remarkable concurrence of views on the controls programme, its effectiveness and on the causes of inflation. The book suggests policies best suited to give Canada a healthy and internationally-competitive economy. It discusses the need for restraint in the public sector; it proposes policies to meet the critical double-headed challenge of low inflation and full employment. Contributors are: **Douglas Auld, Jack Carr, Louis Christofides, Thomas Courchene, James W. Dean, John Floyd, Herbert Grubel, John Helliwell, Stephan Kaliski, David Laidler, Richard Lipsey, Michael Parkin, Simon Reisman, Grant Reuber** and **Michael Walker.**

376 pages	5 charts	9 tables	$4.95 paperback	ISBN 0-88975-010-6

Books on Labour Market Issues

UNIONS AND THE PUBLIC INTEREST
Collective Bargaining in the Government Sector

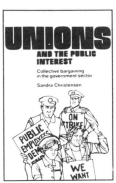

This timely and thought-provoking book is the first in a series of Fraser Institute publications dealing with unions in society and the second in the Labour Market Series. In this volume, Collective Bargaining in the Government Sector, **Sandra Christensen**, an economist at Simon Fraser University, examines the growth and development of public sector unions. She provides a useful analysis of the determination of public sector rates of pay and offers provocative but practical suggestions for ways to cope with dispute resolution.

If you are concerned about the relative power of public sector unions and the public sector's role in the wage spiral, this book is must reading for you.

128 pages   11 tables   bibliography $5.95 paperback   ISBN 0-88975-022-X

UNEMPLOYMENT INSURANCE
Global Evidence of its Effects on Unemployment

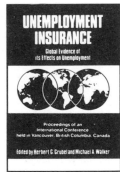

This book contains thirteen papers originally presented at an **International Conference** held in Vancouver. The proceedings begin with a broad, non-technical examination by the two editors, **Herbert G. Grubel**, Professor of Economics, Simon Fraser University and **Michael A. Walker**, Director of the Fraser Institute, of the relationship between "moral hazard", unemployment insurance and the rate of unemployment.

In Parts One and Two, the participating economists examine, empirically and theoretically, contemporary experience of national programs for dealing with unemployment in nine countries: in the **United States (Daniel S Hamermesh)**; **Canada (Ronald G. Bodkin** and **André Cournoyer); New Zealand (Geoff P. Braae); Sweden (Ingemar Stähl); Belgium (M. Gerard, Herbert Glejser** and **J. Vuchelen); Ireland (Brendan M. Walsh); France (Emil-Maria Claassen** and **Georges Lane); Federal Republic of Germany (H. Konig** and **Wolfgang Franz); and Italy (Paolo Onofri** and **Anna Stagni)**.

In Part Three , to add an historical perspective, two papers examine British social insurance systems — the 19th century Poor Laws (**Stephen T. Easton**) and the unemployment relief of the 1918-1939 inter-war period (**Daniel K. Benjamin** and **Levis A. Kochin**).

400 pages   21 charts   18 pages of extensive bibliographical references and notes
82 tables $14.95 paperback   ISBN 0-88975-008-4

Housing & Land Economics Series

ZONING:
Its Costs and Relevance for the 1980s

This provocative book raises a number of questions about zoning, specifically about recent variants of land-use controls. It forthrightly challenges underlying assumptions and principles at the root of the zoning philosophy and is required reading for all those concerned with the future of cities.

Authors are **Michael A. Goldberg**, Visiting Scholar (1979/80), Harvard University and Professor, Urban Land Economics Division, Faculty of Commerce and Business Administration, University of British Columbia, and **Peter J. Horwood**, a Vancouver Planning Consultant; with **Roscoe H. Jones**, Director of City Planning, Houston, Texas (the only North American city with no zoning regulations) and **David E. Baxter**, a British Columbia Urban Land Economist. Editor is **Walter Block**, Senior Economist, the Fraser Institute.

168 pages   3 maps   6 photos $4.95 paperback   ISBN 0-88975-032-7

PUBLIC PROPERTY?
The Habitat Debate Continued

Essays on the price, ownership and government of land. Edited by **Lawrence B. Smith**, Associate Chairman, Department of Political Economy, University of Toronto and **Michael Walker**, Director of the Fraser Institute.

Twelve Canadian economists examine the operation and importance of land markets and the impact of government regulation, control and ownership on the supply and price of land. Essential reading for all those concerned with the future of landownership in Canada.

Contributors include: **David Nowlan** of the University of Toronto (on the land market and how it works); **Larry R. G. Martin** of the University of Waterloo (on the impact of government policies on the supply and price of land for urban development); **Stanley W. Hamilton** and **David E. Baxter**, both of the University of British Columbia (on government ownership and the price of land); **Jack Carr** and **Lawrence Smith**, both of the University of Toronto (on public land banking and the price of land); **James R. Markusen** and **David T. Scheffman**, both of the University of Western Ontario (on ownership concentration in the urban land market); **Stuart McFadyen** of the University of Alberta and **Robert Hobart** of the Ministry of State for Urban Affairs (on the foreign ownership of Canadian land) and **Michael A Goldberg** of the University of British Columbia (on housing and land prices in Canada and the U.S.).

278 pages   7 charts   20 tables $9.95 hardcover   ISBN 0-88975-017-3

ANATOMY OF A CRISIS
Canadian Housing Policy in the Seventies

In this book **Lawrence B. Smith**, Associate Chairman of the Department of Political Economy at the University of Toronto, and one of Canada's leading urban economists, considers the content and objectives of Federal housing policies from 1935 to the present. His conclusions that 1) housing policy is more and more being used as a vehicle for redistributing income in Canada and 2) that this policy is at the same time destroying the private sector's incentive and ability to supply housing, make the book required reading for everybody concerned with housing in Canada today. The book contains a comprehensive bibliography.

| 55 pages | 7 tables | $3.95 paperback | ISBN 0-88975-009-2 |

THE DO'S AND DON'TS OF HOUSING POLICY
The Case of British Columbia

Economist **Raymond Heung's** book is a case study of housing in British Columbia. As well as taking vigorous issue with the methodology and conclusions of the Jaffary and Runge reports, (issued as a result of a B.C. government-funded Interdepartmental Study), Heung's book provides a useful and detailed framework for housing market analysis, together with an examination of the costs of adopting a housing allowance scheme for British Columbia. This scheme, guaranteeing access to basic accommodation for all residents in the province, would cost less than half as much as current government outlays on housing in the province. The book, written by a former staff member of the government study team, has a message applicable to every province. As such, it should be of interest to everyone concerned with Canadian housing economics.

| 145 pages | 4 charts | 28 tables | $8.00 paperback | ISBN 0-88975-006-8 |

PROFITS IN THE REAL ESTATE INDUSTRY

A controversial question never far from the headlines is the subject of profits in the real estate industry. In this book, **Basil Kalymon** of the University of Toronto's Faculty of Management Studies concludes that profits in real estate do not significantly deviate from those earned in investments in other industries. Kalymon examines the question in a scholarly and highly readable manner and vigorously enters the debate on equity compensation and the comparative performance of publicly-owned real estate companies and developers vis-à-vis other sectors of Canadian industry.

| 59 pages | 8 tables | $2.95 paperback | ISBN 0-88975-016-5 |